White
Lake District

Detailed information and maps on 110 rivers in Cumbria, Lancashire and Western Yorkshire.

Stuart Miller

Rivers Publishing U.K.

Photographs are as credited.
Front Cover: Wallabarrow Gorge, River Duddon. photo Mark Leicester collection.
Back Cover: Carlisle Canoe Club playing on the Sands rapid, River Eden. photo Dave Biggs.
Surfing on the Eden, photo Dave Biggs.   Open Canoes on the Eamont, photo Jim Wilson.

Cover Design by Leon Reichel.

Sketch Maps were drawn by Stuart Miller and are based on Crown Copyright Ordnance Survey Maps first published 1947.

Cartoons by Dario Mussoni   **Wildlife Drawings** by Julie Hicks

ISBN: 0-9519413-8-0

A CIP catalogue record for this book is available from the British Library

Printed by Cambrian Printers, Aberystwyth, Wales.

Trade Enquires

* **U.K. and Europe:** to Cordee Outdoor Books and Maps,
  3a De Montford St., Leicester, LE1 7HD, UK,   Fax 0116 247 1176

* **Other Countries:** to Rivers Publishing U.K.
  Blencathra Business Centre, Threlkeld Quarry Park, Keswick, Cumbria, CA12 4TR
  Fax: 01768 779977

Warning
Kayaking, canoeing and water sports of any variation can be dangerous. Risk cannot be eliminated. This guidebook is not an instruction manual, or suggestion of a right of way nor should it take the place of good judgement. The rivers described in this guide can kill you. They can kill you on your first day out on the river with your shiny new dry cag and boat. They can kill a seasoned "River Master" with a thousand runs under his belt. If living under the threat of death is less than appealing to you, please find another sport. Heads do pop off. Lungs do fill with water. People drown. Families will lose favourite members. Rescue people will be forced to scoop some into vile green vinyl bags. Remember, you made the choice to kayak. Have the guts to take responsibility for what you are doing, be it drowning, quasi mutilation, or something as simple as just losing your mind. If you intend to weasel out of your obligation to be responsible, and see laying blame on the publisher or author as an alternative to your ineptness, please do not use this guide. Please, close your wallet and go away now, before it's too late. Goodbye. See ya.
But if you want to have fun:- Be accountable, Be responsible, Be alive.
Try it sometime.
Have a nice day!

Rivers, rapids and obstacles change while humans compiled the book so there are bound to be errors. All advice and information should be treated with caution and checked locally. The publisher and author can accept no responsibility for any loss, injury or inconvenience sustained by any person as a result of information or advice contained in this guide

The Author conducting a descent of Whillan Beck !

The Author

Stuart Miller was born in the Lake District and fell into a life of adventure and exploration as a ruse to avoid full time employment. He has been rock climbing since the age of 15 and is responsible for many new climbs in the area. This passion for the outdoors turned into a profession in 1985 when he gained his International Mountain Guides qualification and started his own business to guide clients climbing and skiing around the world. In the last twenty years this has taken him to many great places, from the deserts of Iran to the summits of the Himalaya and helicopter skiing in Canada.

During a very wet summer in the Lakes he discovered canoeing by accident while running becks and rivers in a kids rubber dinghy. It soon became apparent that here was another sport to divert attention away from serious work. He has managed to keep his paddling activities strictly amateur in an attempt "to be as irresponsible as I like", while his thirst for travel has seen him fit paddling trips in to France, Corsica, Norway, Nepal and New Zealand between his hectic climbing schedule as well as nipping out every time it rains.

He considers himself lucky to live in the centre of the Lake District, close to Keswick, with so much to do on his doorstep. For Stuart the lakes is a big back garden which he is happy to return to time and again.

Note from the Publisher
*When we first saw Stuart's guidebook we were really impressed with it, and happily agreed to publish it for him. This has been an enjoyable and satisfying project and I hope you enjoy the fruits of our work. If **you** have a book you would like to publish – we would be very happy to advise - please contact me via our website,*

Peter Knowles.   *www.riverspublishing.co.uk*

4 INTRODUCTION

CONTENTS

NORTH WEST ENGLAND

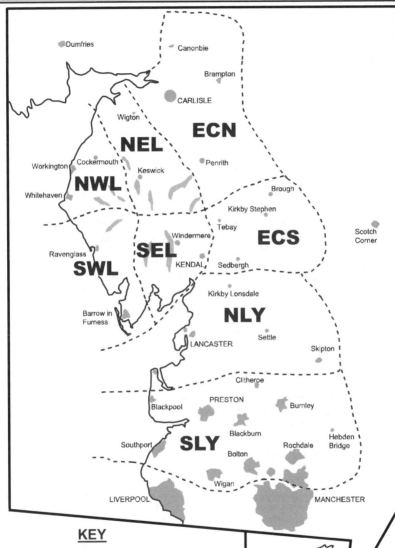

Dumfries

Canonbie

Brampton

CARLISLE

Wigton

ECN

NEL

Penrith

Workington Cockermouth
Keswick

NWL

Whitehaven

Brough

Kirkby Stephen

Tebay

ECS

Scotch
Corner

Windermere

Ravenglass

SEL

SWL

KENDAL Sedbergh

Kirkby Lonsdale

Barrow in
Furness

NLY

Settle

LANCASTER

Skipton

Clitheroe

Blackpool

PRESTON

Burnley

Blackburn

Hebden
Bridge

Southport

SLY

Rochdale

Bolton

Wigan

LIVERPOOL

MANCHESTER

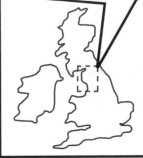

KEY

ECN - East Cumbria North.
ECS - East Cumbria South.
NEL - North East Lakes.
NWL - North West Lakes.
SEL - South East Lakes.
SWL - South West Lakes.
NLY - North Lancashire & Yorkshire.
SLY - South Lancashire & Yorkshire.

FOREWORD

When we first launched off into the River Greta in a plastic inflatable dinghy from Woolworth's in the very wet summer of 1985, I had no idea where it would lead. In fact the dinghy got me hooked on the excitement of both white water and beck exploration. Our naivety showed when after only two trips down the Greta we thought our climbing experience qualified us for more adventurous things. We overheard some canoeists we knew describing a first descent they had done which they had protected by ropes. We presumed this meant they tied themselves to ropes like climbers before setting off down a hard rapid so if they capsized they could be pulled out. "Softies ", we thought, "I bet we can do it in our dinghy without ropes".

The next time it rained we set off on the beck without a clue what lay below or that we should scout rapids. The canoeists had done it so it must be OK. In what I now know to have been flood conditions we were swept at an amazing speed around corners, through tree branches, over several small falls and ducked under a footbridge. The beck then seemed to narrow considerably and our two people in the dinghy one sitting on each side approach had to be quickly abandoned to save our legs being squashed on the rocky walls of the gorge we were about to enter. I threw myself on top of Pam and buried her face in a foot of water at the bottom of the dinghy as the sides folded up around us to squash us like a sandwich. It all went quiet and we fought our way out of our vinyl tomb to gasp at our luck in surviving. However it then seemed that what had passed for a boat a moment ago now resembled something more like an incontinence blanket and we hastily leapt for the shore before being totally enveloped in a large sheet of deflated vinyl. This sinking of the dinghy was actually a stroke of luck as only 10 m below where we made the bank was an ugly tree blockage making a very spiky and deathly strainer which we would never have avoided. So lessons learnt ? Yep, but the seed was sown.

Boating in the Lake District had always had an air of mystery and as more and more becks were explored and as canoeing became more popular it became apparent that the existing guides did not show the areas full potential. Richard Evans produced a useful mini becks guide in 1995 which gave a pointer as to what had been developed in this active period but it missed several important runs in the North Lakes and highlighted the need for a new guide. This guide was therefore born out of a desire to see all the current information from various sources together with descriptions of becks only recently descended. An appeal was also heard from those wishing more information on easy rivers which were often overlooked in the search for white water excitement. I eventually realised that no-one else was about to take on the task of producing such a guide and so started this project myself. Apart from the Lake District it soon became apparent that Lancashire was not covered by any guide book either and it became a North West England Guide.

I have attempted to give a realistic and broad perspective of all the rivers (hard, easy, good or bad) available for canoeing, in the North West of England, so people can make equally informed choices on which rivers to avoid as well as those they wish to do.

Taking a year out to write the guide became two, but eventually I had no more excuses to go out to research and all the information got fed into the computer to miraculously get spat out in the form you now see. In all there has probably been 10 years of research gone into this bright idea! Of the 150 sections of river covered I have paddled, swum, walked and climbed down 110 of them and personally visited the start and egress points of all the others. A labour of love perhaps but an enjoyable and worthwhile experience which has left me even more amazed at the amount of adventure to be had so close to home. While I have tried to keep up to date with current roads, footpaths and parking areas it is the nature of a guide such as this that it becomes out of date on the day it is printed, so sorry if things have changed by the time you get there but let me know for the future and at least you are out there exploring.

Stuart Miller
July 2003

AKNOWLEDGEMENTS

There are many people who have helped and contributed to this guide in some way over the years and I would especially like to thank the following and apologise to anyone whom I may have missed.

Paddling companions:- Pam Andrews, Fraser Dooley, Carwyn Dwyer, Richard Evans, Paul Hill, Dave Kwant, Steve Rogers, Iain Turnbull,
and especially Guy Austin who was always ready to walk or scrape down some remote valley and who kept the faith when everyone else turned to play boating.

Contributions to the Text:- Eric Bradbury, Pete Carter, Chris Foster, Gaz Pat (The Madyaker), Richard Evans, Nigel Timmins, Ian Wilson.
and especially Andy Plimmer who added considerably to our knowledge of Yorkshire Becks

Drawings & Cartoons:- I am especially indebted to Dario Mussoni and Julie Hicks for providing such brilliant drawings under short notice.

Engravings:- The Thomas Allom prints were kindly provided by Carlisle Library.

Photographic Contributions:-Guy Austin, Dave Biggs, Dorine Botteril, Frank Cope, Bob Evans, Dave Kwant, Sue Humphries, Mark Leicester, Andy Plimmer, Steve Rogers, Trevor Suddaby, Simon Wiles, Ian Wilson, Jim Wilson.

Previous Guide Book Authors:- Mike Haywood, Richard Evans, Nick Doll, Tony Tickle,
and of course Mark Rainsley for his excellent on line guide and all the contributors to it who have inspired me to explore further afield.   See www.ukriversguidebook.co.uk.

Proof Readers:- Guy Austin (for checking the river info). Tim Carruthers (for checking my English and punctuation, with special consideration for the semi-colon ; !).

Publisher:- A special thanks to Pete Knowles of Rivers Publishing for showing such enthusiasm for the project and helping with design even before becoming involved as publisher.

Equipment Suppliers:-   Nick Mallabar for Eskimo boats
The Madyaker for paddles and clothing
Jim Wilson of Carlisle Canoes

Lifestyle Guru:- A very special thanks to Pam Andrews for being such an amazing companion on so many journeys, sharing my life, keeping me chilled and teaching me to paddle.

Rafting the Greta 1985

ACCESS

Disclaimer

The inclusion of a river in this book is no evidence whatsoever that there is any agreement of right to navigate that river.

The laws of England and Wales allow many rivers to be privately owned. The owners may or may not give permission to canoe along the waterways passing through their land and the canoeist has no legal right to paddle where they desire.

The descriptions in this book tell of what is physically, or was historically, possible to canoe or navigate and should not be taken as advice to trespass.

It is the responsibility of each canoeist to determine the current state of any access arrangements or to seek permission from landowners.

The Unfortunate Truth

The amount of rivers that have agreements for access or canoeing are actually pitifully few and far between and the sport of recreational canoeing would not exist if we were reliant on such rivers.

Over the years being chased away from rivers has given many canoeists the feeling that they are somehow undesirable anarchists of the outdoors, whereas in reality it is hard to find a more ecologically unobtrusive pastime. With a bit of care, consideration for others, judgement and planning it is possible to kayak almost anywhere you want without conflict. In fifteen years of regular paddling I have only had three conflicts with landowners in this area and after polite and reasonable conversation I have always been allowed to carry on my way. Now if you go to a highly sensitive area, that is easily visible, with a large, noisy group, on a weekend in the middle of the fishing season then you are inviting controversy, but if you paddle in a small group, quietly and out of busy times it is often possible to enjoy runs unchallenged.

A lack of information can also be responsible for crowding the many canoeists onto a few popular rivers so creating honey pot runs that then develop problems from overuse. By including all the rivers in the area I hope that paddlers will start to spread themselves out and seek out new challenges. Many of the smaller becks that are described in this text have no access restrictions, as they are on open fells, above farmland, not fished and often on land owned by the National Trust. There is generally free access to rivers on National Trust land and many of these becks can be enjoyed at anytime, even throughout the summer when sudden downpours offer the rare luxury in this country of a warm paddle.

The Law

Unfortunately (or fortunately) the law on the legal rights of use of the water in a river still appears unclear and contradictory. Under what are called `Riparian Rights` landowners whose land includes the banks of a river normally have the right of ownership of the river bed, or to the centre line of the river if they only own one bank. If no right of access exists the landowners permission must be sought to access their land, or water on their land. If is not obtained then a legal trespass occurs. However the landowner's rights do not extend to ownership of the water and it has been stated in court that *"water in a watercourse is in public and common ownership in that all may reasonably use it who have a right of access to it, and that none can have any property in the water itself"*.

What is unclear is that if a right of access exists to a river above private land and a canoeist stays on the water to egress at a right of access below private land have they trespassed?

Where a trespass occurs the landowner has the right to request those who are trespassing to leave their land by a route of their choosing. This request must be obeyed, but it is obvious to most that the quickest and most direct route for a canoeist and his equipment is often to continue by the water downstream rather than tramping across fields.

Normally `Trespass` is a civil wrong which means you **cannot** be prosecuted and is it not often pursued through the courts by landowners unless some sort of damage has been done . However The Criminal Justice Act of 1994 introduced the new criminal offence of `**Aggravated Trespass**`. To commit aggravated trespass you must first be trespassing; whilst trespassing you must also have the intention of obstructing or disrupting a lawful activity (such as hunting, shooting or fishing) or intimidating those engaged in such lawful activities. Canoeists should not fall foul of this new law if they canoe in a peaceful and considerate manner.

Anyone who finds themselves threatened with a firearm should report the incident to the police.

ACCESS

The Canoeist's Code
To promote harmony and respect from other countryside users and residents it is always important to abide by the `The Canoeist's Code`, which should really be common sense but is unfortunately overlooked by some of our sport's participants.

Be friendly and polite to local residents.
Drive slowly with care and consideration.
Park sensibly without causing any obstruction.
Be as quiet as possible.
Unload kit tidily and take all litter home.
Get changed out of public view.
Get permission before going onto private property.
Avoid wildlife disturbance and environmental damage.
Be considerate to other water users.
Avoid being an intrusion on local life.
Support local businesses if you can.
Say "Thank You" for any help you receive.
Leave no trace of your visit.

and of course let us not forget The Country Code:-

The Country Code
Enjoy the countryside and respect its life and work.
Leave livestock, crops & machinery alone.
Guard against all risk of fire.
Take your litter home.
Fasten all Gates.
Help to keep all water clean.
Keep your dogs under close control.
Protect wildlife, plants and trees.
Keep to public paths across farmland.
Take special care on country roads.
Use gates and stiles to cross fences, hedges & walls.
Make no unnecessary noise .

Up to date Information
It is impossible for a book such as this to include current or meaningful information as access agreements are forever changing with negotiations taking place continually and new agreements emerging as others are lost.
All we can hope to do is guide you in the right direction to find this information.
The British Canoe Union (BCU) is continually working towards better rights of access and has a network of Local Access Officers who voluntarily negotiate for a river or rivers in their area. This information is for the good of all canoeists and is not restricted to those with BCU membership.

The main offices of the BCU are at British Canoe Union,
John Dudderidge House, Adbolton Lane, West Bridgford, Nottingham, NG2 5AS
Tel   0115 982 1100
Website http://www.bcu.org.uk

There are two websites specific to Cumbria and Lancashire which have some more information on access and the current Local Access Officers for particular rivers.

For The Lake District and Cumbria :- Cumbria Canoeists
http://www.cumbriacanoeists.org.uk

For Lancashire:- BCU North West Region
http://northwest.bcu.org.uk

GRADING

I make no apology for using the standard international grading system as used by most paddlers throughout the world. Arguments will always abound as to the accuracy and relevance of this simple system to try and evaluate what are complicated and forever changing natural problems, but it appears to give us enough of an idea if the run is suitable for our abilities. How the grades relate to different areas around the world or even around the country can only be determined by personal experience. The local interpretation of the grading system must be discovered and allowed for by choosing to paddle at a comfortable level to establish a point of reference and so avoid any nasty surprises.

I   Easy: Moving water with occasional disturbances such as small rapids or waves with few or no obstacles.

II   Moderate: Slightly faster water with more frequent rapids and rocks. Waves and small stoppers are found but the route is always obvious.

III   Difficult: The current is swift with the possibility of big irregular waves and stoppers capable of holding boats firmly. Rapids are more continuous with rocks and hazards that must be avoided. Although the route is usually fairly obvious it is necessary to be able to manoeuvre the kayak well and inspection may be needed.

IV   Very Difficult: Large rapids or falls with powerful water, holding stoppers and rock obstacles which can follow each other in quick succession or be continuous . The route may not be obvious from the water, so bank inspection and protection are often necessary. A mistake or swim could be serious.

V   Extremely Difficult: Complex and difficult rapids where even with inspection from the bank it is difficult to recognise a route. Large falls, dangerous hydraulics and serious rock obstacles will present a challenge to any canoeist with substantial danger always a possibility. Inspection and protection essential.

VI   Limit of Navigation: Grade V carried to the extreme . A line down only just exists and luck may play a part. Only favourable water conditions coupled with considerable experience, skilful paddling, advanced protection and an ability to pick the ideal day will be involved in a successful descent. Most of the time they will be too dangerous to canoe and there will always be a serious risk to life.

In practice it can be very difficult to put rapids and rivers into this simple table as there are many other factors which affect our ability to make a successful descent, such as how much beer was consumed the night before. However, the following notes should also be taken into account:

1)   Many of the rivers are not of a sustained nature and have long easy sections between harder rapids or falls. This can give the impression that the rivers are a soft touch compared to rivers of the same technical grade in the Alps, where things are often more continuous. If a section is sustained or continuous then it is mentioned in the text and paddlers will be aware that just because they paddle a short grade IV rapid it does not necessarily mean they can survive a long continuous section of grade IV. Sometimes this means that the river can be run at a lower grade than the main falls by portaging. This is shown in the text by giving the overall grade of a section as the lower grade and the grade of the harder falls in **brackets**. Sometimes the easier sections of rivers are not suitable for mixed ability groups. Just because the grade is easier it may still be serious and unsuitable for those at the limit of their ability. In these cases the overall grade of the section is given as the harder rapids.

2)   There may still be highly dangerous obstacles (such as weirs) on rivers with an easy grade. The river is graded without the obstacle but with the danger clearly highlighted within the text and maps.

GRADING

3)   On many of these rivers and becks the water level can be quite critical to the grade and it is impossible to describe all eventualities. One must use a large portion of common sense and discretion. High water may increase dangers from trees, fences, waterfalls and stoppers while it may decrease dangers from pinning rocks. The grade given is for what is usually regarded as a **normal** level for that river and comments relating to this are mentioned in the text under the **Indicators** section.

4)   **Trees** pose a problem on most of the rivers in this area to a greater or lesser extent. Overhanging branches can be a problem in high water and they can form complete blockages or strainers when they fall down. These hazards are constantly changing, coming and going overnight in storms and floods, and can occur just as easily on a grade I as a grade V. It is therefore impossible to account for this in the descriptions or grading and paddlers must be aware that any river can be blocked at any time by a fallen tree and must be prepared to take evasive action to avoid it. However in instances where there are long established blockages reference has been made in the text. Rivers with continuous problems are highlighted with a tree icon.

How the grade is represented in the different parts of the guide

The **Icon bar** is for quick reference and usually shows the grade of the hardest rapid on the section, however in a few cases where the hardest rapid is a one off the grade at which the river is normally paddled is used.

The **Information box** shows the variation of grades over the different parts of the river.

II,III,IV will mean the river has significant parts at the grades represented.

III (IV) will mean the section is mainly of the lower grade with rapids that are easily portaged at the higher grade.

III / IV will mean the grade is borderline and likely to be easier at lower water levels and harder at higher levels.

Lastly + and - signs are used occasionally where rapids seem hard or easy for the grade but not enough to be put into the next category.

The **Description** has an overall grade for each section.

The **Individual rapids** have a specific grade with + or - used occasionally.

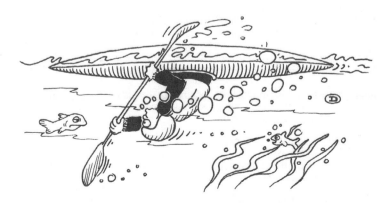

USING THE GUIDE

The purpose of this book is to serve as a source of reference to all the rivers, streams and becks that have been paddled by canoeists and kayakers in the north west of England.

I have attempted to give clear and easily read information on each river irrespective of its popularity, quality, or access problems. There are however **summary tables** at the start of each area chapter which give a star rating for both paddling quality and scenic quality of the rivers.

GENERAL

The design of the book is so that it can be used on several levels depending how much information different people require. It can be used purely as a visual information source with the maps and diagrams along with the icons on the edge of the page to give a quick idea of where each river is and what sort of hazards to expect. The written description then gives more detailed information for those that want it.

The rivers have been grouped for convenience into 8 sub areas as chapters. At the start of each chapter is a map of the rivers included in that area and a summary table of the runs. The rivers are then listed in alphabetical order. Each river has been split into convenient sections that are most usually paddled. Some of the longer rivers run through two or more areas and these are then split and described with the relevant sections in the areas in which they are found.

CHAPTER HEADINGS

The area chapter heading is given on each page.

THE RIVERS

The rivers are listed alphabetically within each area.

RIVER SECTIONS

The rivers are broken down into sections. The sections are chosen from experience of the most usually canoed parts or by suitable access and egress points. Each section of river is given a sketch map which is often sufficient to find your way to the rivers start and finishing points, although in some instances the relevant Ordnance Survey map can be of additional help.

ICON BAR

On the starting page of each river section an icon bar is found running down the right side of the page along with the name of the river. At the top of the icon bar are three boxes which appear for every section giving an idea of the type of river, grade of river and water levels required. At the bottom of the icon bar are the hazard symbols which give an idea of the type of hazards encountered on that section. The grade given in the icon bar will normally show the hardest rapid on that section of river.

INFORMATION BOX

There is an information box at the start of each river section giving the basics needed to get on and off the river: grid references of start and egress points, length of the section, grade of the river, reference to Ordnance Survey maps and stars for both white water quality and scenic quality. The grades given in the information box show the different grades of different parts of the section.

WRITTEN DESCRIPTION

The description for each section of river is meant to stand alone without too much cross referencing. While it gives useful information to get the reader to a river and give them an idea of what to expect it does not attempt to dictate how to paddle particular rapids or falls. Things change, different people approach each problem in a different way, different water levels require different tactics. Descriptions of how to do things can encourage some to run rapids they should not be on. So the decision and element of adventure is left to the individual. This is how experience is gained.

The main description has the following headings.

SUMMARY:- An overview of the section which may give a general feeling for the river and its ambience or mention points of interest.

USING THE GUIDE

INDICATORS:- A guide to the water level required. This is one of the most difficult things to describe as most of the rivers in this guide can be run at a wide variety of levels giving a wide variation in grade. What I have tried to do is to give a general idea of when a river becomes possible to paddle and a useful marker to judge this by, if known. As most of the time in this country we are running around trying to guess when there is enough water to go paddling the markers usually refer to the minimum water requirements for an enjoyable paddle. This is usually when the river has risen after rain and flowing at what I would call normal or low to mid spate levels. It is for these normal levels that the grade of the river is given. It is usual to assume that the higher the water level the more difficult and dangerous a river will become, although in some instances high water can wash out and hide some rapids.

START:- Where to put on and descriptions on how to get there if not obvious.

DESCRIPTION:- Each section of river is further divided into parts that are roughly of a constant grade and are given a brief overview. These parts listed as A,B,C etc are indicated on the sketch maps along with any specific points of interest numbered 1,2,3 etc.
Specific points of interest on the river can vary from falls and rapids to bridges, weirs, fences etc.
It has not been possible to personally check every section of every river and while I have been indebted to the many people who have helped with descriptions there are some which have not been corroborated and should be treated with extra caution. These I have marked in the text with three question marks next to the description heading. **???** .

Abbreviations used are as follows,

W - Weir. These are not graded as they can change very rapidly from easy to impossible depending on water levels. They can have strong tow backs, contain spikes or be undercut.
I have mentioned known dangers on several weirs and marked those that are definite portages but only experience can let you be the judge of whether to run one or not and that is outside the scope of this book. If in doubt portage a weir as its not worth getting into trouble just to run 2 m of concrete.

B - Bridge. This could be either a hazard or a useful marker on the river, including aqueducts or pipes.

F - Fence. These can vary from single strands of barbed wire to meshed wire to heavy wooden sheep fences.

T - Trees. Used where there is a significant hazard from trees that is unlikely to change.

SS - Stepping Stones

X - Portage. These are usually definite portages although over the years as standards and boldness increase what was once regarded as a definite portage may become the test piece of tomorrow. Any way they will always be dangerous sections of river to be inspected and treated with great respect.

Grade - The grade given in the written description of the section is the overall grade at normal levels. Where a section is given two grades such as II / III it will mean that the river is borderline and will be the lower grade at lower flows and the higher grade at higher flows.
If a section is mainly one grade with a single fall at a higher grade it is shown as II (III). Each fall or rapid is then noted and given an individual grade.
Occasionally I have used the + and - signs after a grade where a rapid seems hard or easy but not enough to put it into the next level. (See more about grading, page 10).

EGRESS:- Where to take out with any relevant descriptions on how to get there.

THE RIVER ICONS

I have developed the system of river icons shown on the margin of each description to give a quick visual appraisal of each river and its hazards. The symbols are split into two blocks.

At the top of the page margin there are always three icons showing: the type of river, the amount of rain required and the grade.

At the bottom of the page margin the icons refer mainly to the type of hazards that appear on the river, but they also show information such as rivers with play spots or walking approaches.

TYPE OF RIVER

Lake Fed River

Main Valley River

Steep Rocky Beck

Small River / Stream

WATER LEVELS

All the rivers in this guide are rain dependent and are possible at a wide range of water levels with the grade changing accordingly. This purpose of this icon is to give an idea at what level a run will come into condition. For instance a high water icon will show that a great deal of rain is needed for a run to have enough water in it to be possible. This may not necessarily mean that the run itself will be a wild flood run but that only in high water will it be worth going for a look. If a run has a low water icon it does not necessarily mean that it is only possible in low water but that these runs are the first to come up and the last to dry up and if conditions are low these are the ones to check out. Most rivers fall into the middle category of needing a fair amount of rain to start running and keep their flow.

High Water Levels

Medium Water Levels

Low Water Levels

GRADE

The grade shown in the margin is the overall grade that a particular section of river is given. This will usually be the grade of the hardest rapid but in occasional circumstances if the hardest rapid is usually portaged then this grade may refer to the rest of the river. It is only meant as a quick reference and more detailed information on the grade of individual rapids can be found in the text. I have not used + or - signs in these boxes.

OTHER RIVER INFORMATION

 Tree Danger   This is used to show any danger from trees and varies from branches growing over the river to whole fallen trees blocking the river. This seems to be a particular problem that paddlers in this area grow accustomed to. A high sense of tree awareness is needed on rivers with this symbol and the ability to make micro breakouts at a moment's notice and egress onto the bank with the agility of a water rat to avoid a strainer.

However nearly all the rivers have trees on their banks somewhere and just because a river does not have this symbol is no guarantee that it is free of tree hazards, so keep aware at all times.

 Fences   This shows if there are likely to be fences across the river. These can be single strands of barbed wire, wire mesh or heavy wooden sheep fences. More detail will be available in the text. The position and number of fences on a river can often change and it is impossible to mark them all. It also does not guarantee that a river without this icon is free of fences.

THE RIVER ICONS

 Rocks   This is to show if there are likely to be rock formations to avoid. These could be anything from an abundance of boulders in the river bed to rocky gorges or channels through bedrock.

 Large waterfalls   This shows that there are large falls that have a significant height drop that need inspecting or portaging.

 Strong Stoppers   This indicates that there are often strong stoppers that need particular caution to avoid being held.

 Weirs   This shows there are weirs. No attempt has been made to grade weirs and they should all be inspected on the day to asses their particular danger. Where particular problems are known they are referred to in the text.

 Undercuts   This is to show there are significant undercut rocks in places to be aware of which will be referred to in the text.

 Pinning   This shows there is a significant problem of pinning on the section. If it is one particular spot it will be referred to in the text or it may apply to the whole section of river.

 Siphons   This indicates that there are siphons in places to be aware of. These will usually be referred to in the text.

 Flat water   Possibly the worst fear of many white water paddlers. This means you will have to do some work and actually paddle forwards with a degree of effort involved to reach the next rapid !

 Portage   This highlights dangers that are normally portaged. These can be weirs, falls, trees, factories etc. which will be referred to in the text. Grade VI falls may sometimes be referred to as portages for most people.

 Dubious Water Quality   This is to show rivers where the water quality may leave something to be desired and it would be best to avoid swallowing it.

 Short Boats Advised   Several of the steep narrow becks are best run in specialist creek boats which are more rounded and less likely to pin than modern play boats.

 Play spots   This is to show that a river has good natural features for playing such as friendly holes, eddy lines or rock splats.

 Accessed On Foot   This shows the river can only be accessed on foot and boats will need to be carried for a significant distance.

 The Black Spot   Rivers that are particularly unpleasant and not recommended but included for completeness and to save you the trouble of exploring.

THE MAPS

A sketch map is included for each section of river. These are not drawn exactly to scale although a rough indication of distance is shown on each map in kilometres. They have been kept as simple as possible to show the general position of rivers, lakes, roads, towns and coastlines. They do not claim to show every feature, either on or off the water. They are intended to help the paddler locate the river, the start and finish of each section and the main hazards. In particular trees and fence problems can change regularly and the maps are not accurate enough to pinpoint rapids or features exactly, so use them as a guide not as gospel.

In a few instances it has not been possible to check every part of every river personally and there are some sections which have not been corroborated so the position of hazards on the maps should be treated with extra caution. These I have marked in the text with three question marks next to the description heading (???).

If further detail is required the relevant sheet numbers for the current Ordnance Survey maps are noted for each river in the information box. The first numbers in the box refer to the 1:50,000 Landranger series while the second numbers are for the 1:25,000 Explorer series. These may be particularly helpful when trying to locate paths and routes to becks and rivers away from the road and in finding public rights of way.

Direction of flow of the rivers should be apparent from the start and egress points marked on each diagram.

KEY TO MAP SYMBOLS

The following symbols and fonts are used on the individual river maps. The area maps should be self explanatory.

Roads

Lakes and Place Name

Towns and Rapids

River Sections, Start and Egress

Rivers ....Other rivers that are included in the guide.

1 ....Rapids and other notes in the text.

A ....Section split in text.

Start   Egress ....Start and Egress points

RIVER NAME ....Heading showing river and section

KEY TO MAP SYMBOLS

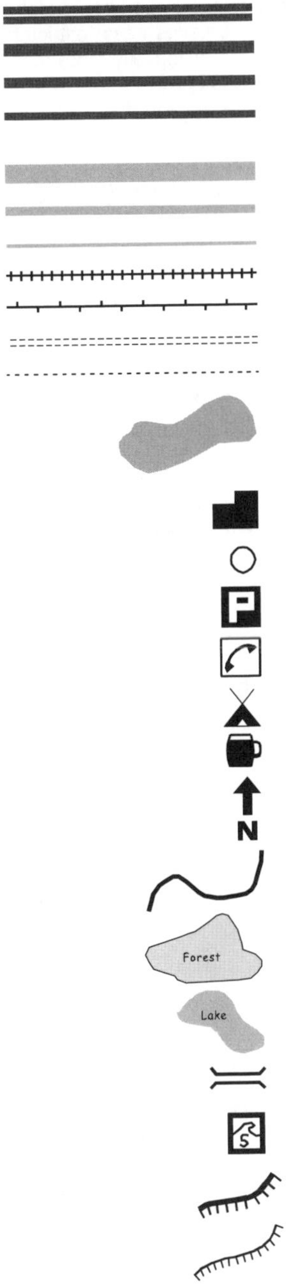

........Motorway or Dual Carriageway

.........Main Roads

.........Secondary Roads

.........Minor roads

.........Large Rivers

.........Small rivers, becks and navigable streams

.........Small un-navigable streams

.........Railways

.........Disused Railways

.........Private roads, un-metalled roads and tracks

.........Footpaths

.........Built Up areas

.........Isolated Buildings

.........Railway Stations

.........Car Parking

.........Public Telephone

.........Camp Site

.........Public House

.........Direction of North

.........Coastline

.........Woodland or Forest

.........Lakes

.......Foot Bridges or Pipe Bridges

........Surf Spots

........Large Cliffs

........Steep ground or small cliffs

LAKE ACCESS

When in the Lake District many people wish to do some flat water paddling either for training, introduction to canoeing or just to relax on a sunny day. Several of the Lakes have restrictions while others enjoy free access. As these access restrictions seem to be historically more stable than agreements on the rivers I have felt able to give details for the main lakes.

Usually there is no charge for canoes if launched from public access points. However, some lakes do require permits and have restrictions on the number of craft in one day.

LAKE	Canoeing Allowed	Special Notes	Permit obtained
Bassenthwaite	Yes with Permit	Restricted nature reserve areas	National Park Office. Pheasant Inn, Peel Wyke. Keswick Tourist Office. Derwent Water Marina.
Buttermere	Yes with permit	Maximum of 10 in one day	National Trust, Permit from Dalegarth, Buttermere.
Coniston Water	Yes	No charge from public launch sites	
Crummock Water	Yes with permit	Maximum of 10 in one day	National Trust, Permit from Wood House, Buttermere.
Derwent Water	Yes	No charge from public launch sites	
Elterwater	No	Passing through on a river trip appears tolerated	
Ennerdale Water	Only with permission	Permission must be obtained in advance	Contact United Utilities.
Grasmere	Yes	No charge from public launch sites	
Rydal Water	No	Passing through on a river trip appears tolerated	
Thirlmere	Yes	Access from Armboth Car Park	
Ullswater	Yes	No charge from public launch sites	
Wastwater	Yes	Maximum of 15 at one time	
Windermere	Yes	Free at public sites	Launching Fee charged on National trust sites

Useful Telephone Numbers:
Bowness Tourist Information..015394 42895
Coniston Tourist Information 015394 41533
Keswick Tourist Information..017687 72645
National Park Office..015397 24555
National Trust North West Regional Office.................................015394 35599
United Utilities Environment and Community Office...................017687 72334

SEA & SURF SPOTS

The Irish Sea on the west coast of Cumbria is not known for its reliable surf conditions as the position of Ireland restricts the swell that has built up across the Atlantic. Therefore any waves that do form tend to be from strong onshore winds locally rather than from offshore storms. Because of this the waves tend to be small, close together and break quickly making it very hard to paddle out through the surf on occasions. Despite this, when the rivers are dry many paddlers do take to the sea for a bit of fun and exercise and if the proximity of all the beaches on the west coast to Sellafield and its radioactive discharges doesn't deter you then the odd day of good conditions can be found.

PARTON   GR 979 208
The most northerly spot regularly surfed. A break forms off the rocks on the south edge of the bay. It works on South to South Westerly winds and an incoming tide. This can be good place during strong southerly winds as St Bees Head gives some shelter so the waves form better.
        Turn off the A595 and descend to either end of Parton Village. In the middle of the village go through an arch under the railway to a car park overlooking the south edge of the bay.

WHITEHAVEN HARBOUR WALL   GR 972 186
Another spot that can be sheltered from southerly storms. A good break can form off the end of the Northern Harbour wall although pollution has been a problem here at times.
        Accessed from parking on the sea front from a road going around Tesco supermarket at the northern end of the town.

St BEES   GR 961 117
The nicest of Cumbria's beaches and possibly the only one that can be called a resort. At low tide a large sandy beach is exposed which stretches a long way south. The northern end of the beach runs abruptly into the red sandstone boulders and cliffs of St Bees Head.
        This is the most popular beach for surfing and can work with anything from a southerly to a north westerly. However it is quite a messy beach break with uneven sandbars creating random breaks which keep changing and always seem to be better 100 m from where you are. South Westerly winds usually provide the best waves on a low to mid incoming tide and again on the ebb. High tides dump badly on the steep shingle at the top of the beach and wooden groins are a hazard near the car park.
        On a calm day a tour north from the beach can give some entertaining playing amongst the rocks while a trip around to Whitehaven harbour is about 8 km.
        From St Bees village follow the signs to a large car park on the sea front, where there are cafe and toilet facilities.

SILECROFT   GR 120 811
A large open beach with flat sand exposed at low to mid tide and steep sand and pebbles at the top. Waves can form with any onshore wind from south to westerly although again South Westerly is best. The waves seem to increase in size as the tide comes in but then dump badly on the pebbles at high tide.
        Turn off the A5093 four kilometres west of Millom where a road leads through Silecroft to a car park and toilets at the sea front.

WALNEY ISLAND   Earnse Point GR 170 699   Bent Hawe Scar GR 183 663
A large open beach with small pebbles. Faces south west and can form good surf with onshore winds. There are two areas on the island that are used. Earnse Point is to the north of Vickerstown while Bent Hawe Scar is to the south.
        From the centre of Barrow in Furness follow the A590 to Vickerstown and Walney Island. After crossing Walney Channel either turn right and follow signs to North Walney and Earnse Point where there is the West Shore car park, or for Bent Hawe Scar keep on the main road across the island to where it comes to an end and meets the beach road, turn left along Biggar Bank road and follow this to a car park and large grassy area above the beach.

continued on next page ⇨

SEA & SURF SPOTS

⇨ *continued from previous page*

ARNSIDE   GR 455 787

Arnside is not a surf beach but on spring tides a bore sometimes forms on the incoming tide while waves, holes and whirlpools give potential for playing as the flood rushes through the arches of the railway viaduct. Both these features are usually accessed from the promenade on the seafront of the village. It is best to **avoid the car park** which can often flood in the high tides which are necessary. Tides of over 9.7m at Cavendish Dock in Barrow are needed before it is worth a visit and even then the features are not consistent and sometimes do not appear at all. They seem to be affected by the wind strength and direction, moving sand bars and the volume of water coming down the river Kent. The best chances of catching a bore are to set off from Arnside at least 2½ hours before high tide and paddle south west towards Blackstone Point where the wave may be found and caught for a surf of about 1.5 km back to the village. The viaduct is just north of the village and contains some fifty small arches giving constantly changing waves, boils and whirlpools. Nothing can be relied on here except the power of the water rushing through the viaduct. This is not a place for beginners.

PARK AND PLAY SPOTS

With the increasing development of Freestyle or Rodeo paddling there is a demand for places to go and practise the moves without paddling the full length of a river. These holes or waves which are convenient places to play in have become known as `Park & Play` spots. While the North West is not renowned for its high quality park and play spots the following will be of interest to those searching for the holy grail.

Workington Fish Counter Weir   `Wooky Weir`

A entertaining site with something to play in at all but very low levels. Consists of four channels divided by concrete walls. The nearest chute to the road has a forever surf wave that is very forgiving, safe and always easy to exit. It is a good place to gain confidence with 360s, blasts, back surfs, blunts and cartwheels all possible. The next chute towards the centre is much rougher and more grabby, but at some levels it can be good for cartwheels although it can be hard to exit. It is easier to exit at higher water levels but vertical moves or capsizing usually gets you clear, The farther two chutes are usually too shallow for much more than sideways surfing. In very high water when the concrete walls are covered a good river wide wave appears. This is a fairly safe play spot but there is only a small eddy up against the near bank so any swims or slow rolls often mean being washed a good way down stream.

It is found on the edge of Workington at the egress from section 5 of the Lower Derwent and should only be paddled outside the fishing season. Page 157.

Brathay Skelwith Force Pool   `The Looping Pool`

A fast hole where the river is squeezed between rocks as it exits the pool at the bottom of Skelwith Force. Good for old skool pop-outs and cartwheel moves. Longer boats tend to hit a rough rock on the left side in low water. It is possible to park close to the Skelwith Bridge Hotel and carry boats 100 m up the road to the pool. Page 172.

Wetheral Weir

A high water play spot on the Eden near Carlisle. Initially it looks similar to Workington weir with three channels divided by concrete walls, but it is very different as the two side chutes contain concrete blocks just below the surface and the centre chute which looks to form a nice green wave in low water is actually impossible to enter without bank support from someone standing on the concrete walls. Best avoided until high water is up to or above the concrete walls. Page 38.

PARK AND PLAY SPOTS

The Leven Brick Chute Weir
The first weir on the Leven has a centre channel where it is usually run. This forms a fast surfing wave at its exit where 360s and blunts can be pulled off but often end up crashing into the walls. Pop-outs and one off cartwheels are possible but the centre channel is not very retentive. The rest of the weir, however, should be treated with caution as it becomes very retentive in high flows. Access restrictions mean this is not a very useful play spot unless running the river. Page 199.

Padiham Weir Project
This is being built as a canoeing facility and fish pass to replace the large weir on the river Calder at Padiham. It is planned to contain three drops and will be found behind the Shuttleworth Mead Business Park which is on the A687 Blackburn Road out of Padiham, close to junction 8 on the M65. There will be coaching, car parking, toilets and changing facilities. Page 309.

The Irwell Burrs Site
The Burrs Outdoor Centre manage this training site on the river Irwell close to the centre of Bury in the Burrs Country Park and for a small fee the changing, toilet, and shower facilities can be used. The site has had some manual sculpting and is a good resource for introducing basic white water skills with a few surfing waves and play spots available. Page 325.

Halton Rapids
Halton rapids are situated on the Lune on the outskirts of Lancaster. They are a few hundred metres long and are formed by a series of stone walls sticking out into the flow from both banks. They can be paddled at all water levels and vary from a good introductory training ground for beginners in normal flows to a full on epic surf spot in spate. The holes formed by the walls are only playable at low to normal levels and form dangerous stoppers as the level rises. Severe access restrictions limit paddling to November, December and January. Page 289.

The Looping Pool, River Brathay.   *Stuart Miller*

SUMMARY TABLE

Name of Run	Page	Grade	WW Stars	Scenic Stars	Km	Water	Notes
Border Esk	25	3	✳	❀	10	Low	level stays up well
Caldew (Lower river) - Section 2	27	2		❀ ❀	12.5	Med	tree hazard
Caldew (Lower river) - Section 3	29	2		❀	19	Med	pleasant tour + weirs
Eamont - Section 1	31	2		❀ ❀	11	Med	weirs
Eamont - Section 2	33	1		❀	11	Low	flat
Eden - Section 1	35	1(3)		❀	10	Low	flat, 1 fall
Eden - Section 2	37	3	✳	❀ ❀ ❀	8	Low	classic intro
Gelt	**41**	5	✳ ✳ ✳	❀ ❀	8	High	sandstone gorges
Irthing - Section 1	43	3(5)			11	High	flat with 2 big falls
Irthing - Section 2	45	3	✳ ✳ ✳	❀ ❀ ❀	5	Med	Classic mid grade
Irthing - Section 3	47	2(3+)		❀	10	Med	remote gorge
Leith	**49**	3			6	High	many fences
Liddle Water	**51**	3+	✳ ✳	❀ ❀	0.6	Med	short but sweet
Lowther	**53**	3	✳	❀ ❀	9	Med	woodland park
Lyne	**55**	1(2)		❀ ❀	19	Med	quiet and remote
Lyvennet	**57**	2		❀	10	High	farmland tour

River Eden near Armathwaite.   *Jim Wilson*

RIVERS OF EAST CUMBRIA NORTH

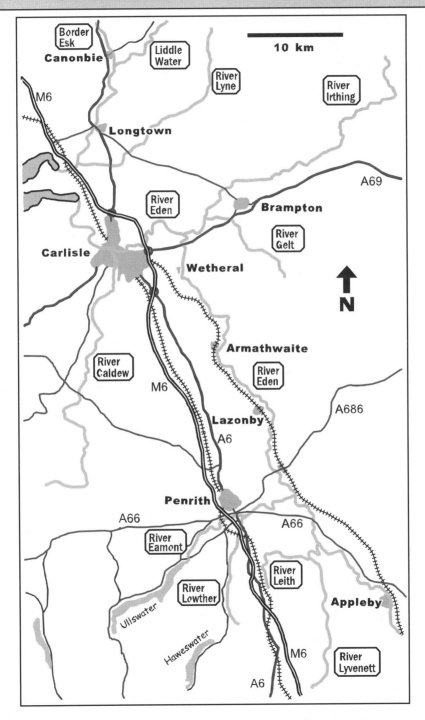

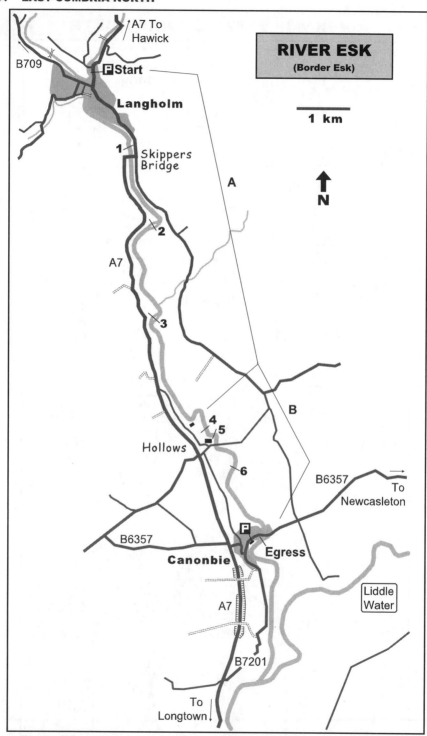

ESK (Border Esk)

From :	Langholm 363 849	Grade :	III / IV
To :	Canonbie 394 764	Maps :	O.S. 79 & 85, Explorer 323
Distance :	10 km	Stars : ✱ Scenery : ❀	

SUMMARY
A Scottish river that has sneaked into this guide by virtue of the fact that it finishes in Cumbria and is close enough to the Lake District to make a quick cross border raid feasible. It holds its water well so a trip up here can be worthwhile when everything else appears dry. It starts high in the southern uplands and above Langholm there is a 15 km long stretch of grade I paddling which can be found by following the B709 north to Enzieholm Bridge and returning to Langholm. The section described here is the more popular trip which is mainly grade I / II paddling dotted with a few harder rapids. There are some long flat sections which can be hard work if there is a head wind but the rapids are pleasant with Hollows Mill giving an excellent finale which can become quite fearsome in high water.

INDICATORS
This is a large river which holds its level well for several days after rain. If the shingle rapids down to the bridge at the egress are navigable without scraping then the rest should be ok. At Langholm there is a large rock behind the sewage works just above the first rapids and if this is showing then it is a low level and should be just covered for a good medium level.

START
Start in the car park of a picnic site off the A7 on the north edge of the town. Put in onto the Ewes Water which flows past the car park and joins the Esk in 100 m. For a slightly easier start it is possible to put in at Skippers Bridge from the lane on the east bank.

DESCRIPTION
A) III The first rapid comes at the exit from the town then the river is mainly flat with a couple of rapids past islands.
1) III+ Skippers rapid starts a few hundred metres above the bridge and runs down to a rocky constriction beneath the bridge. It contains a couple of fun play waves and varies quite a lot with water level, becoming a long stretch of daunting rapids at very high levels.
2) II / III Dog Island. From the A7 bridge a kilometre of easy water leads to a sharp but wide bend right followed immediately by the island. Normally run on the right side but keep alert for a rock in the main flow near the bottom.
3) II / III Irvine House Island. The rapids past the next island are again usually run on the right where another large rock needs to be avoided

B) III / IV A tower on the right bank where a large loop in the river swings first left then back right signals the approach to Hollows Weir This final section of rapids starts with the weir followed closely by a complicated series of rapids down to Hollows Bridge.
4) W Hollows Weir. This large semi natural weir has several lines depending on water levels and should be inspected.
5) III+ Hollows Mill rapid. This follows the weir almost immediately and consists of a series of slabs and stoppers followed by a sharp turn right into confused water. This can go up a grade in high water but a chicken shoot appears river left. Under the bridge there is another short section of rapids with a surf wave.
6) II / III Byreburnfoot. A small reef on this corner forms a rapid on the left of the river.

EGRESS
Egress to the right bank below Canonbie bridge. Park 100 m away at the village hall.

RIVER ESK (Border Esk)

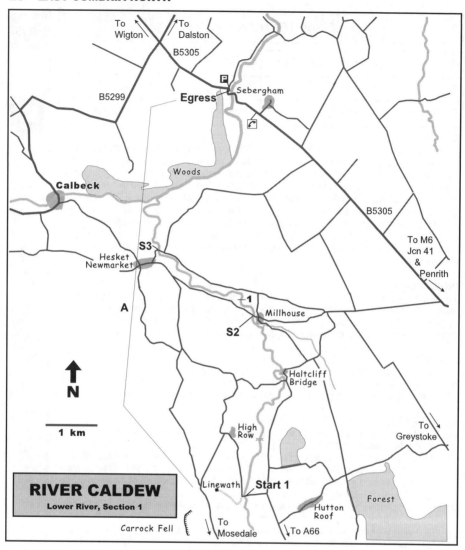

To Wigton

To Dalston

B5305

B5299

P

Egress

Sebergham

Woods

Calbeck

B5305

To M6 Jcn 41 & Penrith

S3

Hesket Newmarket

A

1

Millhouse

S2

Haltcliff Bridge

N

1 km

High Row

To Greystoke

Linewath

Start 1

Forest

RIVER CALDEW
Lower River, Section 1

Carrock Fell

To Mosedale

Hutton Roof

To A66

CALDEW (Lower Caldew)

The Lower Caldew is a pleasant trip which is often overlooked in favour of its more well known neighbours but it offers a long section of easy grade paddling in lovely scenery down to the outskirts of Carlisle. It is in condition more often than is first thought as it has a large catchment area with many small streams increasing its volume by the time it flows through Dalston.

The source of the Caldew is the area of fells in the north east corner of the Lake District known as the Back o' Skiddaw and a short sharp spate run in Mosedale is described in the North East Lakes chapter of the guide. The river then runs for a short while through some flat farmland where trees and fences are the main ingredients before it is worth considering paddling again at Linewath Bridge. Down to the confluence with the Cald Beck gives fairly continuous but straightforward rapids. The river then becomes bigger and gentler for its journey to Carlisle with only a couple of large weirs to look out for.

SECTION 2   Linewath to Sebergham

From : Linewath Bridge 360 342	**Grade :**	II
To : Sebergham Bridge 367 418	**Maps :** O.S. 90 & 85, Explorer OL5	
Distance : 12.5 km	**Scenery :** ❀ ❀	

SUMMARY
Much underrated, this section of the river follows a delightful valley with a feeling of remoteness away from the road for most of its course and below road level when it is nearby. At the start the river is still quite small and trees lining the banks are a major hazard on the way to Millhouse. The rapids are easy and mainly over shingle beds but they are continuous and there are many boulders which need steering around in places making the first part of this run quite awkward for its grade and serious for beginners especially in higher water. There are a couple of alternative access points for a shorter or less tree threatened trip.

INDICATORS
Heavy rain in the northern fells brings this into condition quite often as the bed of the river channels the water well. A look from any of the bridges along its length will give an indication if it is flowing and navigable. There is a gauge under the bridge at Sebergham which should read 0.10 m as a minimum level, which will require a scrape in places. 0.15 m will be medium, while above 0.20 m will be a good high level.

START
The best place to start when there is a good water level is at the bridge close to Linewath, below Carrock Fell. This is found by driving past Mosedale and Carrock Fell to High Row where the road doubles back towards Hutton Roof via Linewath Bridge **(S1)**.
Alternatively the worst of the tree lined banks can be avoided by starting at Millhouse Bridge GR 361 376. Park by the village hall in the centre of the village and carry down to the bridge where the right bank can be gained just below the bridge **(S2)**.
Hesket Bridge GR 343 388 is another access point for a much shorter trip **(S3)**.

DESCRIPTION
A) II   Continuous small and easy rapids with tree lined banks. Beware as there may be the odd fallen tree completely blocking the river. After the confluence with the Cald Beck the river becomes wider and easier with more flatter sections.
1) W   A few hundred metres below Millhouse Bridge there is a broken weir.

EGRESS
Egress just below Sebergham Bridge to the left bank where there is a small car park.

RIVER CALDEW 2 (Lower Caldew)

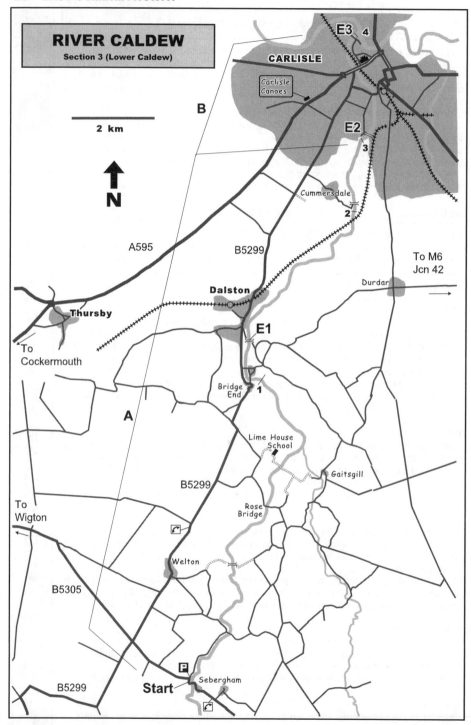

RIVER CALDEW
Section 3 (Lower Caldew)

2 km

N

E3   4

CARLISLE

Carlisle Canoes

B

E2

3

Cummersdale

2

A595

B5299

To M6 Jcn 42

Durdar

Dalston

E1

Thursby

To Cockermouth

Bridge End   1

A

Lime House School

Gaitsgill

B5299

Rose Bridge

To Wigton

Welton

B5305

B5299

Start   Sebergham

SECTION 3   Sebergham To Carlisle

From :	Sebergham Bridge	367 418	Grade :	I / II
To :		Bitz Park 395 567	Maps :	O.S. 85, Explorer OL5
Distance :	19 km			Scenery : ❀

SUMMARY
The river is quite large and broad now with many flat sections and occasional shingle rapids suitable for beginners and lazy open boat trips. It follows still pleasant countryside and farmland down past Dalston and on to the outskirts of Carlisle at Denton Holme. The section through the centre of Carlisle is somewhat bleak but soon passes to egress back in pleasant surroundings in Bitz Park, at the confluence with the river Eden.

INDICATORS
Rain in the northern fells brings this into condition quite often and the many tributaries help build the volume until by the time it reaches Dalston it is a large river. From Sebergham the river is fairly flat with sections that hold the water well, while the short shingle rapids often have a channel that is navigable. There is a gauge under the bridge by the car park at Sebergham which should read 0.10 m as a minimum level. This will require a scrape in places. 0.15 m will be medium, while above 0.20 m will be a good high level.

START
Start just below Sebergham Bridge on the left bank where there is a small car park.

DESCRIPTION
A) I / II   Most of this section flows gently with a few riffles over shingle beds. There are **two large weirs that need portages**. The first is on the approach to Bridge End just above Dalston, while the second is at Denton Holme as the river enters Carlisle.
1) W   Bridge End Weir. The horizon line of this weir should be obvious on the approach as the river bends left 200 m above the bridge. It is a large 4 m weir containing sloping steps which can be run almost anywhere in low to medium flows but the stopper at its base must be treated with caution and portaged in high water. Inspect and portage on the left. A small rapid then follows the weir on the run down to the bridge.
2) W   Cummersdale Weir. This small 30 cm is found 100m after passing under the railway bridge and will wash out in higher flows. However at certain levels it can produce a strong tow back between enclosed banks and should be inspected and portaged if in doubt. Inspect and portage on the right bank.
3) X   Denton Holme Weir. As the river approaches the outskirts of Carlisle this large and dangerous weir is found beside the first buildings on the left bank. It drops 3 m vertically onto concrete and should be portaged on the right bank.

B) I / II   The traverse of the city is all below road level between red brick walls and is accompanied by the railway for some of the way. However the bed of the river is quite broad giving plenty of room to dodge the odd bits of litter and industrial waste that may be found. After passing under the railway near the end the brick walls give way to parkland for the last few hundred metres to the river Eden confluence.
4) W   A final small 30 cm weir just before the confluence. Most will egress above this.

EGRESS
E1)   Many groups finish the trip in Dalston where a road runs down from the village centre to a footbridge and small car park on the green.
E2)   It is possible to egress at Denton Holme weir by walking down the right bank for 100m to a footbridge. This leads to an area where there is parking at the end of Denton Street by Denton Holme School.
E3)   The egress in Bitz Park is found behind the Castle where a road runs down to an area of playing fields and a large car park at the Sheepmount grounds.

RIVER CALDEW 3 (Lower Caldew)

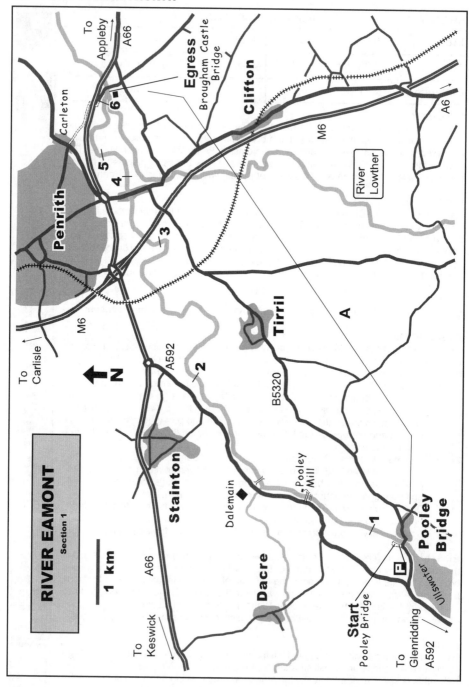

RIVER EAMONT
Section 1

1 km

N

To
Carlisle

To
Keswick

A66

Stainton

Dalemain

A592

Dacre

Start
Pooley Bridge

To
Glenridding
A592

Ullswater

P

Pooley
Mill

B5320

Tirril

1

2

A

River
Lowther

Penrith

To
Appleby
A66

Carleton

6

5

4

3

M6

M6

Clifton

Egress
Brougham Castle
Bridge

A6

EAMONT

The Eamont flows out of Ullswater and is a fairly placid river running through pleasant farmland scenery to join the river Eden near Penrith. Although it drains the second largest lake in the area it still needs a wet spell to make the shallow parts of the first section navigable. At Brougham Castle the river is joined by the River Lowther for the last 7 km to the Eden and this may be possible most of the time.

SECTION 1

From :	Pooley Bridge	469 244	Grade :	I / II
To :	Brougham Castle	538 290	Maps : O.S. 90, Explorer OL5	
Distance :	11 km		Scenery : ❀ ❀	

SUMMARY
A popular introduction to moving water and a pleasant open boat trip. The main hazards are trees overhanging the banks and several weirs which are all navigable with caution. However, in high water these make the whole section quite serious and unsuitable for beginners.

INDICATORS
This is a quite large river fed by Ullswater and can keep its flow for several days after rain. However there are some fairly shallow sections and it is best to check these before a trip is started. The best place to check is at the footbridge and ford to Pooley Mill (GR 476 259). The A592 runs right next to the river here and if it looks navigable the rest of the river will be ok.

START
It is possible to start from the car park on the west bank at Pooley Bridge, or by launching onto Ullswater.

DESCRIPTION
A) I / II The river is quite straightforward at normal levels with occasional small rapids and weirs
1) W The first small weir is only a few hundred metres from the bridge and the two concrete uprights of the central chute are visible from above.
2) W At about 4 km Stainton Island is reached. The left side is clear, whereas the right side has a small weir.
3) W 1 km after passing under the Railway viaduct the river takes a sharp loop left followed by another weir. This is easy angled, but gives a fast slide through some rough water.
4) W A couple of hundred metres below Eamont Bridge there is an awkward weir. This is a sharp drop with rocks at the bottom in places, and can have a strong tow back in high flows. It is difficult to inspect due to trees on the banks.
5) W Now flowing through more open farmland round a long left bend another weir is reached before the river swings back right. This weir can form a stopper across the whole river at certain water levels, and can provide some play potential for the experienced.
6) W The final weir at Brougham Castle is at the confluence with the River Lowther. This can be quite intimidating, but a safe route is usually available down the left channel.

EGRESS
Egress is can be made on the right bank just after the confluence with the Lowther at Brougham Castle Bridge.

RIVER EAMONT 1

Open canoes on the Eamont   *Jim Wilson*

Poling up the Eden. *Jim Wilson*

Low Gill. *Bob Evans collection*

Mosedale Beck.   *Trevor Suddaby*

Mad Mile, Mosedale Beck.   *Trevor Suddaby*

Fighting to keep on the line on Crammel Linn, Irthing.   *Dave Kwant collection*

Picnic Pool, Upper Caldew.   *Stuart Miller*

Lemmings Fall, Upper Clough. *Mark Leicester*

Upper Kisdon Force, Keld Gorge, Swale. *Guy Austin*

SECTION 2

From : Brougham Castle 538 290	Grade :	I / II
To : Langwathby Bridge 566 335	Maps : O.S. 90, Explorer OL5	
Distance : 11 km	Scenery : ✿	

SUMMARY
The river now meanders gently through open fields to its junction with the Eden, and on to Langwathby Bridge with no particular hazards of note. However a point of interest is the legendary Giants Cave. After a long loop to the left a sharp right bend indicates Honeypot Farm. Just after the farm on the left bank look out for the cave in the sandstone escarpment. After the junction with the Eden it is another four kilometres to the egress at Langwathby bridge.

INDICATORS
This lower section of the river is navigable for long periods after rain. If the river looks navigable at Brougham Castle Bridge then the rest will be ok.

START
Start at Brougham Castle Bridge.

EGRESS
Egress just after the metal bridge at Langwathby to the left bank, where a short track leads up to the road by the traffic lights.

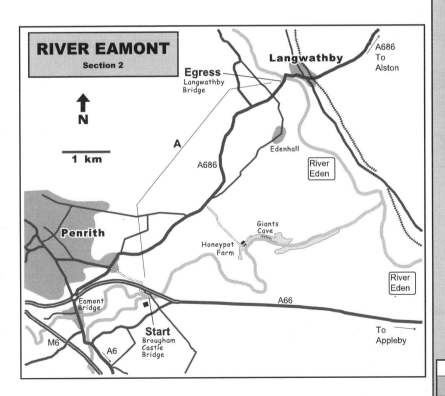

RIVER EAMONT 2

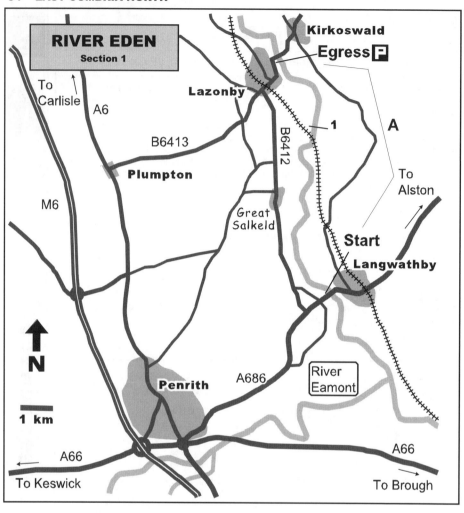

EDEN

Starting high up at Hellgill on the North Yorkshire border this major river flows north-wards for 100 km collecting all the water from the east of the Lake District and the west of the Pennines on its way down the Eden Valley, through Carlisle and out to the Solway Firth. With such a huge catchment most of the river is navigable at any time of the year except in prolonged dry spells or at the upper reaches by the source. Although a complete trip can give an excellent multi day tour, for much of its length the Eden is flat, has access problems, and is of little interest to white water canoeists as it winds its way through prime farmland and zealously guarded fishing grounds. However there are several sections where both access is allowed and the rapids are of interest. The Upper Eden is a spate run at the source above Kirkby Stephen, and this is described in the *East Cumbria South* chapter of this guide.

1) Langwathby to Lazonby. A grade I flat section through farmland, except for a large natural sandstone weir at Eden Lacy.
2) Lazonby to Armathwaite. A section of outstanding beauty with mainly grade I / II water and a few grade III rapids. The best of the Eden.
3) Wetheral Weir. A high water play spot only.
4) Sands Rapid in Carlisle. Inner city boating in surprisingly pleasant surroundings. One small bouldery drop creates a wave train and strong eddy lines in low water, But a useful resource for the local club and testing demo boats from Carlisle Canoes.

SECTION 1

From : Langwathby Bridge 566 335	Grade : I (III)
To : Lazonby Eden Bridge 550 402	Maps : O.S. 90, Explorer OL5
Distance : 10 km	Scenery : ❀

SUMMARY
A flat section of river through pleasant farmland with one river wide bedrock fall to portage.

INDICATORS
If you can float at Langwathby bridge then the trip is possible, but better if all the rocks in the river bed are covered. If the river is bank full or in flood then Eden Lacy Fall will be dangerous.

START
At Langwathby bridge a track on the left bank leads to the river from beside the traffic lights.

DESCRIPTION
A) I (III)   Flat all the way except for Eden Lacy falls.
1) III Eden Lacy falls are found after 6 km, just after a railway viaduct crosses the river. After the viaduct the river bends left, then land to inspect a line on either the far left or far right. The falls are by some sandstone outcrops and are a natural extension of the outcrops forming an undercut river wide sill. This can be quite dangerous in high water but adds a bit of excitement to an otherwise dull trip at normal levels. 200 m after the falls at the next bend left there are some interesting old historical caves in the woods on the right bank.

EGRESS
On the approach to Lazonby the buildings of the swimming pool can be seen on the left bank. Egress a couple of hundred metres below these just before the river begins to steepen for a grade II rapid leading down under the bridge. A scramble up the left bank leads to a car park.

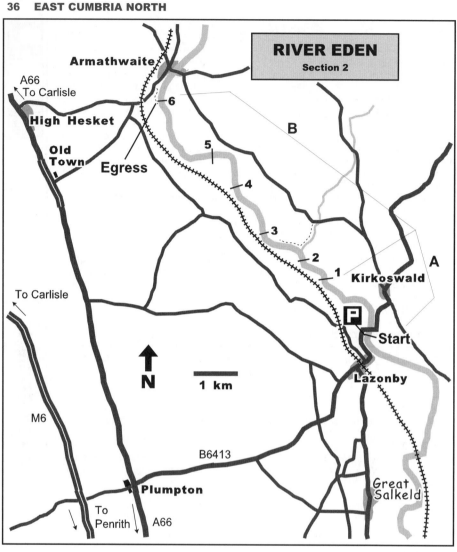

SECTION 2	Lazonby to Armathwaite	
From : Lazonby 550 402	**Grade :**	II / III
To : Armathwaite Weir 503 453	**Maps :** O.S. 86, Explorer OL5	
Distance : 8 km	**Stars :** ✶ **Scenery :** ❀ ❀ ❀	

SUMMARY
Although there is still a great deal of fairly flat water on this section several long rapids spice things up a bit as the river winds it way through a lovely wooded gorge, dotted with sandstone cliffs, offering a scenic voyage through the heart of the Eden Valley. A popular open canoe trip and suitable for beginners as the rapids tend to wash out at higher levels rather than get harder. The access agreement only allows canoeing with prior arrangement or on organised open days, which tend to get quite busy.

INDICATOR
Possible at most levels except in severe drought. If the first 100 m down to the bridge from the put in is a scrape with shingle showing then its not worth getting on. If there is a small surf wave forming near the left bank halfway to the bridge then it is a good mid level and the rapids will be at their best. At high flows all the rapids wash out and the only problem would be recovering swimmers where there are trees on the banks and Armathwaite weir at the end which can grow to the size of a roaring Zambezi raft gobbler.

START
There is car park just before Lazonby Eden Bridge, with access to the bank.

DESCRIPTION
A) I / II The first two kilometres are flat with only a shingle rapid leading to a right hand bend which may contain a few boulders.

B) II / III The river enters tree lined banks with several long but straightforward rapids.
1) II / III An `S` bend signals the first rapid which is between the bends. Rocks on the left of the river can form stoppers and give some playing at certain levels.
2) II   A slight steepening with large sandstone slabs on the left bank gives a narrowing effect which increases the power of the water and forms a nice surf wave at certain levels. Just below here Croglin Water enters from the right through a narrow chasm and a footpath is cut into the sandstone cliff. This is a popular walk to view the waterfalls a short way up from the confluence.
3) II / III A large cliff on the left bank signals the next rapid as the river swings right. The main channel leads through rocks or standing waves near the right bank.
4) II / III A confused section of water with many large boulders.
5) II / III Another slight steepening with most of the water channelled left towards the bottom giving a stopper cum standing wave which many people try to play in but with most being swept quickly on.
6) W   Armathwaite Weir. At most levels this can be shot far right or far left. Left is the safer option, if it is not too rocky, as the right side involves a bold route past a dangerous hole formed by an undercut sill next to the right bank. All the more dangerous for coming at the end of an otherwise easy section, this weir must be treated with great respect and most should stay left to egress above it.

EGRESS
In fact the present agreement is for all to egress above the weir to the left bank close to a stone shed. A path then leads past the shed and through the next field following the fence until a short track leads up to the road at GR 502 457.
Car parking can be a problem here on busy open days, and care must be taken not to block the road at all, or the track on the corner leading to Mill Farm. It is usual to park further south on the road towards the railway viaduct.

RIVER EDEN 2

SECTION 3	Wetheral Weir	
Put In:	Lay By 467 554	**Maps :** O.S. 86, Explorer OL315
	Park and Play	

SUMMARY

A high water park and play spot close to Carlisle. At the right water level this can give some entertainment if you live locally or are passing by.

At low water it can be seen to be made of several channels separated by concrete dividers forming small closed stoppers, and the central channel forms a nice looking green wave. However, the green wave is hard to access and the side channels have concrete blocks like stepping stones just under the surface in the stoppers which make paddling and rolling at best awkward and often hazardous. The weir is better and safer at high water when these features are buried deeply so a river wide wave or stopper is formed.

The weir is easy angled and the stoppers can usually be exited without too much trouble.

INDICATOR

High water is needed to bring this wave into condition, but as the Eden has a vast catchment area and this weir is quite a way down it so stays in condition for a while after rain. Go look as it is easy to see from the road. The man made shelf at the bank by the put in should be covered to give a good level. In low water the stoppers contain blocks just under the surface and are best left alone.

DIRECTIONS

Coming from Carlisle on the A69 towards Hexham turn right just before crossing the Eden at Warwick Bridge, onto the B6263. Follow this road south along the side of the river for 1.5 km to a large lay by just beyond the weir. Park and play, or look and go on your way.

RIVER EDEN 3

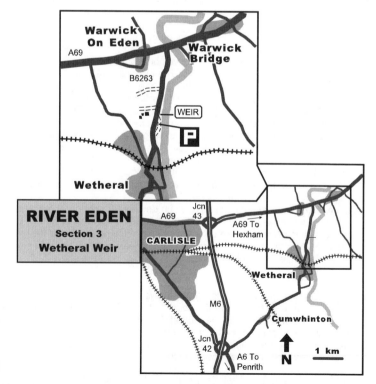

SECTION 4 — Sands Rapid

Put In :	Sands Leisure Centre	Maps : O.S. 90, Explorer OL5
Distance :	100 m	

SUMMARY
This is only really a useful resource due to its inner city proximity and ease of access. The rapid lies in a public park which actually belies its city surroundings. Not really a rapid or a play spot, more of a strong eddy line where the river drops through a small man made shelf of boulders. In low water this produces a 50m section of strong currents which give a good introduction to moving water for beginners. It is also possible when the water is low to do a short tour downstream on flat water below the bridge and then return by paddling back upstream as the flow is so slow.
In higher water the shelf tends to wash out to give some small waves.
Used regularly by the local club, it is also a useful spot to give a quick try out to demo boats from Carlisle Canoes.

DIRECTIONS
From any main road near the centre of Carlisle follow the signs for The North. These will lead you to Hardwick Circus, which is a large roundabout with traffic lights on it just south of the Eden Bridge and next to a large sports and leisure centre `The Sands`. Take the exit off the roundabout which leads to the car park of the Sands centre and park in the car park. Walk around to the right of the centre to a lane at the side which leads to the river. The shelf is about 100m upstream.

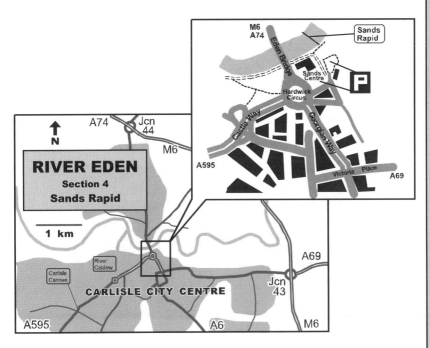

RIVER EDEN 4

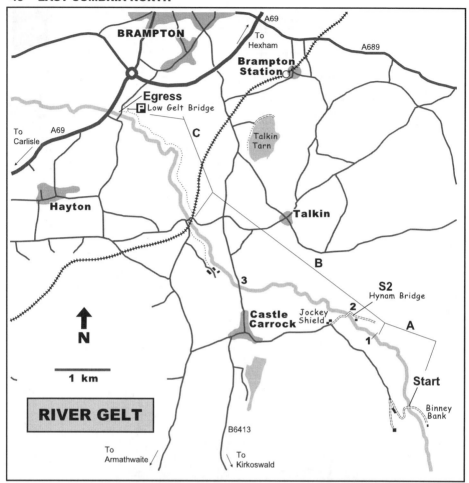

BRAMPTON

A69

To Hexham

A689

Brampton Station

Egress
Low Gelt Bridge

C

Talkin Tarn

To Carlisle

A69

Hayton

Talkin

B

Start

S2
Hynam Bridge

A

2

1

Jockey Shield

Castle Carrock

3

N

1 km

RIVER GELT

Binney Bank

B6413

To Armathwaite

To Kirkoswald

Gelt Pool   *Tom Botterill*

GELT

From :	Binney Bank 571 541	**Grade :**	IV / V
To :	Low Geltbridge 520 591	**Maps :** O.S. 96, Explorer OL7	
Distance :	8 km	**Stars : ✶✶✶** Scenery : ❀❀	

SUMMARY
An exciting, fast and furious spate run through narrow sandstone gorges with some interesting falls and overhanging trees. Love it or hate it, adrenalin is guaranteed due to the lack of eddies and almost certain tree blockages at awkward moments. Survive and it was fun, come to grief and it was nasty. The grade is very much dependent on where the tree blockages occur and what reaction is needed to avoid them. Several gibbering wrecks have emerged from the depths of this run wondering what they have just experienced.

INDICATORS
In places when it is dry the Gelt flows through long narrow gaps only 30 cm wide and looks an impossible boating trip, however when it rains hard it comes up quickly to fill these gaps and create a more feasible run. At its best when bank full, brown and fast but equally at its most dangerous. Still possible at slightly lower levels when it may be easier to avoid trees but some of the gorges will not be as full increasing the pinning potential. A look at the egress will show if its flowing well and if you want to check one of the narrow sections look underneath the road bridge at GR 541 562 where the grade V can be found. At the Hynam Bridge starting point there is a gauge by the weir which should read above 0.90 m for a good level to fill up the gorges.

START
It is possible to put in at the bridge to Binney Bank, which is found at the end of the road into Geltsdale, above Castle Carrock. From the end of the road a track leads down to the river, but parking up here is a problem. An alternative is down a track from a sharp bend at Jockey Shield (GR 555 555), 2 km before the end of the road. This leads to Hynam Bridge and the narrow gorge rapid missing a chance to warm up on the upper beck.

DESCRIPTION
A) III   Fast continuous boulder rapids with tree lined banks.

B) IV / V Continuous rapids with occasional falls amongst narrow sandstone gorges and **constant danger** from trees.
1) III / IV Gelt Pool. This L shaped fall is found 100 m below where the main flow hits a concrete wall and rocky outcrop on a bend.
2) IV / V The river becomes channelled as it passes under Hynam Bridge and over a small weir. A narrow defile follows immediately containing three drops to end in a large pool. The first drop is very constricted and not possible in low water. The whole section should be inspected by landing on the right bank above the bridge.
3) V   Under the road bridge a large block of sandstone guards the entrance to a right angle bend. Recent rock fall has filled the bend with blocks, potential siphons and a nasty stopper. Most will portage on the left along a slippery shelf.

C) III / IV The final gorge through Gelt woods is channelled between smooth sandstone banks where any form of rescue would be problematic. It is best to inspect this for trees before starting by walking up the footpath through the woods from the bottom car park.

EGRESS
A final wave shoots you under Low Gelt Bridge to a possible egress on the right. There is a car park just upstream from the bridge on the right bank.

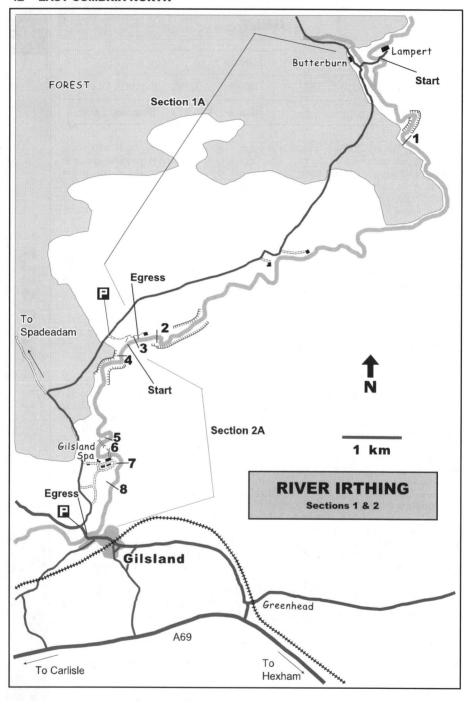

FOREST

Butterburn

Lampert

Start

Section 1A

1

Egress

P

To
Spadeadam

2

3

4

Start

Section 2A

N

1 km

5

6

Gilsland
Spa

7

8

Egress

P

RIVER IRTHING
Sections 1 & 2

Gilsland

Greenhead

A69

To Carlisle

To
Hexham

IRTHING

The Irthing drains a large area of upland forest in the Borders region north of Hadrian's Wall between Brampton and Haltwhistle. It can therefore come up quite quickly and, as it often receives different weather patterns to the central Lakes, it may provide good paddling when the lakes are dry, or vice versa. Starting high in moorland forest it then falls over the mighty falls of Crammel Linn, the largest waterfall in the region, before entering a deep twisting valley for some 15 km. The central section is by far the most continuous and popular part of the river but the sections above and below can be added to give a longer trip.

SECTION 1   Butterburn to Crammel Linn

From :	Lampert Bridge	680 741	Grade :	II, III, (IV) (V)
To :	Crammel Linn	640 696	Maps : O.S. 86, Explorer OL43	
Distance :	11 km			

SUMMARY
Starting off quite flat the river soon enters a small valley as it cuts through a band of rock with a **large fall** at the end. Another long flat section across open moor land follows before the banks rise up again to build anticipation for the **monster falls**.

INDICATORS
Sometimes brought up from rain that sweeps north of the Border the Irthing is in condition more often than may be realised. The best place to get a feel for the level is at Gilsland Bridge. Looking upstream from the bridge all the boulders in the river need to be covered.

START
From Gilsland take the B6318 over the bridge then turn right up the road to Spadeadam. Follow this road to the entrance to the Spadeadam works site, where a turn off right over a cattle grid leads up a hill through forest plantations and soon crosses another cattle grid to enter open moor land. Keep going across the moors, through a section of woods and down a short hill to Butterburn where there is a turn off right. Turn right here and cross the first bridge over the burn to put in at the bridge over the main river.

DESCRIPTION
A) III (IV)(V) Flat to start with the river soon cuts into a small steep sided valley containing some falls before turning west and becoming flat again for several kilometres as the valley sides open out. It begins to cut into the moor land again on its approach to Crammel Linn.
1) IV / V Moss Catherine Waterfall. Soon after the start the river turns sharply left then bends in a U turn back right through a gorge below some outcrops. These 3 m falls are found at the end of the gorge where it bends left again. Shoot a slabby rapid on the corner then get out on the left to inspect and portage.
2) III   As the river winds through the moors an `S` bend signals this 1.5 m shelf which in high water can have a grippy stopper in places to wake you up. Some large boulders follow in the run down to the building which marks the next fall.
3) V   Crammel Linn. The previous rapid is your warning to watch out for this huge roaring drop which follows in a few hundred metres, and is marked by a small building on the right bank. Big and awkward, as an ugly hole guards the obvious main flow on the left. High water, some technical moves and a bold approach allow this to be skirted. Get out in good time to inspect and portage on the right.

EGRESS
As you egress to portage these falls on the right bank a path leads up and across the moors to the road in about 400 m. However most will want to put back in below the falls for the next excellent section.

Gilsland Falls, River Irthing. *Guy Austin*

SECTION 2		Crammel Linn to Gilsland	
From :	Crammel Linn 640 696	**Grade :**	III+
To :	Gilsland Bridge 632 664	**Maps :** O.S. 86, Explorer OL43	
Distance :	5 km	**Stars : ✶✶✶ Scenery : ❀❀❀**	

SUMMARY
An excellent and entertaining section of river with some good rapids through large boulders in an attractive wooded gorge. The pool below the falls provides an atmospheric starting point and the rapids are fairly continuous. Many consider this to be the best grade III in the area.

INDICATORS
Looking upstream from Gilsland bridge it will be at its best in spate and flowing well with all the boulders in the river covered, and when bank full touching on flood it will wash out all the rocky rapids but produce some powerful water, standing waves and extra tree hazards.

START
From Gilsland bridge follow the road to the entrance of the Spadeadam works site, turn sharp right over the cattle grid and up the hill as for section 1. Park on the right 100 m after the 2nd cattle grid, at the start of a footpath which leads in 400 m down to the river, **below** Crammel Linn. If you want to shoot the falls it is an easy contour round left to put in above.

DESCRIPTION
A)   III+ From the pool below the falls the river is immediately flowing through a twisting valley with rocky outcrops and trees along the banks. Several boulder fields produce some technical rapids and at certain levels the water runs into the outcrops which have small undercuts in places. The first kilometre is the most sustained then the river gradually eases towards Gilsland.

4) III+   The first left bend starts a technical route amongst a long boulder field leading back right around the next corner and ends with the main flow heading close to a cliff on the right bank.

5) III   Small rock bands produce rapids down to the first footbridge.

6) III   A diagonal shelf under the second footbridge.

7) W   A very easy angled natural weir can be a scrape in low water.

8) W   A easy angled weir made of pebbles should not be a problem leading round the right side of a tree covered island

EGRESS
Egress to the right bank just above the bridge. There is a large lay by 200 m from the bridge on the left where the road up to the put in turns right.

⇦ Map on previous page

RIVER IRTHING 2

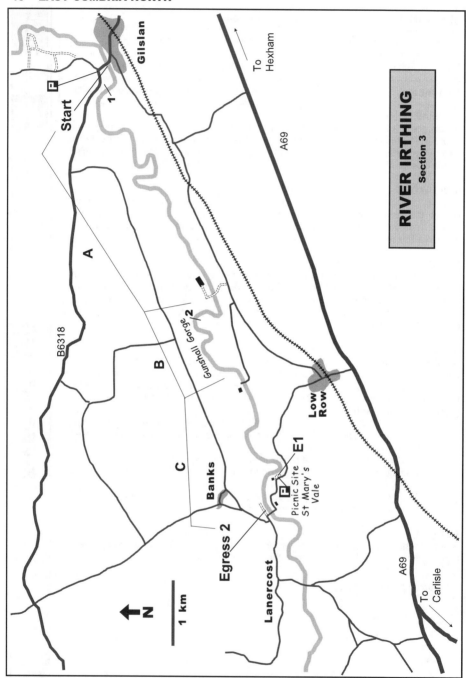

RIVER IRTHING
Section 3

To Hexham

A69

Gilslan

Start

P

1

B6318

A

B

Gunshall Gorge 2

C

Banks

Low Row

E1

Picnic Site
St Mary's
Vale

P

Egress 2

Lanercost

N

1 km

A69

To Carlisle

SECTION 3   Gilsland to St Mary's Vale

From :	Gilsland Bridge 632 664	Grade :	II (III+)

To : St Mary's Vale Bridge 564 639	Maps : O.S. 86, Explorer OL43

Distance :	10 km	Scenery : ❀

SUMMARY
Although the river continues to flow through a narrow valley it has lost most of its gradient and with the exception of two falls it meanders gently, rarely exceeding grade II, through some nice countryside. At normal levels, if the two falls are portaged, it gives a pleasant beginners trip with some strong currents in the Gunshall Gorge. For those who have enjoyed the technicalities of the upper river this lower section may feel a bit tedious, but in higher flows most paddlers will enjoy the two falls and the flat water between should pass reasonably quickly.

INDICATORS
Looking upstream over Gilsland bridge the river should be flowing with all the boulders covered, but bank full will help speed up the flat sections and make the two falls quite fun.

START
Park at the lay by 200 m north of Gilsland bridge, at the sharp bend and road junction on the B6318. Walk back to put on by the bridge.

DESCRIPTION
A)   II (III+)   After the initial fall the river meanders through flat flood planes, fields and woodland with the occasional shingle rapid at the base of a steep sided valley, eventually reaching a long straight with a bridge.
1) III+ Gilsland Falls. 200 m from the start, around the first bend, is a large fall. On the right it is a large step which can develop quite a hole in high water while the left is a longer series of smaller steps. Inspect or portage on the right.

B)   II (III+)   Gunshall Gorge. After the long straight the river bends right then broadens into a wide flat bend back left, before dropping into the gorge. The entrance fall is the only rapid of note but strong currents in the gorge and steep cliffs may hinder rescues.
2) III+ A sandstone shelf and large boulders form this twisting drop into the gorge, producing some powerful water in high flows. Inspect and portage over the boulders on the right bank

C)   II   The last 3 km are straightforward down to St Mary's Vale bridge.

EGRESS
There is a picnic site just under a kilometre upstream from the St Mary's Vale bridge which provides good parking but access to the river is hindered by thick bushes and a small shingle rapid on a corner making egress awkward **(E1)**.
The easiest egress is just upstream of the bridge to a track on the right bank **(E2)**.

RIVER IRTHING 3

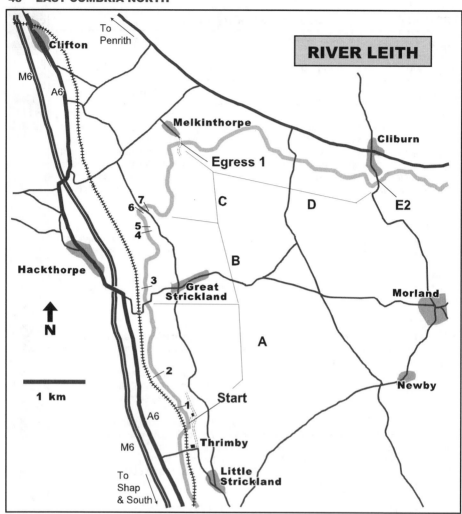

RIVER LEITH

To Penrith

Clifton

M6

A6

Melkinthorpe

Cliburn

Egress 1

C

D

E2

7
6

5
4

Hackthorpe

N

3

Great
Strickland

B

Morland

1 km

2

A

Start

Newby

1

A6

M6

Thrimby

To
Shap
& South

Little
Strickland

LEITH

From : Thrimby Bridleway 558 206	Grade :	III
To : Melkinthorpe 557 250	Maps : O.S. 90 & 91, Explorer OL5	
Distance : 6 km		

SUMMARY
Hidden in a tiny valley alongside the M6 just south of Penrith, this small and isolated beck becomes an entertaining spate run in high water conditions. Some nice rapids, but spoilt somewhat by trees and fences.

INDICATORS
Needs quite a bit of rain but comes up quickly as it is such a small beck. Best place to judge it is the bridge at Strickland Mills, just off the A6, between Hackthorpe and Great Strickland. Needs to be in spate and bank full.

START
Just east of Thrimby bridge there is a bridleway from the sharp corner by some houses which leads down to some barns by the river just below a railway bridge. This is the best place to start as there is a fence directly under the railway bridge above here which is extremely hard to portage in anything but low water conditions.

DESCRIPTION
A) III The run starts off with some fun water through a small tree lined ditch next to the railway line. Some low footbridges and tree blockages add to the interest.
1) III A low footbridge signals the start of continuous rapids through the woods.
2) W A large easy angled sloping weir.

B) III The woods open out and the river relaxes slightly, except for two small drops, but there is still considerable hazard from branches and there are **10 sheep fences** in this section which can cause a lot of hassle. However at the time of writing and in medium water conditions it was possible to avoid any portages by pushing the swinging sections of the fences up and overhead. This practise can not however be safely recommended.
3) F The first of many sheep fences.
4) III Two L shaped falls with fast chutes, complicated by having a sheep fence in between them. This 6th fence is visible from above the first fall and it is advised to inspect before shooting the fall.
5) III The third rapid on this section is a straightforward but fast chute, soon followed by two more fences.
6) F The final two fences are just by the Waterfalls Road bridge, the second of which can be awkward to portage as it is under the bridge with no banks.

C) III More easy but entertaining rapids lead down through a scenic wooded gorge with occasional rocky outcrops to Melkinthorpe. Again beware of tree blockages.
7) F A single strand of barbed wire in the trees just below the bridge could cause problems in high water.

D) I/II It is possible to continue to Cliburn through fields and woods but there are no more rapids

EGRESS
The best egress is to the left bank at the ford in Melkinthorpe, just below the footbridge, where there is parking **(E1)**.
If you continue it is possible to egress to either bank just after the bridge at Cliburn **E2)**.

RIVER LEITH

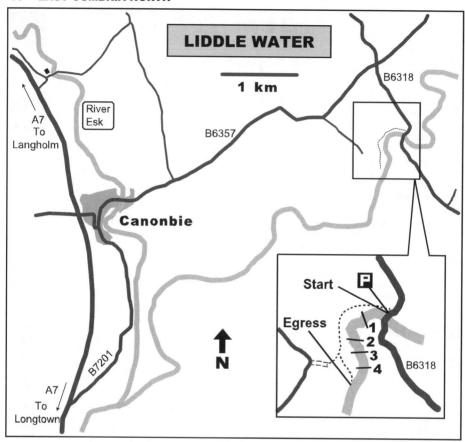

LIDDLE WATER

1 km

B6318

River Esk

A7 To Langholm

B6357

Canonbie

B7201

A7 To Longtown

N

Start

P

Egress

1
2
3
4

B6318

LIDDLE WATER

From :	Bridge 432 774	Grade :	III / IV
To :	End of Rapid 431 770	Maps :	O.S. 85, Explorer 324
Distance :	600 m	Starts : ✷ ✷	Scenery : ✿ ✿

SUMMARY
The true Border river with the right bank in Scotland and the left bank in England, most of the Liddle is flat and hard to access. However this short section is worth a look if you are in the area doing the Border Esk, find good water levels and want an extra thrill. It consists of one good long set of rapids amongst spectacular rock scenery containing several small bedrock falls and boulders which can produce some challenging holes in high water. There are some nasty large rock formations normally above the water line on the right bank to be wary of in flood. This river can also offer a pleasant and easy scenic tour between Newcasleton and Longtown if this section is portaged,

INDICATORS
From the bridge at the start a track follows the right bank of the river to view the whole section. if you have enjoyed a medium to high water run on the Esk then it is worth a look over here but if the Esk is low this probably will be too and not really worth the effort.

START
From Canonbie take the B6357 over the Esk and after 4 km turn right at a crossroads onto the B6318 which soon leads to the bridge. Park at the bridge where there is a small car park for the forest path. Steps lead down from the car park to a sloping slab of rock under the bridge.

DESCRIPTION
A)   III / IV   The whole of this 600 m section cuts through a rocky band producing four small drops and a bouldery rapid amongst strange rock formations and steep cliffs. In low water these are straight forward except the last drop which contains large flakes of rock in the main flow. The grade increases quite dramatically with the water level and it is an awesome sight in flood with all the drops merging into one long rapid with large holes.
1) III / IV The first two drops are just as the river bends left .
2) III / IV A 100 m of flatter water leads to the third drop close to the cliff on the left side.
3) III / IV The fourth drop contains some large vertical flakes of rock as the river twists
      through the rock formations.
4) III   The river suddenly eases off but has a last rush over a bouldery rapid into a
      short narrow gorge between the final cliffs.

EGRESS
Gain the right bank immediately after the last narrow gap to a beach before another broad bouldery rapid leads to flat water. From here a good path leads back up above the cliff on the right bank to join the forest path back to the car park in 650 m.
Beyond here the river is flat, joining the Esk after 6 km and has no other egress until Longtown some 14 km away.

LIDDLE WATER

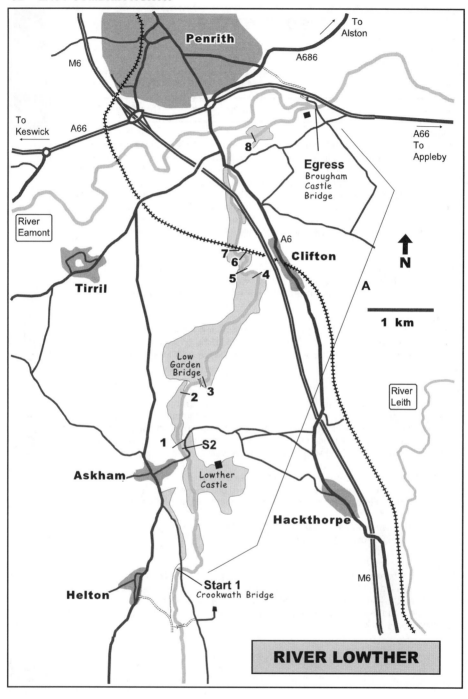

To
Alston

Penrith

M6

A686

To
Keswick

A66

A66
To
Appleby

8

Egress
Brougham
Castle
Bridge

River
Eamont

A6

7 6

Clifton

Tirril

5   4

A

N

1 km

Low
Garden
Bridge

2 3

River
Leith

1   S2

Askham

Lowther
Castle

Hackthorpe

Helton

M6

Start 1
Crookwath Bridge

RIVER LOWTHER

LOWTHER

From : Crookwath Bridge	517 222	**Grade :**	III
To : Brougham Castle	538 290	**Maps :** O.S. 90, Explorer OL5	
Distance :	9 km	**Starts : ✷**	**Scenery : ❀❀**

SUMMARY
The Lowther has quite a large catchment area from the eastern fells around Shap and Haweswater but much of its water is held back by dams and for most of its length it is flat and slow flowing. However the last few kilometres from Askham to Penrith steepen slightly and rush through a beautiful wooded valley in Lowther Park, giving pleasant and fairly straightforward grade II / III boulder strewn rapids.

INDICATORS
Their is a small broken weir just below Askham bridge and if this is navigable then the rest of the river will be ok.

START.
Many people start by parking at Askham Bridge and put into the pool just above the weir **(S2)**. However it is worth starting at further 2 km upstream at Crookwath Bridge **(S1)** for a warm up. At Crookwath Bridge a public footpath leads down to the left bank just above the bridge in some trees.

DESCRIPTION
A) II / III   Pleasant boulder-strewn rapids
1) W   The weir just below Askham bridge is easy angled but cluttered with trees.
2) II   The first island is best past on the left.
3) W   Immediately below Low Gardens Bridge there is a small vertical weir.
4) III   At the end of a caravan site on the left bank the river takes a sharp left bend. There is an island on the bend with a clear route on the right, while the left channel needs a bit of control to steer around shingle banks and a small man made wall. There is a natural shelf just below the island which can be taken anywhere.
5) III   Around the next right bend their is a short slightly steeper rapid.
6) II   Either side of the next island can be taken but there are less tree branches in the left channel.
7) II   Avoid the left channel under the railway viaduct as it is blocked by trees.
8) T   Beware of large trees in the river and take the main channel left of the last island by Brougham Hall farm.

EGRESS
Take out on the right bank just above Brougham Castle Bridge.

RIVER LOWTHER

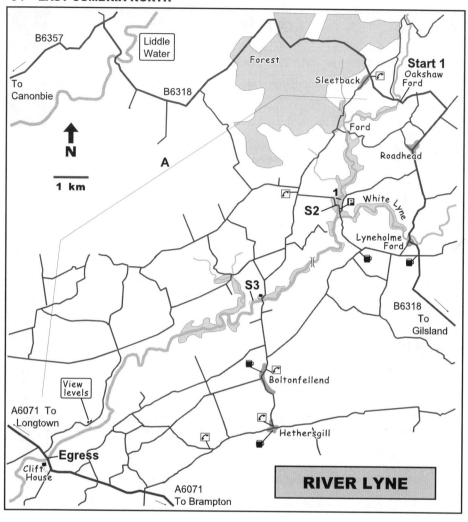

LYNE

From :	Oakshaw Ford	513 762	Grade :	I / II
To :	A6071 Bridge	413 662	Maps : O.S.85/86, Explorer 315/324	
Distance :	19 km		Scenery : ❀ ❀	

SUMMARY
A quiet and remote river that has cut a channel through rich farmland. This is a long easy trip with few access points as the river winds its way along a small wood filled valley beneath the level of the surrounding countryside giving it a great feeling of isolation and commitment. Not many rapids but a few bedrock sills near the start form occasional small stoppers. It is not possible to access the river other than at the points marked as the valley is surrounded by farmland with few roads.

INDICATORS
A difficult one to get right as the river is flat and slow flowing at the egress making it awkward to judge the level. But a good deal of rain is needed to cover the bouldery bed of the river which starts quite small at the put in and grows considerably along it length. If you drive up the minor road on the north side of the river for 2 km there is a grassy track down to the river opposite some cottages GR 426 672. The river here should be flowing and covering the rocks to a navigable level. If its obviously flowing and paddleable at the start without a scrape then the rest will be ok.

START
A maze of small roads lead up to the bridge at Oakshaw Ford **(S1)** on the B6318. There is limited parking here but it is possible to access the river just down stream of the bridge on the left bank via some large concrete shelves.
The next road bridge downstream **(S2)** GR 496 733 which is just above the confluence with the White Lyne gives easier access with parking and is also a better option in low water. However, it misses out the pleasant top gorge and a few rocky shelves. Parking is in a lay-by on the east side of the bridge towards a road junction while a path leads to the right bank of the river upstream on the other side of the bridge.
It is also possible to access / egress the river from the final bridge **(S3)** GR 475 707 for a shorter trip but again there is limited parking and the river can only be gained by following a public footpath for 300 m down the right bank through the gardens of a house and the adjacent field until it reaches the river.

DESCRIPTION ???
A) I / II Initially the river is small and the bedrock channels the water in places and causes small stoppers as drops over occasional steps, but soon the White Lyne joins to double the volume and there is then very little to disrupt the flow on the long journey through the valley. The valley sides drop away to reveal fields only a kilometre above the egress.
1) II A series of small steps with stoppers lead down to the first road bridge.

EGRESS
Egress to the right bank just above the A6071 road bridge where a stile leads up to the road. It is possible to park on the bridge.

RIVER LYNE

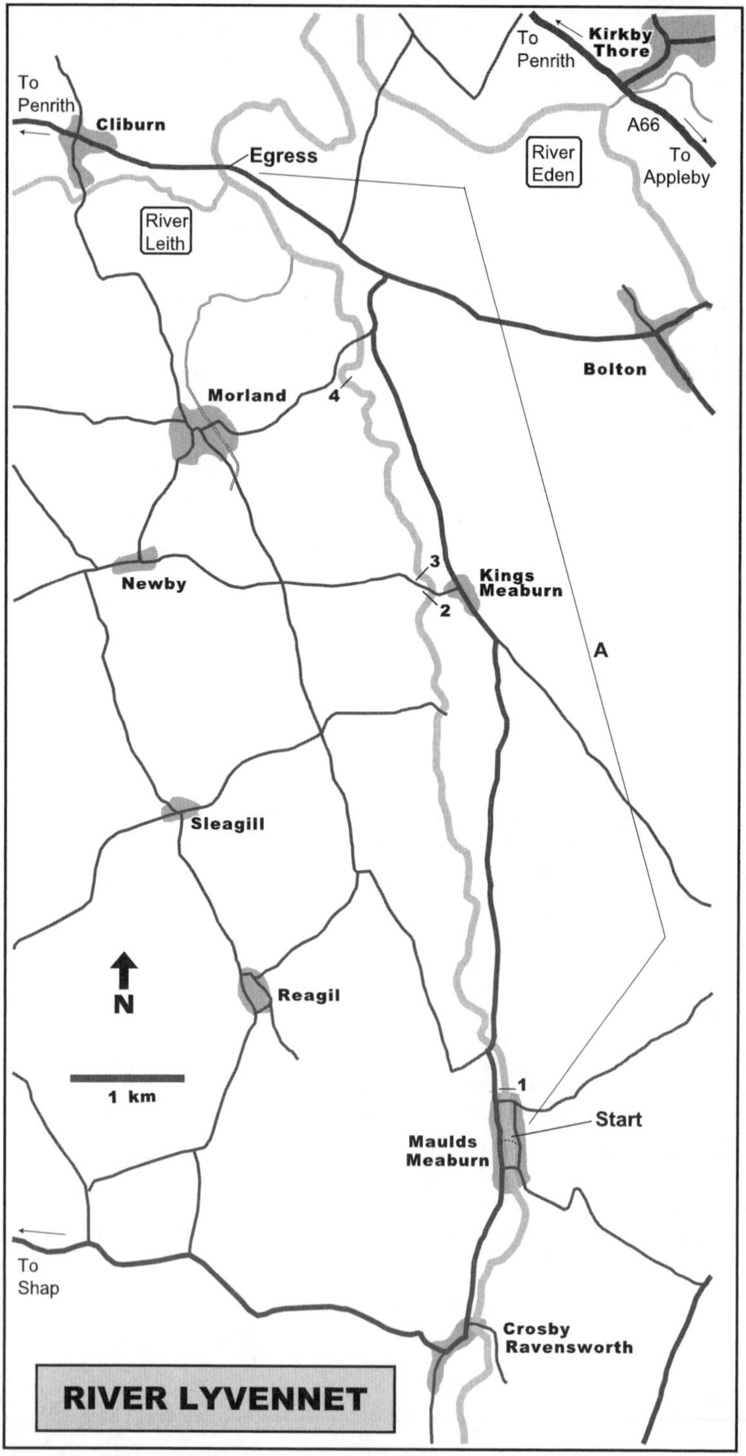

To Penrith
Kirkby Thore

To Penrith

Cliburn

To Penrith

Egress

River Eden

A66

To Appleby

River Leith

Bolton

Morland 4

3

Kings Meaburn

2

A

Newby

Sleagill

↑ N

Reagil

1 km

1

Start

Maulds Meaburn

To Shap

Crosby Ravensworth

RIVER LYVENNET

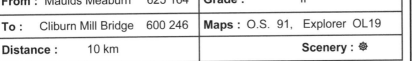

LYVENNET

From : Maulds Meaburn	625 164	Grade :	II
To : Cliburn Mill Bridge	600 246	Maps : O.S. 91, Explorer OL19	
Distance :	10 km	Scenery : ✿	

SUMMARY
A small tributary of the Eden which flows through a pleasant valley with weirs fences and trees to avoid and only possible in high water. More notable for the hidden rural retreats you will discover than any white water action, and therefore really an esoteric diversion for local paddlers.

INDICATORS
If it looks as though you can float a boat at the start it is paddleable.

START
At Maulds Meaburn. Park and start anywhere from the common in the centre of the village. There is an angled weir near a footbridge in the centre of the common, which beginners may wish to avoid.

DESCRIPTION
A) II Nowhere very steep or fast the river passes through farmland and woods with some small but fun rapids and the main hazards being tree branches and fences.
1) W A small weir is encountered shortly after the start.
2) II A ford and small drop at Kings Meaburn
3) II A small wood follows with some pleasant rapids
4) W A large sloping weir near the road at Woodhead farm is normally a simple shoot.

EGRESS
Egress to the right bank at Cliburn Mill Bridge.

RIVER LYVENNET

SUMMARY TABLE

Name of Run	Page	Grade	WW Stars	Scenic Stars	Km	Water	Notes
Belah	61	5	★★★	❀❀	5	High	sustained gorge
Birk Beck	63	4(5)	★★	❀	3.5	High	Big fall
Borrow Beck	65	4(5)	★	❀	7.5	High	fences
Clough - Section 1	67	4	★★	❀	8.5	High	strong stoppers
Clough - Section 2	69	4	★★★	❀❀	6	Med	fun classic
Crookdale Beck	71	4	★	❀	1	High	short & sustained
Dee	73	5	★★	❀	6	High	waterfall gorge
Low Gill	75	4	★	❀	0.3	Med	short & steep
Lune (Upper river) - Section 1	77	2(4)		❀	8	Med	1 off rapid
Lune (Upper river) - Section 2	79	3+	★★★	❀❀❀	8.5	Low	classic mid grade
Rawthey - Section 1	83	5	★	❀	2	Med	hard rocky gorge
Rawthey - Section 2	85	3+(4)	★★★	❀❀❀	10	Med	classic pool drop
Rawthey - Section 3	87	3 (4)	★★	❀❀	6	Med	
Scandale Beck (Ravenstonedale)	89	2		❀	8	Med	many fences
Swale (Keld gorge)	91	5	★★★	❀❀❀	7.5	Med	big waterfall classic
Swindale Beck	95	5+	★★	❀	5.5	High	big fall, hard rapids
Upper Eden - Section 1	97	4	★★	❀	1.75	High	flume ride gully
Upper Eden - Section 2	99	2 (5)		❀	13.5	High	portage danger falls
Wasdale Beck	101	5	★★★	❀❀	2	High	steep & sustained
Whitsundale Beck	103	3	★★	❀	3	High	pleasant gorge

Pearly Gates, River Belah.   *Guy Austin*

RIVERS OF EAST CUMBRIA SOUTH

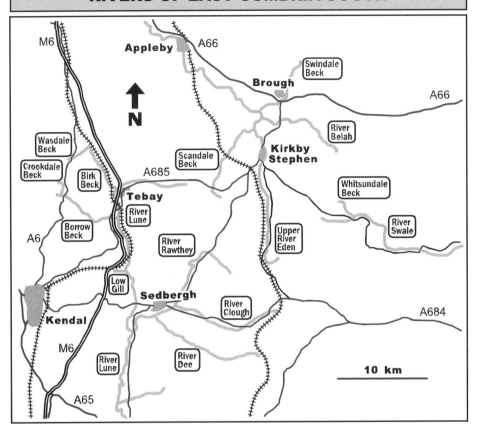

M6

Appleby   A66

Swindale Beck

Brough

A66

River Belah

N

Wasdale Beck

Crookdale Beck

Birk Beck

Scandale Beck

A685

Kirkby Stephen

Whitsundale Beck

Tebay

River Lune

A6

Borrow Beck

River Rawthey

Upper River Eden

River Swale

Low Gill

Sedbergh

River Clough

A684

Kendal

M6

River Lune

River Dee

10 km

A65

Heron

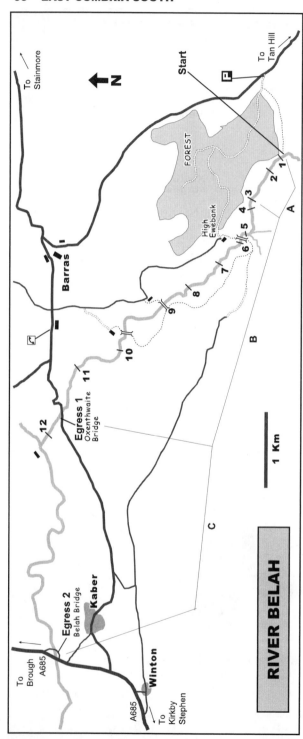

To Stainmore

N

Start

To Tan Hill

P

FOREST

High Ewebank

A

1
2
3
4
5
5
6
7
8
9

Barras

B

10

11

Egress 1
Oxenthwaite Bridge

12

1 Km

Kaber

Egress 2
Belah Bridge

Winton

To Brough
A685

To Kirkby Stephen
A685

C

RIVER BELAH

⇦

continued from opposite page

EGRESS
E1   Egress on the left bank just below Oxenthwaite Bridge.

C) II / III   If you hunger for more you can carry on for another 4 km down to Belah Bridge.
12)   III   There is a fall 300 metres below Oxenthwaite Bridge which slopes into a small drop and which could form a river wide stopper at high levels, then the river continues swiftly through farmland with tree lined banks in places.

E2   Get out between the old and new bridges to a large lay by beside the A685.

BELAH

From :	Woofer Gill Scar 857 090	**Grade :**	IV, V
To :	Oxenthwaite Bridge 824 119	**Maps :**	O.S. 91, Explorer OL19
Distance :	5 km	**Stars :** ✶✶✶	**Scenery :** ❀❀

SUMMARY
A well-kept secret tucked into a remote corner of Cumbria, below the western slopes of Stainmore near Brough. If you get the water right for this remote trip then I hope you're ready, for there is no flat water in the whole section and the central gorge can be one continuous grade IV rapid of over 3 km interspersed with hard falls and constant danger from trees, all in splendid isolation.

INDICATORS
High water is needed to cover the continuous jumble of boulders in the gorge. The best place to judge the level is at the Egress at Oxenthwaite Bridge. Look upstream over the bridge. The river needs to be covering the whole bed across to the bottom of the bridge supports and flowing well. However flood conditions should be avoided due to the high risk of blockages from tree branches and the stoppers on the big falls. An idea if it is flowing can be gained by looking at the river lower down as it passes under the A685, at Belah Bridge, halfway between Brough and Kirkby Stephen. If it looks to be swollen and flowing well here then further investigation upstream is warranted.

RIVER BELAH

START
A high start is made by taking the road to Tan Hill from Brough via Barras. Park at GR 867 093 where a track leads down into the woods by a small stone bridge. Follow the track a short way but before entering the wood head off down the hill following the wall across some boggy ground to join the river as it exits a gorge below Woofer Gill Scar (1 km). The gorge just above this access point could be paddled if the water is high enough but don't worry as there is plenty of excitement below and it will soon feel irrelevant.

DESCRIPTION
A) III A small beck at the start where the water is collected off the moors with some of the water running underground and resurfacing at the first small fall by the barn.
1) F   A sheep fence soon after the start.
2) III   A small fall by a barn.
3) F   A wire fence. This is awkward to spot but lies where a wall comes down to meet the left bank and there is a stile with a small information board. Portage this and then inspect the large fall below.

B) IV (V) A large fall marks the start of the continuous steep descent through the long series of gorges littered with large boulders, several vertical sills of bedrock and trees. 3 km of hard paddling with no respite. With so much rock in here only the larger vertical falls are noted.
4) V   Belah Falls. A big multi tiered 6 m drop with no plunge pools.
5) F   A wire fence at the confluence and entrance to the gorge.
6) III A 2 m stepped fall, just after the footbridge.
7) IV The Pearly Gates. A gap between two enormous boulders shoots over a 2.5 m vertical fall. The following rapid leads to a tree blockage.
8) IV Right Angle Fall. Slabs of mossy rock on river left indicate this awkward fall where the water hits the right wall and turns back onto rocks at the base of the fall.
9) III The next horizon line is a large easy angled chute below Powley Close Bridge.
10) F   A fence made out of metal sheets. Portage
11) IV The last 1.5 m fall should be inspected for lines over the rocky projections.

↩ *continued on opposite page*

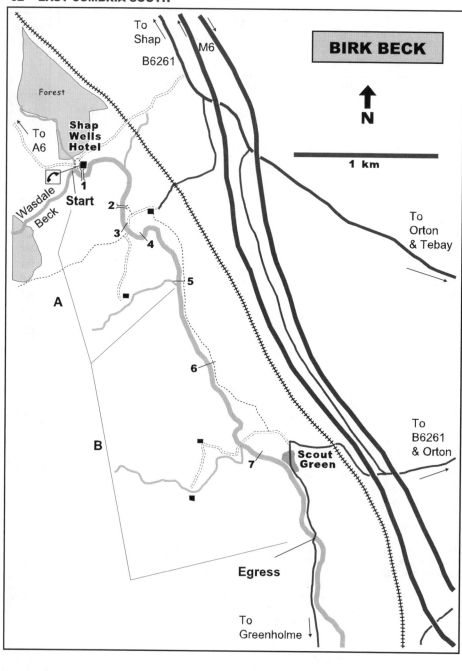

BIRK BECK

N

1 km

To
Shap

B6261

M6

Forest

To
A6

Shap
Wells
Hotel

Wasdale
Beck

Start

1

2

3

4

5

A

6

B

7

Scout
Green

To
Orton
& Tebay

To
B6261
& Orton

Egress

To
Greenholme

BIRK BECK

From :	Shap Wells Hotel 578 095	Grade :	III, IV (V)
To :	Scout Green Bridge 595 071	Maps : O.S. 91, Explorer OL19	
Distance :	3.5 km	Stars : ✶✶	Scenery : ❀

SUMMARY
A nice section of river in a remote tree-lined valley setting. Although much of this run is fairly flat the current remains channelled and swift with surprising power in places. With one **large fall** and two other long stepped falls the interest is maintained to the end, making it a logical addition to Wasdale Beck.

INDICATORS
Wasdale Beck really needs to be running to make this worthwhile. The best place to check the level is at the start by Shap Wells Hotel where Wasdale Beck becomes Birk Beck. The last big fall on Wasdale Beck (seen easily from the road at the hotel entrance) should be well covered, and the wide shallows from the falls to the corner by the road easily navigable.

START
The Shap Wells Hotel is reached from either the A6 or the B6261 just south of Shap. If you get permission from the hotel it is possible to park beside the river at the entrance to the hotel car park. Otherwise park as for the start of Wasdale Beck and run them both.

DESCRIPTION
A) III (V) Negotiate the fence under the footbridge by the put in, which is soon followed by some more debris in the river around the first corner. The river is then straightforward down to a footbridge near a farm where there is a fence which needs portaging. Soon after this it swings left and a single strand of barbed wire has caused problems in the past. Swinging back right the river then enters a tree lined valley with a small stopper on a bend. A straight avenue of trees then runs down to Docker Force, be ready and inspect.
1) F Fence under bridge at start.
2) B Footbridge
3) F Fence at farm.
4) F A single strand of barbed wire may lie hidden around the left bend. Take care as this can cause problems in high water.
5) V Docker Force. A large 4 m drop. The right side is horseshoe shaped and has a shallow landing, while a rocky ramp on the left leads past the stopper into deeper water. Care is needed to make the break out on the lip of the fall as the current is fast and the eddies small. Portage through the trees on the left bank.

B) IV Mostly grade III the river runs through tree lined banks with occasional boulders and two falls which would be awkward to portage.
6) IV A long series of stepped drops, contained between tree lined banks.
7) IV Some angled shelves in the bedrock lead down to a large flat pool.

EGRESS
Just beyond the large pool the houses of Scout Green appear on the left. The road then runs along the left bank for 500m to a bridge. Egress can be made anywhere along here to the road, although the trees and steep bank are probably most easily tackled by the bridge. There is plenty of room to park at the side of the road just beyond the bridge. Below here the river remains flat until its confluence with the Lune at Tebay in 3 km.

BIRK BECK

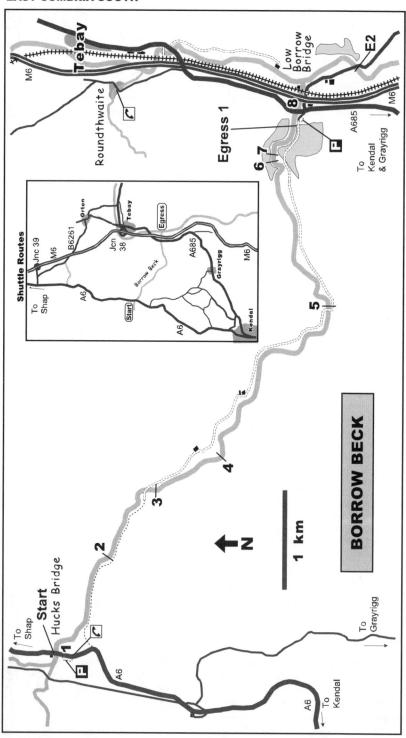

BORROW BECK

BORROW BECK

From :	Huck's Bridge 552 039	Grade :	II, III / IV, (V)
To :	Low Borrow Bridge 606 014	Maps :	O.S. 91, Explorer OL19, OL7
Distance :	7.5 km	Stars : ✱	Scenery : ✿

SUMMARY
Borrow Beck runs from the A6 to the M6 through a remote valley and although there may be no flat water for its whole length, it is really only in the last two kilometres that it starts to get interesting. For most of the way it is one long continuous grade II / III rapid interspersed with fences. Towards the end the rapids pick up a bit and a **difficult fall** signals the start of the final harder run through a wood. The shuttle can be done north or south but seems to take ages either way.

INDICATORS
This needs a lot of rain to make it worthwhile as the first five kilometres would be very tedious if it is not flowing well. Inspect at the start and you really want the bouldery bed of the river to be completely covered.

START
There is a lay by on the A6 only a hundred metres south of Huck's bridge. For a bit of added interest have a look at the short Crookdale beck which flows into the confluence just above the bridge.

DESCRIPTION
A) II / III   The first five kilometres is one long bouldery but straight forward rapid. The only hazards being several fences which need portaging. These tend to occur in awkward places amongst swift water with no eddies.
1)   W   A weir right at the start under Huck's Bridge. Usually presents no problems.
2)   F   Fence
3)   F   Fence
4)   F   Fence

B) IV (V) Below the second bridge things liven up a bit down to the main fall.
5)   III+ Large rocks give a good rapid just below the bridge.
6)   V   The river eases slightly as it rounds a sweeping left bend in the run up to the fall where the river turns right again. Get out in good time to a field with a few trees on the right bank to inspect or portage. The fall has an awkward chute, then piles all the water into a wall.
7)   IV   In high water the short gorge immediately below the fall has some powerful boils and currents. This soon eases slightly but trees can remain a problem to the end.
8)   W   The weir underneath the motorway bridge can have an very strong tow back in high water.

EGRESS
E1)   It is possible to egress to the right bank at the entrance to the track up the valley by a parking area just off the A685 (GR 606 014), and so avoid the last weir. This parking area is found by turning off the A685 just south of where it crosses Borrow Beck.
A staggered cross roads leads west to the parking area and east down under the motorway to Salterwath Bridge.
E2)   Salterwath Bridge (GR 611009) . If you choose to shoot the weir, this alternative egress is 500m after the confluence with the Lune . Egress is to the right bank just after the bridge where a footpath and stile lead back to the road.

BORROW BECK

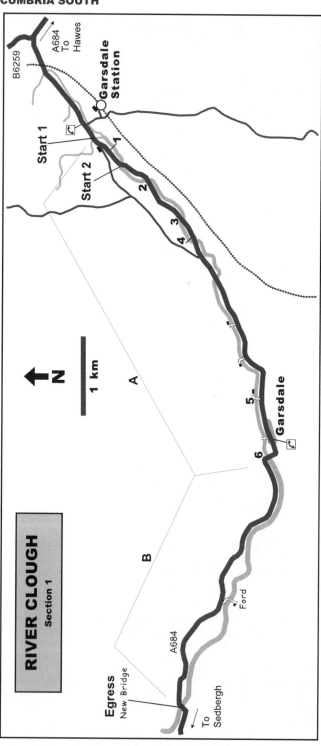

RIVER CLOUGH
Section 1

N
1 km

Egress
New Bridge

To
Sedbergh

A684

Ford

A

B

Garsdale

6

5

4

3

2

1

Start 1

Start 2

Garsdale
Station

B6259

A684
To
Hawes

CLOUGH

The Clough starts above Garsdale Head on the Yorkshire border, only a few kilometres from the source of the Eden. In the 14 kilometres of its course down to Sedbergh it flows over many limestone bedrock sills and through a couple of narrow gorges, giving entertaining paddling for almost its whole length. The upper section is dependent on very heavy rain and contains considerable tree hazards whilst the lower section comes into condition more often and is easily combined with the Rawthey for a good day out.

SECTION 1

From : Garsdale Head	785 918	Grade :	IV
To : A684 New Bridge	713 907	Maps : O.S. 89, Explorer OL19, OL2	
Distance :	8.5 km	Stars : ✶✶ Scenery : ❀	

SUMMARY
This top section of the Clough is characterised by numerous limestone sills forming short vertical drops that give continuous interest and can produce some extremely retentive stoppers in high water. Starting amongst open moor land at first the river soon enters a narrow tree lined valley with the associated problems of blockages and branches. The A684 gives easy viewing and access for most of this section.

INDICATORS
Very heavy rain is needed to bring this section into condition, but there is a fine line between enough and too much. Huge spate makes both the tree and stopper hazard dangerous. As the road follows the river for most of its length a good idea of the conditions can be easily gained. For those who like a marker there is a ford at GR 727 901 which is made of concrete with the water normally flowing through pipes. At paddleable levels the water needs to be flowing over the top of the concrete.

START
In high water the river can be started at Garsdale Head. It flows from the north out of the smaller Grisedale valley and goes under the A684 close to a junction with the old road. It is possible to put in at this bridge which is 200 m below the turning for the station and Cowgill. However the A684 follows the river for most of its length and crosses it above Garsdale some five times giving numerous access points. It can therefore be started almost anywhere you wish depending on the water level.

DESCRIPTION
A) IV Fairly steep and continuous with numerous bedrock falls, bouncy rapids and tree hazards. As this section contains many small shelves only the largest are noted.
1) IV   A large bedrock fall with a series of smaller steps on the left.
2) F   The second road bridge after the start (GR 779 912) has a wire fence. Portage.
3) F   The third road bridge has a single wire that may require portage at certain levels.
4) IV   Lemmings Fall. Below the third bridge the river narrows into a short and exciting gorge ending with a chute over three drops, the last 3m fall being the largest.
5) III / IV After the fifth road bridge the road follows the left bank with a series of three smaller bridges crossing it to properties on the right. Under the third of these minor bridges is another drop, which can be quite grabby in high water.
6) III / IV Another drop under the road bridge in Garsdale.

B) II / III Interesting paddling continues down to the concrete indicator ford. The river then eases for two kilometres to the start of the lower section.

EGRESS
Egress at the New Road bridge or better, continue down the lower section.

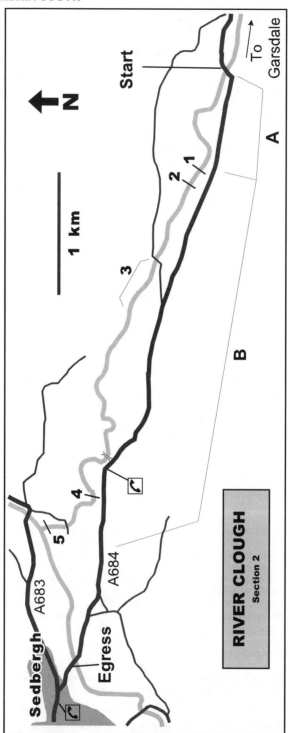

N

1 km

Start

To Garsdale

A

1
2
3

B

4
5

Sedbergh

A683

Egress

A684

RIVER CLOUGH
Section 2

SECTION 2

From :	A684 New Bridge	713 907	Grade :	IV
To : Sedbergh New Bridge		665 919	Maps : O.S. 89, Explorer OL19	
Distance :	6 km		Stars : ★★★ Scenery : ❀❀	

SUMMARY
Below the New Bridge access point this often underrated section of river leaves the road and gives continuously interesting paddling. A great section with several bedrock drops, a boily gorge, some fun rapids and a technical weir.

INDICATORS
Heavy rain is needed but if the Rawthey is flowing this often will be also. At the New Bridge access point there needs to be enough water to float without hitting the river bed. The river is more channelled lower down and so improves. Other places to view the river are at the boily gorge which lies below the bridge on a minor road at GR 698 913, and at Hallbank where the river first meets the road after leaving Sedbergh.

START
Approaching from Sedbergh the first bridge over the river is the New Bridge and start for the lower section. Put in just upstream from the bridge on the right bank.

DESCRIPTION
A) II / III   The first 500 m are flat as the river runs down to a right hand bend before sweeping back left.

B) IV   The river bends right again and runs down a tree lined gorge containing several limestone sills up to 2 m in height which produce strong stoppers in high water. At a bridge a technical rapid leads into a short limestone gorge. Below the gorge continuous rapids keep the interest up all the way down to the confluence with the Rawthey. This is then followed for a kilometre to Sedbergh New Bridge.
1) III / IV   The first sill.
2) III / IV   The second and largest sill.
3) IV   The narrow boily gorge. Beware of an undercut cliff on the left under the
         bridge and other strange rock formations. Also look out for a **strong hole**
         near the bottom.
4) W   The narrow entrance to this large weir hides an easy angled drop but leads
         straight into a pool at the top of a rapid and the stopper may need respect.
5) IV   The final 2 m fall leads straight into the river Rawthey.

EGRESS
Follow the river Rawthey for a kilometre to egress just below the bridge at Sedbergh on the right bank where a path leads to a lay by.

RIVER CLOUGH 2

The Clough Gorge   *Steve Rogers*

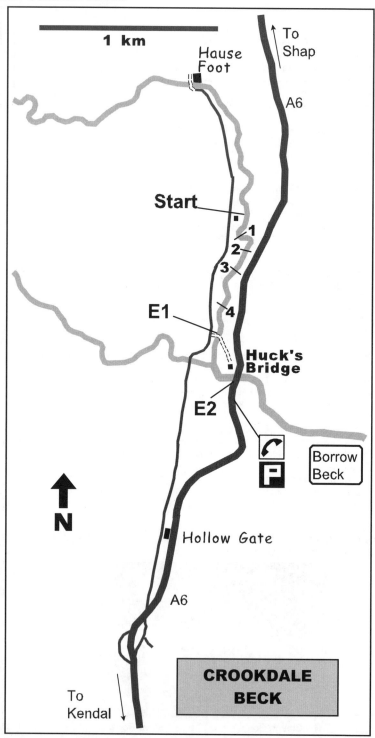

1 km

Hause Foot

To Shap

A6

Start

1

2

3

E1

4

Huck's Bridge

E2

Borrow Beck

P

N

Hollow Gate

A6

To Kendal

CROOKDALE BECK

CROOKDALE BECK

From :	Sheep Fold	553 049	Grade :	IV
To :	Huck's Bridge	552 039	Maps : O.S. 90, Explorer OL07	
Distance :	1 km		Stars : ✶ Scenery : ❀	

IV

SUMMARY
A short steep beck with several narrow rocky falls which gives a good technical start to Borrow Beck.

INDICATORS
Very heavy rain needed for this. The upper reaches can be seen tumbling out of the moors west of the A6 as it climbs the hill north of Huck's Bridge over Borrow Beck. The beck needs to be in high spate and look wild, white and frothy as it comes off the fells.

START
The beck has been paddled from high on the fell by walking up from the end of the road at Crookdale bridge. Although it looks promising from the road, nothing of interest is really encountered until the last kilometre before the Borrow Beck confluence and as the beck passes through a private garden at Hause Foot it should only be paddled from below here for the easily accessible lower gorge.
Either slide down the steep fell side from the A6 to put in at a long flat section just above the final gorge, or drive south from Huck's Bridge on the A6 for 1.5 km to the first road on the right which doubles sharply back to cross Borrow Beck and leads over a hill past the gorge to a flat area. Here the beck comes close to the road without any fences and there is a small stone walled sheep fold.

DESCRIPTION
A)   IV   The beck is fairly flat at first until a small fall leads to a bend left. The beck then bends back right narrows and steepens through 4 falls before calming down to pass under a bridge and join Borrow Beck.
1)   III   The first fall on the corner leads to some boulders in the centre of the river where care is needed due to some protruding old fence posts.
2)   IV   The next two falls merge together amongst the continuous bouldery rapids.
3)   IV   An obvious drop into a narrow slot with back loop potential.
4)   IV   The last fall contains an awkward twisting rocky ramp around an S bend.

EGRESS
Either egress above the bridge **(E1)** across an open field on the right bank to the minor road, continue to Huck' Bridge **(E2)** or carry on down Borrow Beck.

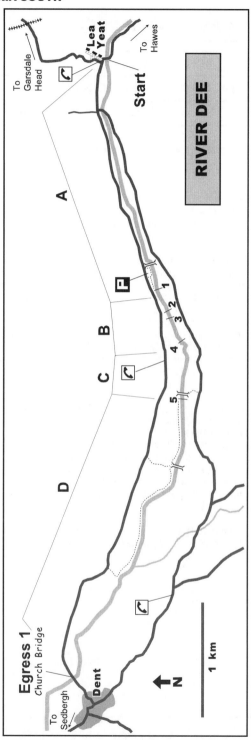

DEE

From :	Lea Yeat	761 868	Grade :	I, II, III, V
To :	Church Bridge	707 872	Maps :	O.S. 89, Explorer OL2
Distance :	6 km		Stars : ✶✶	Scenery : ✿

SUMMARY
A curious river that starts well but soon enters a serious gorge for a short section before easing off completely. The short gorge really needs prior knowledge and inspection by scrambling in dry conditions for a safe descent as there are few eddies or escape routes and a **dangerous fall** that needs portaging. Always an adventure!!

INDICATORS
Heavy rain is required to give high water in the area and start the beck flowing, but not too much is actually wanted in the beck as the gorge becomes a death trap if you can not make the bank below the second fall. The only indicator for this must be prior inspection in dry conditions and your own decision knowing the consequences of what lies in the gorge. The gorge can be found by parking at a lay-by (GR 742 865) close to Ibbeth Peril fall.

START
At the head of Dentdale put in by the bridge in the hamlet of Lea Yeat.

DESCRIPTION
A) III / IV From the start down to the next bridge there are small tight rapids with undercut banks. Below the bridge there are several limestone steps down to where a cliff appears on the right bank just before a footbridge which marks the approach to Ibbeth Peril fall.
1) IV Ibbeth Peril Fall. The fall is a three metre slide into a large pool. Ibbeth Peril Cave is a pothole found in the undercut cliff right of the fall.

B) V The gorge below here contains three large falls of which the middle one requires portaging. Check it is possible to egress immediately below the first fall before committing to the gorge.
2) V The first 2 m fall is 300 m below Ibbeth Peril and contains a protruding shelf on the right and a boily slot on the left. Egress almost immediately to the right bank.
3) X This 3 m fall contains nasty sharp rocks at its base making it a portage. Egress in good time to the right bank where a high mossy shelf leads to a short climb down to the lip of the fall. A ring bolt on the lip aids a further awkward climb down onto rocks below.
4) V The next steepening starts with a narrow slot that needs portaging in low water. This is followed immediately by a short series of steps (with pinning potential) into a large pothole on the lip of the final 4 m fall. The narrow exit channel fires you over this big drop into a deep plunge pool. Inspect or portage on left bank.

C) III The gorge now eases off but boulders and small rock steps give still interesting rapids down to next footbridge.
5) III Just below the footbridge is a last bedrock sill full of channels and potholes.

D) I / II A few more easy ripples down to the next footbridge then all is flat back to Dent.

EGRESS
E1) Egress on the right bank at Church Bridge, Dent.
Below Dent there is 8 km of grade I paddling before a 500 m section of grade III rapids lead past Sedbergh Golf Course and Abbott Holme Bridge (GR 649 658) to a confluence with the river Rawthey .
E2) Abbot Holme Bridge is a possible egress, but parking is a problem here.

RIVER DEE

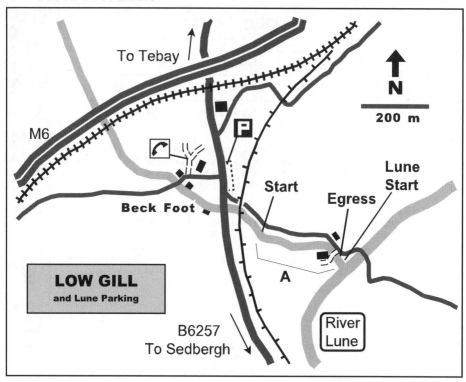

To Tebay

N

200 m

M6

Beck Foot

LOW GILL
and Lune Parking

Start

Egress

Lune
Start

A

River
Lune

B6257
To Sedbergh

LOW GILL

From :	Viaduct	616 964	Grade :	IV	
To :	Lune confluence	619 963	Maps : O.S. 97,	Explorer OL19	
Distance :		300 m	Stars : ✶	Scenery : ✿	

SUMMARY
A short steep little low volume beck which gives an entertaining start to the Lune.

INDICATORS
It needs to have been raining fairly recently to give some flow but too much would make it very serious. Use common sense as always. You will only be doing this on the way down to the Lune put in so, either run it or walk it.

START
Park as for the Lune (Section 2) at the hamlet of Beck Foot. This is found by either driving south on the B6257, off the A685 Tebay to Kendal road, or driving north on the B6257, off the A684 Kendal to Sedbergh road. Park on the verge just above the turning down to the river under the viaduct. Please do not drive down the lane to the Lune as this can cause inconvenience to the residents, especially on busy days, and it is only a short carry. Follow the road under the viaduct and put on 100 m below, where the road meets the beck.

DESCRIPTION
A) IV   The beck soon begins to drop steeply with several narrow falls and slides. After the first short rocky slide the second drop often pins vertically in the main channel on the left, so portage or slide over the less obvious rocks on the right. The next two steepest drops are 2 m each and lead to a split in the beck where a long slide finishes the falls and leads to a bridge. The right side of the slide tends to be more straightforward, as the left channel contains an undercut slot. The bridge may require portaging in high water, but probably not at a level most would consider paddling the beck.

EGRESS
Egress just below the bridge to the left bank, but most will now carry on down the Lune.

LOWGILL BECK

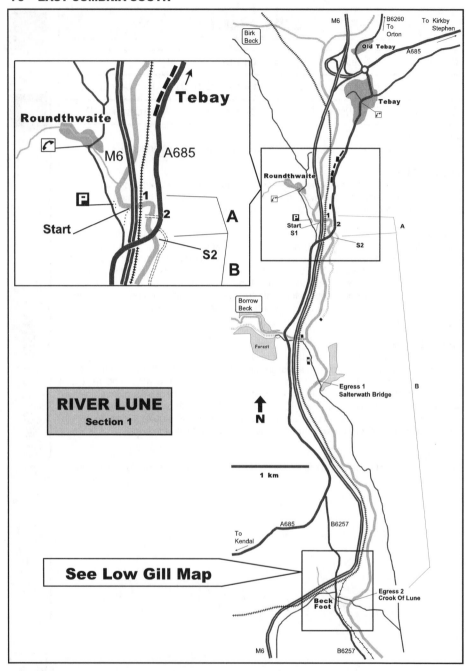

RIVER LUNE

Section 1

LUNE (Upper River)

The Lune is one of the area's big rivers, only beaten in length by the Eden and the Ribble. It flows some 70 kilometres from high in the Howgills down to Lancaster, separating the Southern edge of the Lake District from the Pennines. Being long and flat for most of its length is not the only thing it has in common with these two other great rivers, as prime fishing and farmland are to be had along its banks, making access to parts difficult. Along the northern edge of the Howgills many small streams gather to form the top section of the Lune but the gradient and volume do not really produce anything worthwhile for canoeing until the meeting with Birk Beck at Tebay and the whole lot is then forced through the crowded Tebay Gorge. Here two roads, a motorway, a railway and the river jostle for space in the narrow valley, which has always been an important route from north to south and was guarded in Roman times by a fort at Borrow bridge.

It is through the Tebay Gorge down to Sedbergh where the river loses most of its height and it this part which is of most interest to canoeists, with a good section of grade III rapids and gorges interspersed with a couple of harder falls.

Below here the river enters Lancashire and the lower sections are found in the *North Lancashire and Yorkshire* chapter of the guide. There is a long section of easy touring and just before entering Lancaster the Halton rapids provide a short park and play spot. Below Halton there is a bizarre trip through the centre of Lancaster, which has as its main point of interest a extremely deadly weir to portage, before hitting the tidal waters of the Irish sea for the last few strenuous kilometres to Glasson Dock.

SECTION 1   Tebay Gorge

From : Motorway Bridge 611 029	Grade :	II (IV)
To : Crook Of Lune 620 963	Maps : O.S. 97 & 91, Explorer OL19	
Distance : 8 km	Scenery : ❀	

SUMMARY
All the difficulties here are in the first 500 m with a weir, then a fall and short gorge under the Old Lune Bridge, but things soon settle down for an easy run with occasional boulders. In high water this can pass fairly quickly but most will treat the falls as a one off and then drive to the Crook of Lune for the next section. For those looking for an easy section of river it is possible to put in below the gorge at Lune Bridge.

INDICATORS
This section of the Lune needs recent rain to cover the rocks. It is possible to park at the Old Lune Bridge (GR 613 028) and look over directly at the falls.

START
Access to the river bank by the old bridge is difficult, However a public footpath leads down to the river by the motorway bridge. This is found by following the main road south from the old bridge, crossing the river, railway, and motorway by the new bridge, then doubling back right along the road to Roundthwaite. After 100 m where this road narrows there is a footpath leading over a stile and down to the river just above the motorway bridge **(S1)**. There is parking in a large lay-by 100 m further along the lane. It is best to **inspect the weir** under the railway bridge before you start and possibly put on below this. To avoid the first gorge altogether a steep slope leads down to the river from a track on left bank starting from the new bridge **(S2)**.

DESCRIPTION
A) IV A weir under the railway bridge then leads to the fall under the bridge which you will have had a good look at by now.
1) W The weir under the railway bridge can form a dangerous stopper in high water.

continued on next page ⇨

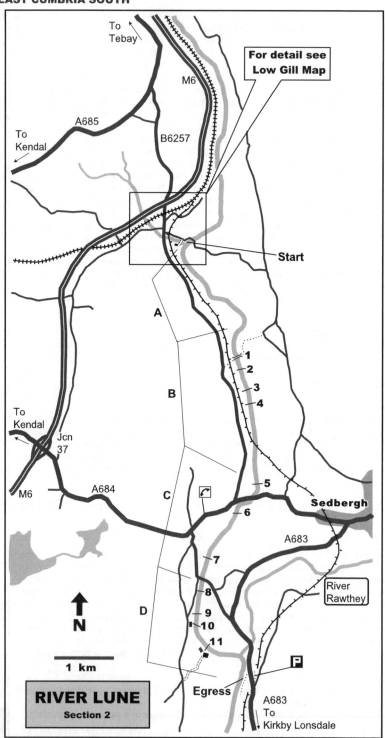

To
Tebay

**For detail see
Low Gill Map**

M6

A685

To
Kendal

B6257

Start

A

1
2
3
4

B

To
Kendal

Jcn
37

M6   A684

C

5

6

Sedbergh

A683

River
Rawthey

7

8

9
10

11

D

N

1 km

Egress

P

A683
To
Kirkby Lonsdale

RIVER LUNE
Section 2

⇨ *continued from previous page*
2) IV Tebay falls contains some narrow pinning rock formations in low water.

B) II From below the new A685 road bridge the river is easy .

EGRESS
E1 Another access / egress point is the right bank below Salterwath Bridge just after the Borrow Beck confluence.
E2 Crook of Lune Bridge. Please see directions for the next section for notes on parking .

SECTION 2   Crook of Lune to Rawthey confluence

From : Crook Of Lune 620 963	Grade : III+
To : Lay-by on A683 630 892	Maps : O.S. 97 & 91, Explorer OL19
Distance : 8.5 km	Stars : ★★★ Scenery : ❀❀❀

SUMMARY
From the Crook of Lune the river steepens again and runs through several narrow gorges in the bedrock giving fairly continuous grade III paddling with a couple of slightly harder falls. This is a brilliant section of river with lovely scenery, entertaining rapids and reliable water levels and is accessible from north or south via the motorway. Unfortunately its popularity has been its downfall over the years and its proximity to the motorway has meant large groups descend on it with little consideration for the environment and property. This has led to overcrowding with severe erosion in places and caused great problems in trying to negotiate access agreements. Please consider coming here in small groups and avoid landing or walking on the banks except in an emergency.

INDICATORS
The river holds its level well and this section can even be paddled several weeks after rain. The narrow gorges are quite fun in low water and if it is possible to float at the put in by the bridge and around the island without scraping too many rocks then the rest will be OK. In high water all the gorges and falls wash out but large boils, strong eddy lines and trees become hazards and Broadraine Weir can become a monster Himalayan style rapid when in flood

START
There is no parking by the river at the Crook of Lune bridge and the local residents have requested that canoeists do not even drive down the narrow lane to drop off boats. So please park at the end of the lane that runs down to the river from Beck Foot above the viaduct, where there is plenty of room on the grass verge, and carry boats down the 400 m to the river. This request does not seem unreasonable when you consider that at times there have been as many as two hundred paddlers on the river. Please respect these wishes to avoid upsetting the sensitive access negotiations. If you find the river busy, consider going elsewhere.

DESCRIPTION
A) II / III The first 1.5 km are a pleasant introduction with shallow rapids and a couple of islands usually taken on the left.

B) III After a large sweeping bend right the river bends back left and narrows as it passes under a footbridge at Hole House. It then becomes channelled into a series of gorges in the bedrock . These are straightforward and don't contain any rocks, but can produce some large waves and unsettling boils. Although intermittent the gorges last for just over a kilometre down to a viaduct.
1) B A footbridge.

continued on next page ⇨

⇨ *continued from previous page*
2)   III   The first gorge is about 100 m long.
3)   III   A chute with play stopper, at lower water levels
4)   III   More gorges.

C)   III+   Just above Lincoln's Inn Bridge is a slightly harder rapid and then about 500 m below it is The Strid.
5)   III+   At normal levels a couple of small shelves with standing waves lead into a narrow slot with a large boulder causing some boily water. At certain levels this can be unsettling and is apparently known as John's Stone.
6)   III+   The Strid. On a left bend the river is wide and begins a rapid over bedrock shelves. It then bends back right and is channelled into a very narrow slot on the right of a river wide reef. This is more technical in low water and has sometimes caused pinning, although it is usually no problem at normal levels. At high water levels a large stopper forms across the whole river. Inspect / portage over reef on the left.
7)   III   Another section through a rocky gorge gives pleasant rapids down to Killington New Bridge, which is often used as an egress point.

D)   III   From Killington New Bridge the river maintains its grade and interest down to the Rawthey confluence, with a couple of weirs and another rocky section which used to be used as a slalom site.
8)   W   100 m downstream from the bridge is a weir. Usually shot far right, but a strong tow back means it is best portaged in high water.
9)   III   A short section of playful rapids lead down to flat water above the next weir.
10) W   Broadraine Weir. This large weir is always awkward to run or portage and has been the scene of many dramas, so get out to inspect in good time. The main weir face is a steeply angled drop with an extremely strong tow back in anything above low water. On the left side of the weir there are a couple of lines which open up at certain levels. Either use a projecting shelf to bypass the main stopper, or go further left down a series of rocky shelves. These lines are hard to spot from the river and there are metal spikes protruding from the river bed in places so caution must be exercised. In very high water this left hand route becomes a good grade IV Himalayan style, big water rapid with massive standing waves and a huge hole which has horrible consequences if you get it wrong but sweet if you hit it right. Inspection and portage of this weir is usually taken over the concrete walls on the right although this is not straightforward either in high water. In low water rocky shelves immediately below the weir may bare their metal spikes. Often called Stangerthwaite weir by mistake. Stangerthwaite is actually the next farm down the river, more appropriately positioned to name the final set of rapids.
11) III   Stangerthwaite Gorge. On the corner below the weir a couple of sloping shelves on the right form playful stoppers before the river enters the final rocky gorge with a series of standing waves which lead down to the Rawthey confluence where the river gets much broader and eases off.

EGRESS
Continue beyond the Rawthey confluence and around the slight right bend for three hundred metres to land in the wood on the left bank. A bridleway leads from here up a track back to the road at a gate just below a large lay by. If in any doubt follow the bridleway down to the river before starting, to find the egress.

Broadraine Weir, River Lune.   *Simon Wiles*

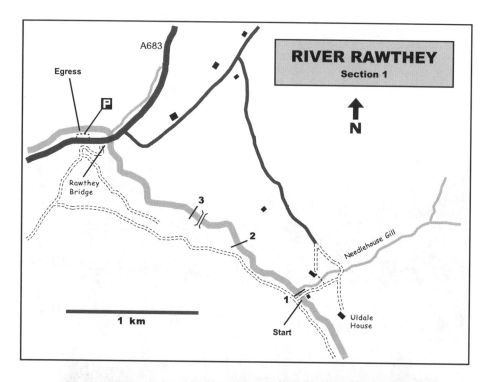

RIVER RAWTHEY
Section 1

Rolling on the Rawthey   *Stuart Miller*

RAWTHEY

A popular and interesting river running along the southern edge of the Howgills. In its higher reaches the Rawthey is a small beck with some large falls and a difficult gorge. Many side streams then add size and volume throughout the main central section, which maintains continuous interest with a variety of falls, rapids and gorges. Below Sedbergh it has grown to become a large and mature river which equals the Lune in its stature.

SECTION 1   Disappointment Gorge

From : Needlehouse Gill 727 967	Grade : III, V / VI
To : Rawthey Bridge 713 979	Maps : O.S. 98, Explorer OL19
Distance : 2 km	Stars : ✳ Scenery : ❀

SUMMARY
Little more than a beck, this section contains the hardest rapids on the river as it runs from the sides of Baugh Fell through some narrow gorges down to the normal starting point at Rawthey Bridge, and makes a worthwhile addition to the standard trip.

INDICATOR
If the river is looking good at the standard put in at Rawthey Bridge and not a scrape then this upper section should be OK as well. However if the river is running **high or in flood then Disappointment Gorge will be a serious grade VI** and is probably best avoided.

START
From Rawthey Bridge carry on up the valley and turn almost immediately right. After a kilometre turn right again and keep going. Where the road forks park considerably and take the left branch through a gate. It leads down to a bridge over Needlehouse Gill and then carry down a bridleway on the left bank of the gill to a bridge on the Rawthey just above the confluence.

DESCRIPTION
A)   **V** Some large falls and a serious gorge before easier rapids to the finish. Trees blockages can be a problem on several of the falls.
1) V   Underneath the bridge at the access point there are a series of steps finishing in a large fall with a powerful stopper. Easier rapids then follow for a short while.
2) V-   A large slide with a drop below it. More easy rapids then lead down to a bridge.
3) V / VI Disappointment Gorge. The stone bridge marks the start and there are four drops in the gorge. The first drop has a very undercut right wall at its base and the exit from the next pool is blocked by a tree. The last drop is the hardest with all the water flowing into an undercut boulder midstream. This should all be inspected prior to entry as it can be a very serious proposition with no break outs in high water.
     Easy rapids then lead to Rawthey Bridge and the normal access point.

EGRESS
Egress is easy back to the main road on the left bank below Rawthey Bridge, but most will want to carry on down the rest of this fine river.

RIVER RAWTHEY 1

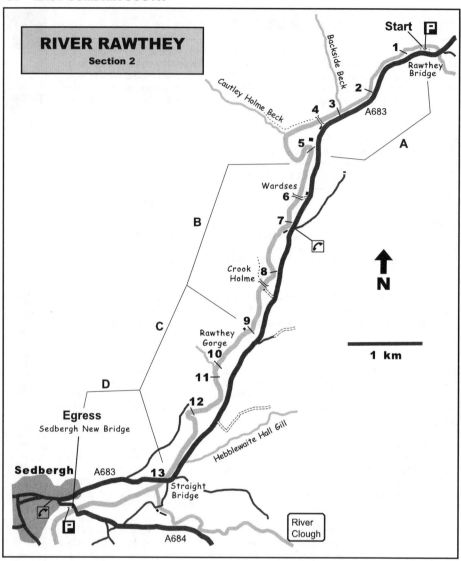

RIVER RAWTHEY
Section 2

Start

Rawthey Bridge

Backside Beck

Cautley Holme Beck

A683

A

Wardses

B

Crook Holme

N

Rawthey Gorge

1 km

C

D

Egress
Sedbergh New Bridge

Sedbergh   A683

Straight Bridge

Hebblewaite Hall Gill

River Clough

A684

SECTION 2	Rawthey Gorges	
From : Rawthey Bridge 713 979	**Grade :**	III, IV
To : Sedbergh New Bridge 665 919	**Maps :** O.S. 98, Explorer OL19	
Distance : 10 km	**Stars : ✱✱✱** **Scenery : ֎ ֎ ֎**	

SUMMARY
A great and popular section of river with continuous and sustained grade III rapids, dotted with several harder bedrock falls. The river falls from the high open countryside near Cautley Spout down through tree lined gorges leading to the Clough confluence and then Sedbergh.

INDICATOR
This river needs recent rain as it rises and falls quite quickly. If you look downstream over Sedbergh New Bridge, at the egress, there is a sand and gravel bank on the right hand side where you get out. If this is covered then it will be a good level. On the way up to the put in the road follows the river for the last 1.5 km and it should be obvious if it is going to be a scrape or a decent level, as this is the shallowest part of the river.

START
Follow the A683 north east from Sedbergh crossing over Straight Bridge. Although close to the road the river is hidden from view amongst the tree lined gorges for most of its length, but becomes open and meets the road again at Cross Keys, where a footbridge leads to a popular path up into the Howgill Fells and Cautley Spout. Continue beyond here, following the river, for 1½ km to a large lay-by 100m below Rawthey Bridge. A steep grassy bank leads down to the river.

DESCRIPTION
A) III+ (IV) At first the river is narrow and rocky with many small drops. A couple of bedrock falls and the addition of more water from two side streams see the river open out for a short shallow section before a large loop leads to it cutting back on itself where with a hard fall it enters more tree lined territory.
1) III+ Soon after the start one of the small drops has a vicious stopper which can back loop boats in high water. It is easy to start above or below this.
2) III+ A wide shallow rocky reef gives a bumpy drop wherever it is taken, and is found next to a bend in the road, from where it is visible on the way to the put in.
3) III+ Backside Beck Fall. Found just below the confluence of Backside Beck this fall usually has a central rock at normal levels with a choice of lines. Complicated rock dodging on the left or a large hole on the right.
4) B A footbridge below where the river becomes broader and shallower with shingle riffle rapids leading past the Cautley Beck confluence.
5) IV Loup Falls. A large loop left sees the river flowing back on itself up the valley before a sharp U turn back right leads straight into this difficult fall. It is a large diagonal 2m drop with three tiers and several lines available. At normal levels a large flat eddy is present on the outside of the bend above the fall on river left, however in high water it may be wise to inspect and portage from river right by landing before the sharp bend.

B) III The river now becomes lined with trees as easier but continuously technical rapids lead down for 2 km to the gorges.
6) B The footbridge at High Wardses. This is used as alternative access in low water.
7) III A large central rock followed by a diagonal stopper at a bend named `In Close`.
8) III A rapid containing sharp rocks leads to Crook Holme footbridge and a small weir formed by a ford.

continued on next page ⇨

RIVER RAWTHEY 2

⇨ *continued from previous page*

C) III+ (IV) A barn on the right bank marks the start of Rawthey Gorge. There are three small falls in the first part of the gorge with continuous rapids in between, and then one harder final fall at the end. Beware of trees, which can sometimes fall completely blocking the river making it quite serious, especially in high water which can increase the grade and become a continuous grade IV. The lower gorge is much easier, but inescapable.

9)   IV   The final fall in the Rawthey Gorge. This is an awkward twisty slot which can be inspected / portaged at most levels on the right.

10)   III   An island is passed on the left.

11)   II / III   The lower gorge starts on a sharp bend left with a fine waterfall cascading from the high right bank. This gorge is lined with steep conglomerate rock and is inescapable but is almost flat with no particular hazards except trees again, which occasionally get trapped.

12)   B   Straight Bridge. This marks the end of the main difficulties and is often used as an egress point in low water.

D) II / III The river then becomes wider and more open as the Clough enters from the left adding yet more water to give a mature feel to the river on the final kilometre.

EGRESS
At Sedbergh New Bridge egress is made to the right bank just under the bridge where a path leads to a large lay-by. Or continue down the next section.

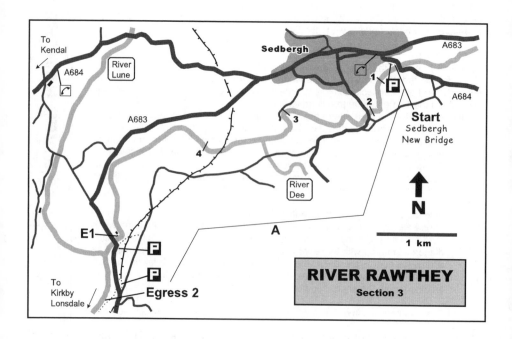

SECTION 3	Railway Falls	
From: Sedbergh New Bridge 665 919	**Grade :**	III (IV)
To : Middleton Bridge 628 896	**Maps :** O.S. 98, Explorer OL19	
Distance : 6 km	**Stars : ✶ ✶**	**Scenery : ❀ ❀**

SUMMARY
Not often done as a separate section in its own right but a very worthwhile addition to the main run with some good rapids and several weirs to negotiate. Most of the interest is in the first 2½ kilometres down to the Dee confluence amongst a scenic tree lined valley as the river by-passes Sedbergh. It then opens out to become broad and gentle with only the final Railway Falls to quicken the pulse before an easy run to the finish.

INDICATOR
If the rest of the river has not been a scrape then this will be OK as well. Although the river is wider the additional water from the Clough and later the Dee compensate for this. Looking downstream over Sedbergh New Bridge the sand and gravel bank at the put in on the right should be covered for a good level.

START
There is a large lay-by at Sedbergh New Bridge where a path leads to the river below the bridge.

DESCRIPTION
A) III (IV) Wide and easy at the start, but the first weir is only 300 m below the bridge. The river then steepens and narrows for a while with interesting rapids lying between two more weirs in the next kilometre. The Dee confluence soon adds even more water for the final broad section through fields, but be ready for the last hard fall beyond the railway viaduct.

1) W   A small vertical weir with an unpleasant fish chute in the middle. It can have a strong tow-back in high water. Easily portaged on the left bank.

2) W   A sharp bend and short rapid lead under a road bridge to this small wooden weir with an outcrop of rock on the right. Usually run without problems.

3) W   Several tight bends and rapids lead down to the final weir on a left bend. The weir is broken and contains wood and spikes, but the river is broad at this point with a clear route usually being available into the grade III rapid which follows it down to a footbridge.

4) IV   Railway Falls. This last rapid lies 500m below the viaduct and varies a lot with water level. An interesting two tier fall in low water becomes an exciting large rapid with a big final hole when in spate. Inspection / portage on the left bank.

EGRESS
After two kilometres through the fields a sharp right bend signals the final rapid down to Middleton Bridge. It is possible to egress, half way down the rapid, upstream of the bridge, on river right where a path leads to the road., and there is limited parking just over the bridge. **(E1)**

If you wish to run the final 50 m of the rapid to the bridge then you must continue on down to the Lune confluence and egress to the bridleway 500 m beyond, as for section 2 of the Lune. **(E2)**

RIVER RAWTHEY 3

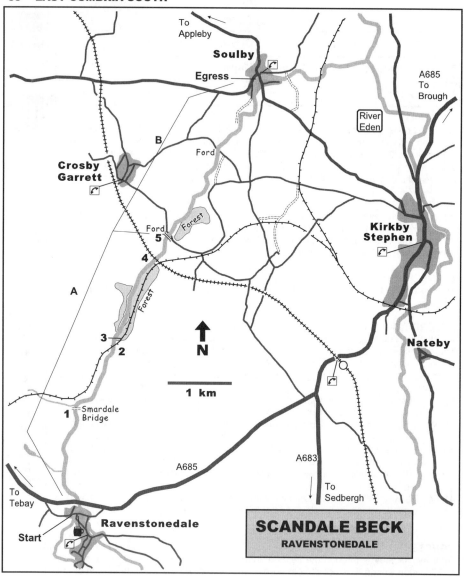

SCANDALE BECK
RAVENSTONEDALE

SCANDALE BECK (Ravenstonedale)

From :	Ravenstonedale	721 045	Grade :	II / III
To :	Soulby	749 109	Maps : O.S. 91, Explorer OL19	
Distance :	8 km		Scenery : ✿	

SUMMARY
One of the source rivers for the Eden, this gives a nice easy grade paddle with occasional rapids through a remote and picturesque valley in a quiet but extremely friendly corner of Cumbria. Unfortunately the run is interrupted throughout by sheep fences and then an abundance of tree branches near the end.

INDICATORS
A good downpour will make this possible in medium spate. However, bank full and near flood conditions will add some much needed interest, producing long series of standing waves in the fast current. This will push the grade up a bit and obviously increase the fence danger requiring quick avoidance reactions. At Soulby the river should really be close to bank full for a good trip. A look at either the start or the finish will give a good idea if it is flowing.

START
Put in at the centre of Ravenstonedale village just above the bridge in front of the Kings Head Hotel is convenient.

DESCRIPTION
A)   II / III   The short section at the start down to the main road bridge is probably the most lively part before the river settles into a straightforward series of wave trains and easy rapids. There are some **8 sheep fences** to portage which makes this otherwise pleasant run a bit tedious. There are also possible tree blockages to watch our for and some single strands of barbed wire.
1)   F   The first of the many fences is just after Smardale Bridge.
2)   F   The fence (4th) under the first railway viaduct is hard to spot but needs portaging on the left, so land in good time.
3) II / III The best sections of rapids are between the two viaducts. But keep a keen eye open for more fences as a couple of them in here are made of wire mesh and are hard to spot.
4)   F   Egress for the fence under the second viaduct in good time on the left bank, where it is necessary to climb up a bit through another arch to portage.
5)   F   A single strand of barbed wire at the first ford is at an awkward level.

B)   II Tree branches start to become a problem amongst the flat stretches. There are also a few single strands of barbed wire between here and Soulby which depending on water levels can be ducked under or paddled over so a good watch is needed to the end.

EGRESS
Egress at the bridge in the centre of Soulby.

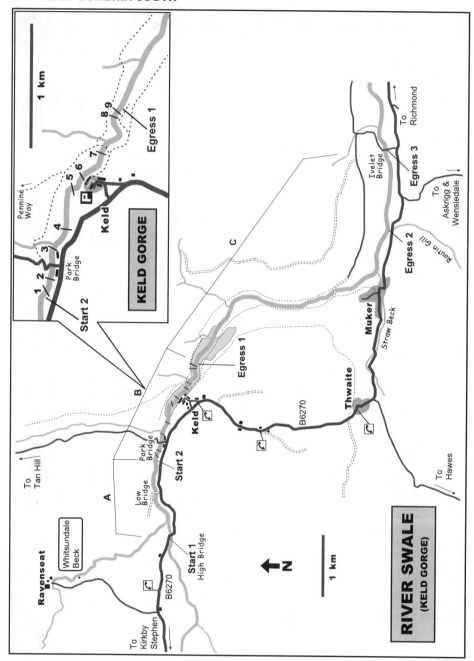

KELD GORGE

RIVER SWALE
(KELD GORGE)

SWALE (Keld Gorge)

From :	High Bridge 871 013	Grade :	III, V
To :	Routin Gill 920 977	Maps : O.S.91/98, Explorer OL19/30	
Distance :	7.5 km	Stars : ✶✶✶ Scenery : ❀❀❀	

SUMMARY

This section of the Swale has appeared in the North East England guide book. It just had to be also included here if for no other reason than it is brilliant and we love it ! However, It is very close to the other becks around Kirkby Stephen, only an hour's drive from the central Lakes, is often possible when other rivers are too low, has fantastic waterfall paddling and is England's answer to the middle Etive. The main part of this run contains 7 large waterfalls within a kilometre and a half of scenic limestone gorge and varies with water levels from a fun plop and drop to a full on scary experience. Only venture forth if you are ready for the challenge as portaging the drops can be as awkward as running them, and I would **not** really recommend this as a grade III paddle with portages as I have sometimes heard it described !!

INDICATORS

To paddle the whole of this section needs quite a bit of rain to bring the river up to middle spate and flowing well to cover the shingle rapids either side of the gorge. However the gorge section can be paddled when the level is slightly lower, with the exception of the large Lower Kisdon Force, as the gorge contains the water well and it is possible to walk back up to Keld after the last fall. The best place to judge the level is Wainwath Force which is right next to the road just above the bridge and road to Tan Hill at GR884 015. If the whole width of the fall is just covered then it is a good middle level with all the falls possible. If there is a good flow covering the whole shelf and the tow back looks strong in places then things will get scary lower down. If parts of the rocky shelf are showing and clear of water but its still possible to get over the shingle rapid out of the plunge pool then it is a low level, Lower Kisdon Force will not be on and a walk back out mandatory.

START

In mid to high flows it is worth starting at High bridge (Hoggarths Bridge) for a bit of a warm up with some shingle rapids down to Wainwath Force. Or even better is Whitsundale Beck, if its flowing, which in high water it should be. In low water it best to put straight on at Wainwath Force.

DESCRIPTION

A)   III   In high flows the shelf just above High Bridge can have a strong tow back, so choose to put in above or below it. The confluence of Whitsundale Beck is soon passed and the river follows the road down to Wainwath Force.

B)   IV / V   Keld Gorge. A beautiful section of river in an atmospheric limestone gorge with seven exciting falls to shoot culminating in the mighty six metre drop of Lower Kisdon Force.

1) IV   Wainwath Force. Strong tow back in places when flowing high.
2) III   Shingle rapids lead into a narrow sculptured gully down to Park bridge.
3) V   Rainby Force. Break out just below the bridge onto slabs on the right to inspect this first big one. The main flow, and the only flow in low water, takes a steep chute on the right onto rocks. However close inspection of these rocks reveals them to be angled at roughly 45 degrees, and if you aim carefully to hit them square on you are sent skittering across the pool below giggling like a loon. Improbable maybe, but much more fun than the slimy climb to portage.

continued on next page ⇨

RIVER SWALE (Keld Gorge)

⇨ *continued from previous page*

4) IV   Not far below is a slightly longer double drop with a twisty line and a nasty protruding rock on bottom left which should be easily avoided.

5) IV   Catrake Force. A large double drop. A steep chute far right on the first drop leads to a huge recirculating eddy which can be hard to escape from in high water. Once escape has been made the second drop goes anywhere and has a bumpy ledge along most of its length.

6) III   Small ledges force most of the flow against a cliff on the left bank.

7) III   A pleasant boulder garden leads down under a footbridge and around the corner below.

8) IV   Upper Kisdon Force. After the boulders the river flattens as it leads to a right bend where the river disappears over a horizon line. Get out in good time to inspect. This top drop has a ledge to avoid protruding in the middle. A meltdown through the main channel on the right sends you way deep, while a line over the far left ledge opens up in high water. This fairly straightforward drop is made more intimidating by the huge lower fall lurking at the exit of the pool below and any rescues should be made extremely swiftly.

9) V   Lower Kisdon Force. The largest and **most serious fall** which is usually portaged. Most of the water on this 6 m fall is channelled down a narrow slot on the left containing a protruding cliff and undercuts, which should be avoided. However, at high water levels a route opens up on the right hand side of the fall with a hard bounce over a 2 m wide ledge half way down. This fall has done plenty of damage to boats, paddles and vertebrae in its time, so be safe. The portage of the fall is also awkward: either climb down slippery rocks on the right or follow the path a short way on the right until a steep gully leads back to the river. Many will choose to finish the trip here and go back up the footpath high on the right which soon leads to Keld.

C)   II / III   3 km of easy but continuous boulder rapids lead down to Muker and the confluence with Straw Beck. 700 m after the confluence another small beck, Routin Gill, joins from the right bank through a patch of trees, and marks the egress.

EGRESS
E1) From Kisdon Force it is possible to climb up to a path on the right bank which leads in 700 m back to Keld (GR 893 011) ,where there is a car park.

E2) On the B6270 a kilometre below Muker the road runs close to the river and crosses a small stream with some trees on the left. This is Routin Gill (GR 920 977), and egress can be made from the river up the side of the stream in only 30 m to the road. There is a lay by 100 m further down the road on the left.

E3) Continue another 1.5 km to Ivelet Bridge.

Rainby Force, River Swale.   *Stuart Miller*

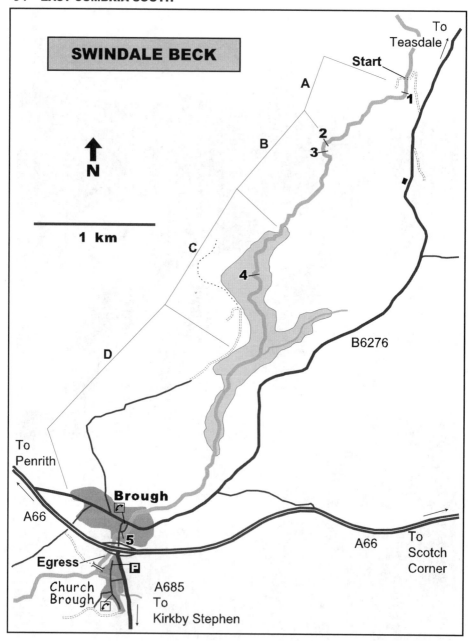

SWINDALE BECK

From :	Ford	818 182	Grade :	III, IV (V+)
To :	Church Brough	793 142	Maps : O.S. 91, Explorer OL19	
Distance :	5.5 km		Stars : ✶✶ Scenery : ✤	

SUMMARY
An excellent beck with a good feeling of adventure as it explores a steep uninhabited valley, with big falls and gnarly boulder rapids, surrounded by trees and rocky outcrops.

INDICATORS
Heavy rain is needed to bring this up and ,as all these small becks, it comes up and down quite quickly. The best place to judge the level is in the centre of Brough village where there is a large sloping weir just above the A685 road bridge. This weir needs to be totally covered with a good flow for the beck to be possible.

START
From Brough take the B6276 Middleton In Teesdale road until it levels off 500 m after a farm called Windmore End. Park at GR 819 179, where a grassy track leads down to the river at a ford. The first and **largest waterfall** is only just below and best inspected before starting to see if you are going to run it.

DESCRIPTION
A) III (V+) The first kilometre is straightforward except for a large fall 100 m from the start.
1) V+   A large double drop of 2 m then 4 m with a tricky line and a small plunge pool. Usually portaged.

B) IV (V) From a second large fall the valley sides steepen and a continuous series of rapids and steps lead down to a short easing where the valley opens out before entering a tree lined gorge.
2) V   The second large fall is a straight 4 m plunge with a large stopper.
3) IV   Continuous rapids and steps.

C) III (V+) Bouldery rapids in the gorge with the threat of rock fall in places from the outcrops followed by danger from trees lower down.
4) V+   On a sharp left bend debris from a landslide forms a nasty set of falls, and the following few hundred metres are ominously overhung by the left bank.

D) III The gradient eases but trees remain a hazard
5) W   The large sloping weir in Brough should be inspected before starting a trip, followed by a short canalled section down to the egress.

EGRESS
Egress is easiest to the right bank just after passing under the A66 dual carriageway. Then walk down 100 m and cross the footbridge to Church Brough. A path leads from a parking area in the village near the school to the footbridge. It may be possible to egress directly to the left bank but it is covered in trees and quite steep in places.

SWINDALE BECK

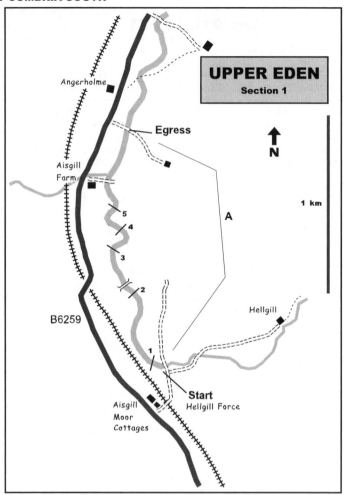

UPPER EDEN
Section 1

N

1 km

Angerholme

Egress

Aisgill
Farm

5

4

3

2

A

Hellgill

B6259

1

Start
Hellgill Force

Aisgill
Moor
Cottages

UPPER EDEN

Below Kirkby Stephen the Eden is flat and uninteresting for many miles down to the Lazonby section described in the *East Cumbria North* chapter, but the first few kilometres from the source in Hellgill on the Yorkshire border down to Kirkby Stephen can give entertaining paddling in high water with the first section although short being a superb rattle down a narrow gorge.

SECTION 1   The Hellgill Flume Ride

From :	Hellgill Force 778 965	Grade :	IV / V
To :	Angerholme 777 981	Maps : O.S. 98, Explorer OL19	
Distance :	1.75 km	Stars : ✶ ✶ Scenery : ❀	

SUMMARY
A short sharp blast in a narrow gorge, with curling waves bouncing off the sides. Cumbria's answer to the Château Queras gorge !!

INDICATORS
Heavy rain needed to bring this up. The river follows the B6259 road almost all the way from Kirkby Stephen so a good idea of the level is easily gained. Inspection of the gorge before paddling is prudent, then decide if it is a level you can handle.

START
The B6259 leads from Kirkby Stephen to Garsdale via the Mallerstang valley along which the Eden flows. Follow the valley up to its highest point just above where it crosses the railway. Park by Aisgill Moor Cottages, where a track leads to the right of the houses crosses over the railway and turns left to a ford at the top of a large waterfall, Hellgill Force. This awaits a descent but the lack of any depth in the plunge pool will probably keep things that way, so make sure to start from the pool below !

DESCRIPTION
A) IV / V   A series of easy angled slabs gradually steepen and lead into the gorge. This is continuously difficult with few eddies and no chance of escape. It is therefore wise to inspect the whole run for any tree blockages before starting, although this is not easy in itself. The only real fall is at the exit from the gorge and this contains some sharp blocks with pinning potential in low water. There is then one last fall after the main gorge before easier water.

1)   IV / V   The start of the gorge
2)   IV / V   The exit fall. This contains rocks which can be a problem at lower levels.
3)   F   A wire fence. Portage
4)   IV   The last slabby fall.
5)   F   A wire fence. Portage

EGRESS
From the last fall continue past the second bridge to where the river splits around a small island. Egress at the bottom of the island where a track leads to the road almost opposite Angerholme cottages.

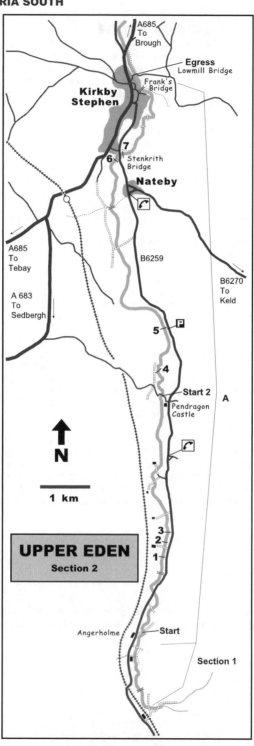

SECTION 2	Mallerstang Valley	
From : Angerholme 777 981	**Grade :**	II (IV) (V)
To : Kirkby Stephen 775 090	**Maps :** O.S. 98, Explorer OL19	
Distance : 13.5 km	**Scenery : ✿**	

SUMMARY
A mostly fairly easy and much neglected run with numerous straightforward shingle rapids through the scenic Mallerstang valley. However there are two **large falls** in the valley which demand caution due to potholes and undercuts and then the **very dangerous fall** under the bridge at Stenkrith which must be inspected before getting on the river and avoided at all costs. Immediately below here a short entertaining rapid then leads down to Kirkby Stephen.

INDICATORS
Heavy rain needed to bring this up. The river follows the B6259 road almost all the way from Kirkby Stephen so a good idea of the level is easily gained and the bouldery bed should look well covered.

START
The river can be started almost anywhere along the valley as the road is never very far away and there are numerous public footpaths and bridges. Its really a matter of deciding how much you want to paddle. Angerholme **(S1)** is the highest access for the easy paddling, where a public footpath opposite the farm leads down to a track to a ford on the river. While Castle Bridge **(S2)** by Pendragon Castle (GR 781 028) gives a good starting point for a shorter 8 km trip.

DESCRIPTION
A) II (IV,V)   Mainly grade II shingle rapids with the occasional fence and a couple of hard bedrock falls which will probably need portaging.
1) F   The first of a series of three fences in close succession.
2) F   A wire with metal sheets.
3) F   A wire mesh fence that may be hard to spot.
4) IV   A jagged bedrock sill produces an angled fall. The main flow is blocked by a tree at the lip but high water allows a bumpy passage on the left. Portage is awkward in very high flows as the river drops into a mini gorge here necessitating a long detour on the left bank.
5) V   A two tier bedrock fall with a big nasty hole at the bottom. Beware of potholes and undercuts. 50 m above this fall a low tree overhangs the river on the right and a concrete pillar on the left act as markers. Egress promptly to portage left.
6) X   Stenkrith Bridge. Portage the horrible fall under the bridge. It is important to walk up the left bank from the bridge to find an egress point before starting as the pleasant looking lead in rapid has no breakouts before suddenly dropping into oblivion. Get out well above the rapid and follow the path down the left bank. Cross the road and follow another path to the bottom of the fall. Either put on immediately for the next good grade IV or walk a further 200 metres down the left bank to where the rapid ends in a large pool.
7) IV   The rapid immediately below the bridge, has one large hole in the middle in low water and turns into a huge roaring roller coaster ride in high flows, with a small playhole at the bottom.

EGRESS
There are several places to egress around Kirkby Stephen, but all have limited parking although there is plenty of parking in the town centre.
Frank's Bridge is a footbridge close to the town Centre, whereas Lowmill Bridge is the stone road bridge just before you leave the town GR 775 090.

UPPER RIVER EDEN 2

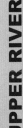

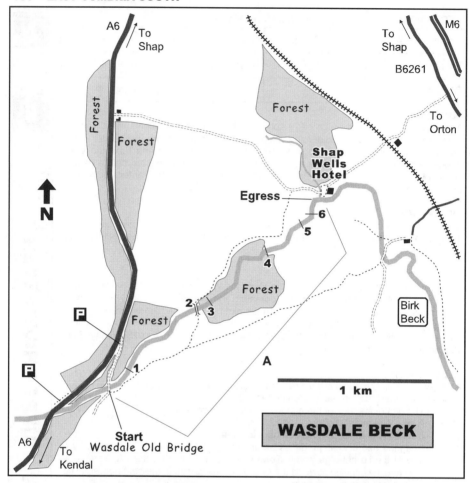

A6
To
Shap

To
Shap

M6

B6261

To
Orton

Forest

Forest

Forest

Forest

Shap
Wells
Hotel

Egress

6

5

4

Forest

2

3

Forest

P

P

1

A

Birk
Beck

1 km

WASDALE BECK

N

A6
To
Kendal

Start
Wasdale Old Bridge

Shap Wells Fall, Wasdale Beck.   *Stuart Miller*

WASDALE BECK

From : Wasdale Old Bridge 564 083	**Grade :**	IV / V
To : Shap Wells Hotel 578 095	**Maps :** O.S. 90/91, Explorer OL07	
Distance : 2 km	**Stars :** ✶✶✶ **Scenery :** ❀❀	

SUMMARY
Although quite short this brilliant beck packs in a lot of clout. If you are up to the challenge and find it flowing then only fools will pass it by without getting on. Or maybe that should be only fools will get on. A very steep and continuous boulder field leads down to a brief respite through the woods before racing down a narrow gorge and over a three tier fall.

INDICATORS
Lots of rain is needed to allow passage around the large boulders. At the start the beck should look in spate and almost bank full. If in doubt walk 500 m down the right bank to view the nature of the boulder field. The final fall at the egress should have all the rocks of the shelves covered.

START
It is best to park just off the A6 where a forest track leads down through a gate to Wasdale Old Bridge. It is also possible to park in a lay-by, 500 m further south along the A6 close to the new bridge over the beck. However getting onto the beck at the new bridge is awkward and immediately a fence has to be negotiated, with only an extra 200 m of grade III rapids down to the old bridge.

DESCRIPTION
A) IV / V   From the old bridge there is about 100 m to get used to the power of the water before the beck tilts dramatically to go up a gear as it tumbles around and over large boulders. Occasional rocky outcrops restrict the flow, and the last drop over a boulder at the bottom has a hidden rock in the pool. A footbridge then a low tree trunk across the river begins a series of pleasant rapids over shelves which lead through the forest before an easier section is reached and a fence at the exit from the woods. A narrow bedrock gorge then leads to a small but **nasty weir** above the final fall.

1) IV / V   Continuous steep bouldery rapids down to the footbridge
2) B   Footbridge
3) F   A fence at bottom of the steep section just after the footbridge has recently collapsed. Beware if it is repaired, but also a low tree trunk in 50 m will need portaging in high water any way.
4) F   Fence and wire at exit from woods. The second single wire to be aware of is only 30 m beyond the fence.
5) W   The narrow gorge section is straightforward but a small nasty weir lurks at its end. Beware of rocks below the centre of the weir which tend to spoil boofs and pin more traditional methods of descent. Portage on the left.
6) IV / V   Immediately below the weir is the run into the Shap Wells Fall. This imposing finale drops 8m over three tiers of slabs and falls.

EGRESS
Egress to the left bank below the last fall and before the corner by the hotel. A fence just around the corner is an incentive not to miss this get out. Or negotiate the fence and carry on down Birk Beck for more waterfall action.

It is usually possible to park at or just outside the hotel car park (best to ask permission and change considerably).

WASDALE BECK

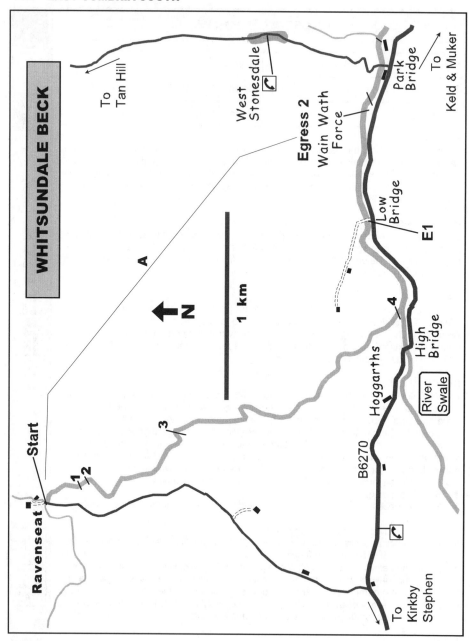

WHITSUNDALE BECK

WHITSUNDALE BECK

From :	Ravenseat	862 033	Grade :	III
To :	Low Bridge	877 015	Maps : O.S. 91, Explorer OL19	
Distance :	3 km		Stars : ✶ ✶ Scenery : ✿	

SUMMARY
This small beck livens up quickly and is much more interesting than first appearances suggest at the put in. Two large but straightforward falls lead to a kilometre of gorge with small shelves, boulders and tight turns. A final rocky rapid spills out into the Swale to which this makes a worthy addition and excellent warm up.

INDICATORS
Heavy rain is needed to bring this up. The best place to see if its running is from the road along the Swale, as it climbs a hill just below the High Bridge put in. The bottom rapid at the confluence with the Swale can be viewed from here and, as it is the most rocky part, if this looks ok the rest will be also.

START
When driving over from Kirkby Stephen to Swaledale there is a road to Ravenseat on the left, opposite a building, and just before a cattle grid where the road steepens. This leads in 2 km to the farm of Ravenseat, where it is possible to put in by the bridge.

DESCRIPTION
A) III Shallow at first, the beck soon narrows and falls over two bedrock steps before the valley sides steepen and it enters a short gorge. Boulders, short rapids and several small weir like steps keep the interest up until the confluence with the Swale.
1) III   The first fall, apart from some bushes on the right, is straightforward although expect to scrape and bounce on the rocky shelves.
2) III   The second fall is similar to the first only a bit bigger at 2.5 m, Again expect to bounce on rocky shelves.
3) III   The start of the gorge.
4) III   This rapid leads to the confluence with the Swale and is visible from the road. A very rocky fall with several lines depending on water level.

EGRESS
Follow the Swale for 500m to egress at Low Bridge **(E1)**, or a further 500 m to just above Wainwath Force **(E2)**.
Much better to continue down the Swale which is probably what you have come over here for.

WHITSUNDALE BECK

SUMMARY TABLE

Name of Run	Page	Grade	WW Stars	Scenic Stars	Km	Water	Notes
Caldew (Upper river)	107	4	★★	❀	3	High	short & sustained
Derwent (Upper) - Section 1	109	4		❀❀❀	2	High	1 fall then boulders
Derwent (Upper) - Section 2	110	3	★	❀❀❀	6	Med	very pretty
Derwent (Upper) - Section 3	111	1		❀❀❀	2.5	Low	relaxing intro
Derwent (Middle)	113	1		❀❀	4	Low	reliable intro
Glenderamackin - Section 1	115	4	★	❀❀	2.5	High	high mountain
Glenderamackin - Section 2	117	2			5	High	too many fences
Glenderamackin - Section 3	119	2		❀	6	Med	
Glenderaterra.	121	4	★★	❀❀	3	High	rocky beck + trees
Glenridding Beck.	123	4(5)	★★	❀❀❀	2.5	High	steep sustained fall
Goldrill Beck	125	2		❀❀	4.5	Med	
Greta (Keswick)	127	3	★★★	❀❀❀	8	Med	popular classic
Keskadale Beck	131	4	★	❀❀	2.5	High	trees
Langstrath Beck	133	4	★★★	❀❀❀	2.5	Med	beautiful pool drop
Mosedale Beck (NE)	135	4+	★★★	❀❀	5	High	Long intense rapids
Newlands Beck.	137	3(4)	★★	❀❀❀	3	High	A mini classic
St John's Beck	139	2		❀	6.5	High	seldom water
Trout Beck (North)	141	4	★	❀	3.5	High	sustained gorge
Wyth Burn.	143	4(5)		❀❀	1	High	short, 1 nasty fall

Final Fall, Langstrath Beck.   *Stuart Miller*

RIVERS OF NORTH EAST LAKES

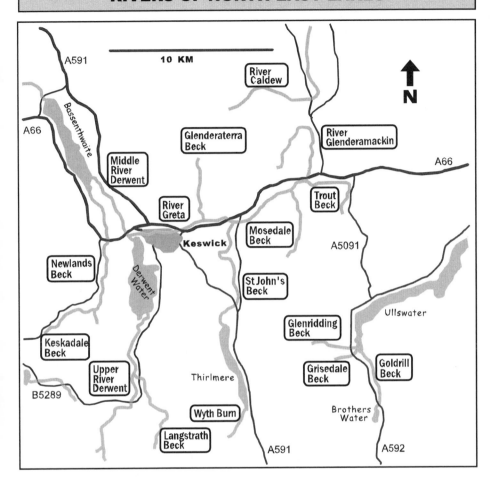

10 KM

A591

River
Caldew

N

A66

Bassenthwaite

Glenderaterra
Beck

River
Glenderamackin

A66

Middle
River
Derwent

River
Greta

Trout
Beck

Keswick

Mosedale
Beck

A5091

Newlands
Beck

Derwent
Water

St John's
Beck

Keskadale
Beck

Glenridding
Beck

Ullswater

Upper
River
Derwent

Thirlmere

Grisedale
Beck

Goldrill
Beck

B5289

Wyth Burn

Brothers
Water

Langstrath
Beck

A591

A592

Herdwick Sheep

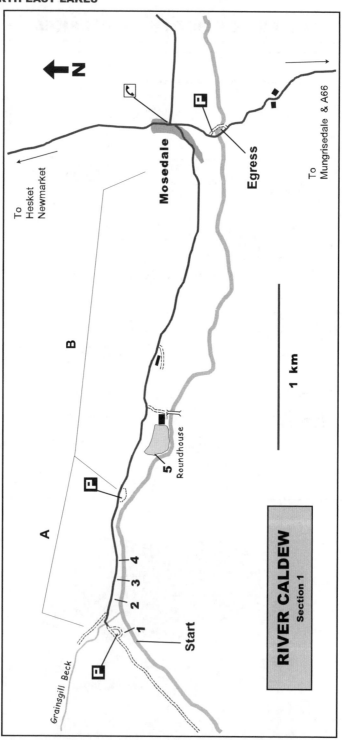

CALDEW (Upper Caldew)

A long river with its source at the Back o` Skiddaw running all the way to Carlisle before joining the Eden. The short top section gives the only major rapids and is an exciting blast in high water, over three falls and sustained bouldery rapids. Parts of the lower river can give good easy grade touring suitable for open boats through pleasant countryside before the rather bleak traverse of the city between red brick walls. The lower river is described in the *East Cumbria North Chapter* while the short top section is described here as it has more in common in both its character and geography to the other rivers of the North East Lake District.

SECTION 1

From :	Grains Gill Beck	327 326	Grade :	IV	
To :	Mosedale Bridge	356 320	Maps : O.S. 90,	Explorer OL5	
Distance :	3 km		Stars : ✶✶	Scenery : ✿	

SUMMARY
A superb blast for the first kilometre with 3 main drops and continuous bouldery rapids giving surprisingly fast and powerful water when in flood. This initial section is right next to the road and can easily be run a second time before the still fast but less hectic lower part to Mosedale Bridge.

INDICATORS
Lots of rain brings this up fairly quickly. Common sense.

START
Drive to the end of the road up Mosedale and park where the road turns into a rough track just after the bridge over Grainsgill Beck.
Put in above the first main fall which is just by the parking spot above the bridge.
It is possible to continue up the rough track for a further 1.5 km to put in higher up but there are no falls of any note.

DESCRIPTION
A) IV   There are three obvious falls in the first 500 m and continuous bouldery rapids for the first kilometre to where the road leaves the river. In high water this whole section runs into one mega rapid and it would be difficult to retrieve a swimmer or boat.
1) IV   Picnic Pool. The first fall is a 5 m slide .
2) IV   A drop into a narrow cleft, guarded by a tree on the left.
3) IV   A 1.5 m drop with a large boulder in the centre on the lip .
4) IV   Continuous rapids round large boulders gradually ease after 500 m.

B) III   From where the road leaves the river the gradient relaxes slightly but remains fast flowing all the way to Mosedale Bridge with low tree branches to be aware of in the lower reaches.
5) III   The only rapid of note is on the first left hand bend as the river passes a wood by Roundhouse Farm.

EGRESS
Get out just after Mosedale Bridge on the right bank.

The next three kilometres are through flat farmland with many fence and tree obstacles which are best avoided. The lower river is worth consideration at a much easier grade from below Linewath and is described in the East Cumbria North chapter.

RIVER CALDEW 1 (Upper Caldew)

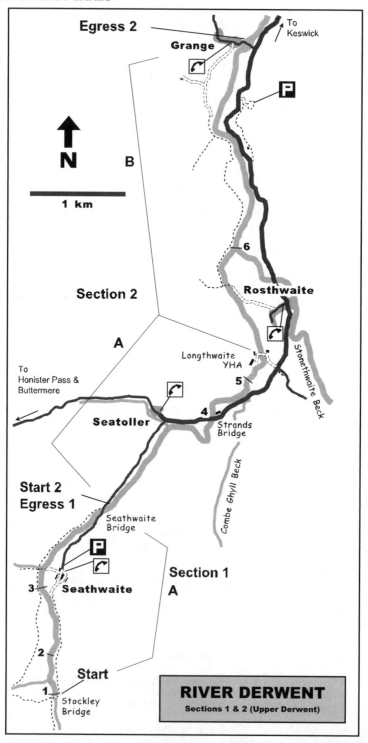

Egress 2

To
Keswick

Grange

P

N

B

1 km

Section 2

6

Rosthwaite

A

Longthwaite
YHA

To
Honister Pass &
Buttermere

5

Stonethwaite Beck

4

Seatoller

Strands
Bridge

Combe Ghyll Beck

Start 2
Egress 1

Seathwaite
Bridge

P

Section 1

3

Seathwaite

A

2

Start

1

Stockley
Bridge

RIVER DERWENT

Sections 1 & 2 (Upper Derwent)

DERWENT (Upper & Middle)

With its source by Great End, high in the central fells and its exit to the sea at Workington, the Derwent at roughly 65 kilometres is the longest of the Lake District rivers. It is also the most varied of the rivers, encompassing in its length: steep narrow falls and beck paddling, beautiful Lake District valley paddling, two lakes, and large lowland river paddling. A trip from source to sea could really not be bettered.

The river is conveniently split into three parts by Derwent Water and Bassenthwaite giving the Upper, Middle, and Lower Derwent, each with a different character and each with different access arrangements. As this river flows through both the northern areas of this guide the Upper and Middle descriptions are found here and the descriptions to the Lower Derwent can be found in the North West Lakes Area of the Guide.

UPPER DERWENT

SECTION 1   Above Seathwaite

From : Stockley Bridge 234 109	Grade : III, IV
To : Seathwaite Bridge 239 127	Maps : O.S. 90, Explorer OL4
Distance : 2 km	Scenery : ✿ ✿ ✿

SUMMARY
Starting high in what is known as the wettest place in Britain this section still needs a lot of rain to make it possible. The fall under Stockley Bridge is an awkward slot which is out of character with the rest of the river and probably not worth the walk unless you have done everything else or you are exploring even higher into Grains Ghyll.

INDICATORS
Only possible in high spate conditions.

START
Park at the road head at Seathwaite farm and carry straight up the valley for just over a kilometre to Stockley Bridge. Start with the crux fall under Stockley Bridge, or put in the pool below.

DESCRIPTION
A)   III / IV   From the main fall the beck runs over a bed of boulders and soon joins Styhead Ghyll to form the Derwent. Another short bedrock rapid leads to more fast and continuous rapids over boulders down to the Bridge at Seathwaite farm.
1)   IV+ The main fall under the bridge
2)   IV- A hundred metres below the confluence there is a short fall on a right hand bend.
3)   W   A small weir shelf made of wire baskets which may have loose strands is found beside the fish farm at Seathwaite.

EGRESS
It is possible to get out at the confluence with Sourmilk Ghyll and follow the footpath from the bridge back to Seathwaite Farm, or carry on to Seathwaite Road Bridge and the next section.

III

RIVER DERWENT 2 (Upper Derwent)

SECTION 2	Seathwaite to Grange

From : Seathwaite Bridge 239 127	Grade : II, III
To : Grange Bridge 253 174	Maps : O.S. 90, Explorer OL4
Distance : 6 km	Stars : ✷ Scenery : ✿ ✿ ✿

SUMMARY
One of the most beautiful sections of river in this guide, and an excellent open boat trip. It starts down a fast flowing corridor between walled banks, twists around some swift but straightforward rapids then eases into a gentle drift through the oak woods of Borrowdale.

INDICATORS
Fairly heavy rain is needed to cover the bed of the river in the channel at the starting point. If this is possible the rest is fine. A trip from Longthwaite Youth Hostel is possible in lower water conditions.

START
It is best to park and start at Seathwaite Bridge.

DESCRIPTION
A)   III   A shallow fast flowing section. The first kilometre is hemmed in by man made walls and the next kilometre is fairly continuous grade II / III- rapids with tree branches possibly causing some problems as far as Strands Bridge. The river then relaxes apart from the main rapid at Longthwaite Youth Hostel.

4)   B   Strands Bridge. Usually no problem except in high water when the low arch can be very low!!!

5)   III   Longthwaite Youth Hostel. Just after the confluence of Comb Ghyll Beck the river bends sharp right and enters a wood. Immediately round this bend is the start of this rapid. The initial drop through a small stopper leads to about 200 metres of bouldery rapids. Nothing nasty but plenty of excitement for those who may find themselves on here as their first grade III.

B)   II   After Longthwaite the river eases to meander through the flat fields and stunning scenery of upper Borrowdale before Stonethwaite Beck joins on the right and a slight steepening in gradient rushes you through the `Jaws of Borrowdale` and the woods down to Grange Bridge.

6)   II   The junction with Stonethwaite beck causes strong currents and eddy lines to catch the unwary.

EGRESS
It is best to egress on the left bank at Grange Bridge, where it is possible to park.

SECTION 3   Grange to Derwent Water

From : Grange Bridge 253 174	Grade : I
To : Kettelwell Car Park 267 195	Maps : O.S. 90, Explorer OL4
Distance : 2.5 km	Scenery : ✿ ✿ ✿

SUMMARY
A flat but lovely part of the river leading to the lake. The open flood plains just before the lake are home to a whole host of wildlife. This section is often paddled in reverse starting from the lake and making headway upstream until the current or shallows force a retreat.

INDICATORS
Fairly recent rain is needed for the first part of this section, the shallowest part of which is visible from Grange bridge. But even in low water it is possible to paddle some way upstream from the lake.

START
There is parking by Grange bridge in front of the Church but this can get very crowded during holidays and weekends

DESCRIPTION
A) I The river is flat all the way to the lake with the possible hazard of tree branches in high water. As the river enters the lake it is possible to cut through a gap on the right before a small island and then head directly to Kettlewell car park.

EGRESS
It is possible to get out on the shores of Derwent Water at several places but the most convenient is at Kettlewell car park.

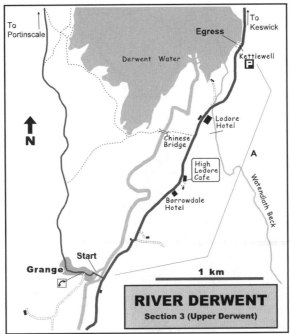

RIVER DERWENT
Section 3 (Upper Derwent)

RIVER DERWENT 3 (Upper Derwent)

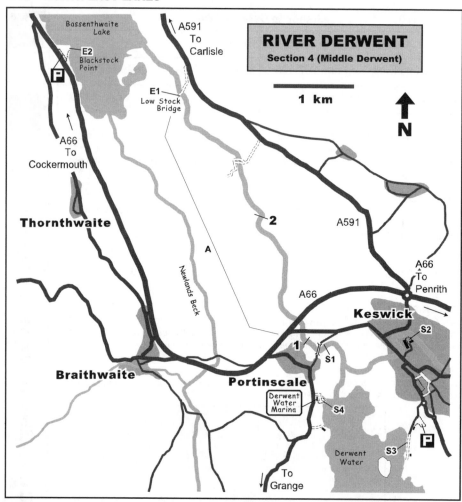

RIVER DERWENT
Section 4 (Middle Derwent)

1 km

N

Bassenthwaite Lake

E2
Blackstock Point

P

A591
To
Carlisle

E1
Low Stock Bridge

A66
To
Cockermouth

Thornthwaite

2

A591

A
Newlands Beck

A66
To
Penrith

A66

Keswick

S2

1
S1

Braithwaite

Portinscale

Derwent Water Marina

S4

S3

P

Derwent Water

To
Grange

Millican Dalton on the Derwent

`The Professor of Adventure`
Originally from Nenthead, near Alston, Millican Dalton was an early protagonist of the outdoor lifestyle. He gave up an office job in the city in 1897, at the age of 30, and came to Borrowdale where he lived in a cave during the summer on the side of Castle Crag. He made a living out of introducing people to rock climbing, sailing and raft building and led many guided trips to Scotland and Switzerland as well as the Lakes right up until his death aged 80. A strict vegetarian who made his own clothes and equipment. He was a caring and patient instructor who famously became known as `The Professor of Adventure`.

MIDDLE DERWENT

The Middle Derwent joins Derwent Water to Bassenthwaite Lake and is possible at most water levels.

SECTION 4 Derwent Water to Bassenthwaite

From : Portinscale Bridge 253 237 or Derwent Water	Grade : I
To : Low Stock Bridge 236 268 or Blackstock Point 222 273	Maps : O.S. 90, Explorer OL4
Distance : 4 km	Scenery : ✿✿

SUMMARY
A fairly flat easy section of river which is often used by groups due to its easy grade, ease of access and reliable water levels. There are many different starting points but it is important to note the egress before exiting onto the lake, as the access agreement for Bassenthwaite Lake requires a permit to be obtained, and a nature reserve to be avoided.
(SEE LAKE ACCESS NOTES).

INDICATORS
Possible most of the year except in severe drought. If there is enough water at Portinscale Bridge then the rest of the river will be OK.

AGREEMENTS AND ACCESS
A good and long standing access agreement is in place which gives me the confidence to publish it, and also in the hope that it may be an example for others. Nothing should be done to jeopardise this.
November 1st - March 1st   Open. No restrictions.
April 1st - - - - - July 31st   Open. Must be off the water by 4 pm.
August 1st - - - October 31st   Closed. No canoeing.
Please note again that **Access to Bassenthwaite Lake is by Permit only** and egress must be made at Low Stock Bridge to avoid this.

START
There are several choices for beginning a trip on this section.
Portinscale footbridge **(S1)** is a good starting point on the river itself and has ample parking on the cul-de-sac leading to the bridge. Leaving Keswick towards the A66 to Cockermouth this is the first road left after leaving the 30 mph area.
It is also possible to start at the Keswick Climbing Wall car park **(S2)** and follow the last easy section of the Greta down to Portinscale Bridge.
However many groups start with a session on Derwent Water before a run down the river. This can be started from the Keswick town boat landings **(S3)** or at Portinscale from Derwent Water Marina, where a launching fee may be charged **(S4)**.

DESCRIPTION
A) I / II There are a few shingle rapids and some sharp bends with strong currents.
1) W A small gauge weir soon after the start usually presents no problems, and soon washes out above low levels
2) I A sharp corner with some exposed old wooden bank support stakes.

EGRESS
E1 - Take out at Low Stock Bridge and walk up the track for 350 m to the A591.
E2 - If you continue to Bassenthwaite then cut straight across the lake to Blackstock Point without deviating back south as their is a nature reserve which is out of bounds below this line. You will also need a permit.

RIVER DERWENT 4 (Middle Derwent)

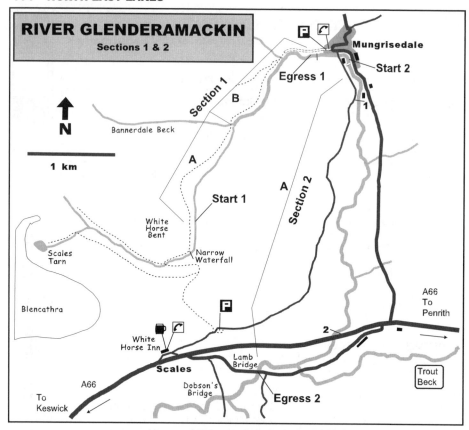

RIVER GLENDERAMACKIN
Sections 1 & 2

Mungrisedale

Start 2

Egress 1

Section 1

B

N

1 km

Bannerdale Beck

A

Start 1

A

Section 2

White
Horse
Bent

Narrow
Waterfall

Scales
Tarn

Blencathra

A66
To
Penrith

White
Horse Inn

2

Lamb
Bridge

Scales

A66

Dobson's
Bridge

Egress 2

Trout
Beck

To
Keswick

Blencathra from St John's Vale.   *J. Harwood 1842*

GLENDERAMACKIN

With its source high up in the heart of Blencathra, at Scales Tarn below Sharp Edge, the Glenderamackin is one of the main feeders rivers to the Greta. It probably deserves more recognition for this than for its canoeing quality but is included for completeness and for the bizarre circular trip which can be undertaken by parking at Scales Inn and combining the first two sections. This gives 8 km of paddling and ends up just below the pub again, at Lamb Bridge, although the steep walk to the start and the many fences on the second section will deter all but the most desperate.

Section three deserves to be more popular as it is a lovely easy grade trip through pleasant scenery, but unfortunately it needs plenty of rain and as most of the banks are lined with trees and reeds it is virtually impossible to land, which can pose problems and make it quite serious for beginners who would otherwise enjoy this section. The whole river is overshadowed by the much more popular, safer, and better Greta.

SECTION 1

From : White Horse Bent 343 279	Grade : III, IV-
To : Mungrisdale 360 302	Maps : O.S. 90, Explorer OL5
Distance : 2.5 km	Stars : ✷ Scenery : ❀ ❀

SUMMARY
Very rarely undertaken this section needs a great deal of water and strong legs. At the start the beck is no more than a metre wide log flume ride, but the second half is a continuous boulder rapid amongst mountain scenery down to Mungrisdale.

INDICATORS
It is best to look at the Egress at Mungrisdale to see if there is enough water covering the boulders.

START.
The start can be reached by a choice of two rather masochistical hikes.
1) On the A66 Penrith to Keswick road there is the White Horse Pub at Scales below the slopes of Blencathra. Turn off to the pub and then follow a small road east around the fell to park at the bottom of Mousthwaite Comb. GR 349 272. Follow the path up the back of the comb and drop steeply down the far side to the beck. Cross the beck and walk down its left bank past a narrow waterfall and two short gorges choked with trees. Put in below the 2nd gorge.
2) The same place can be reached by parking at the Egress at Mungrisdale and walking up the valley following the beck on its true left bank.

DESCRIPTION
A)   III   A log flume ride down the narrow beck with lots of little steps and grassy banks. No break outs but no nasty surprises either.

B)   IV   Halfway down the run Bannerdale Beck enters from the left. This livens things up as the width and volume of the beck doubles, the gradient steepens and many rocks appear. After about 600 m things ease off again on the final approach to Mungrisdale.

EGRESS
Get out onto the left bank just above Mungrisdale after a corner with an eroded bank, as below there is a very low tree branch followed by a weir and then a fence where the beck disappears into the trees and goes through some private gardens, These must all be portaged down to the village hall if you intend to continue on the next section. Parking is found by a phone box on a bend, just after the turning to the pub, where a track leads up the Glenderamackin valley.

RIVER GLENDERAMACKIN 1

Lodore Falls from Derwentwater.   *H. Gastinean 1836*

SECTION 2

From :	Mungrisdale	363 302	Grade :	II
To :	Lamb Bridge	353 267	Maps : O.S. 90, Explorer OL5	
Distance :	5 km			

SUMMARY
An unpleasant section of river which can not be recommended. It winds its way through trees and farmland without much interest except for branches and some 15 fences !! As this is better farmland than canoeing territory it is best to leave it that way and not upset the farmers with the numerous portages necessary to pass the fences. Only included to complete the round trip combined with section 1.

START
Start at the Mungrisdale Village Hall where a small footbridge leads to The Mill Inn.

INDICATOR
Look at the beck at the start in Mungrisdale. If all the boulders are covered here and the beck navigable then the rest will be ok.

DESCRIPTION
A) II A fight with trees is followed by some **15 fences**, including a potentially **dangerous barrier** underneath the A66.
1-2) F 15 Fences between these two points !! Not really worth the hassle.
2) X Their is short canalised section starting with a small weir just before the river goes under the A66. Do not go over this weir as it is then impossible to get out before going under the road and there is a fence in the middle of the tunnel. Portage the whole canalised section on the left bank which necessitates crossing the main road.

EGRESS
Egress at Lamb Bridge, where there is plenty of parking space.

⇦ Map on previous page

Mosedale Beck   *Trevor Suddaby*

RIVER GLENDERAMACKIN 2

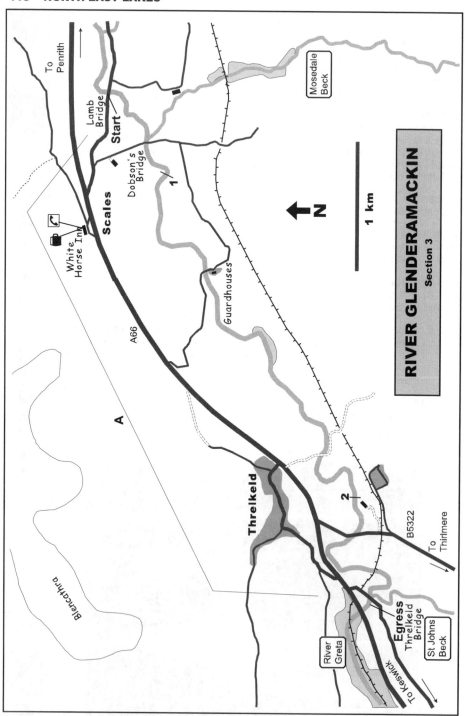

RIVER GLENDERAMACKIN

Section 3

N

1 km

To Penrith

Lamb Bridge

Start

Scales

Dobson's Bridge

1

White Horse Inn

A66

Guardhouses

Mosedale Beck

A

Blencathra

Threlkeld

2

B5322

To Thirlmere

Egress

Threlkeld Bridge

River Greta

St Johns Beck

To Keswick

SECTION 3

From :	Lamb Bridge	353 267	Grade :	I / II
To :	Threlkeld Bridge	314 247	Maps : O.S. 90, Explorer OL5	
Distance :	6 km		Scenery : ✹	

SUMMARY
A pleasant float along through agricultural land with fine views of Blencathra. Although there is only one short rapid much of the banks are lined with reeds and trees giving an air of mystery and seriousness to this section.

INDICATOR
If the river is obviously flowing well at the start then the rest will be ok.

START
Put in at Lamb Bridge.

DESCRIPTION
A) I / II   Mainly flat water between reeds and bushes.
1)   II   After Dobson's Bridge the river swings left then as it turns back right there is a short bouldery rapid.
2)   W   As the river passes close to the housing below Threlkeld Quarry there is a small gauge weir .

EGRESS
Take out on the left just under Threlkeld Bridge where St Johns Beck joins to form the

`The Tunnels of Doom`, Naddle Beck ?   *Stuart Miller*

A bit of detective work for you! BUT be warned, If you do find these tunnels that the left tunnel is littered with iron spikes, hidden in the dark, which hold wooden groins in place and are responsible for pinning and wrecking boats. Then again keep central and you may survive !!!

RIVER GLENDERAMACKIN 3

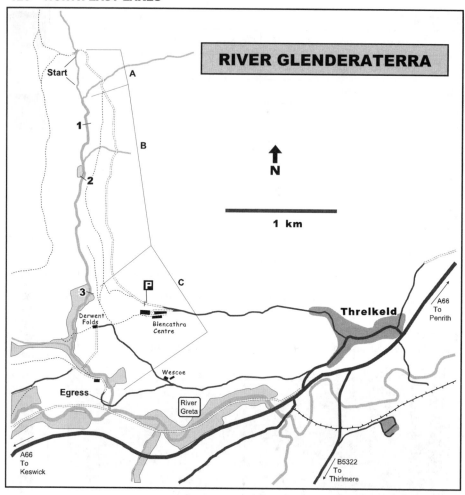

GLENDERATERRA

From :	Footbridge 296 278	Grade :	IV
To :	Greta Confluence 299 247	Maps : O.S. 90, Explorer OL4	
Distance :	3 km	Stars : ✶ ✶ Scenery : ❀ ❀	

SUMMARY
A steep beck with two distinct sections. The start lies on open fell in a dramatic steep sided valley between Blencathra and Skiddaw, and is a continuous helter skelter of twisting rocky rapids. The lower section flows through dense woodland, where easier rapids are constantly interrupted by low and fallen trees. Extreme care is required on both sections as portages become necessary at awkward moments with no eddies. The top section is very enjoyable if caught in the right water level, and escape is possible before the lower jungle!

INDICATORS
Heavy rain is needed for this little gem. The best place to judge the flow is at the egress. If their is a good covering over the boulders here it will be OK higher up.

START
From Threlkeld Village a road runs north west to the Blencathra Centre. Park just beyond the centre in a car park (GR 302 256). From here you must carry boats along the track which contours round to the head of the valley (2.5 km). It is possible to start at a footbridge where the track meets the beck but it is more usual to slide down the grassy bank from the track to start just below this steep section.

DESCRIPTION
A) IV The first 200 m are incredibly steep and contain many sharp rocks. An exceptional amount of water needs to be flowing for this to be possible and there is still a great potential for pinning .

B) IV Continuous rapids demand constant vigilance.
1) F As the beck passes some old mine spoil heaps watch out for a steel pipe which blocks most of the route at certain water levels.
2) F As the gradient eases slightly watch out for a fence at the end of a small wood on the right bank. Below the fence trees begin to line both banks making it more serious.
3) X Just before entering the main forest there is a short section canalised between concrete with no eddies and a fence across it at the bottom.
Make sure you get out above this **perfect trap** to portage .

In high flows of water and adrenalin it is probably best to escape now to a footpath on the left bank which leads back up to the track and the car park.

C) IV Otherwise prepare to run the gauntlet of trees. This needs lots of inspection round fallen trees and blind bends down to the bridge and road at the confluence with the Greta.

EGRESS
The egress is found by following a small lane which leads to Westcoe and Derwentfolds a few hundred metres west of the road to the Blencathra Centre.
At Westcoe turn off left and follow the lane towards Brundholme. There is parking for a couple of cars at the bridge over the Glenderatterra by the confluence with the Greta. Alternatively the Greta can be joined and followed to Keswick.

GLENDERATERRA BECK

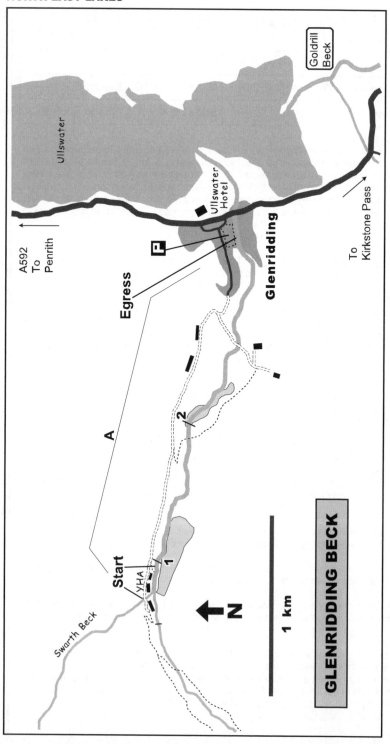

Ullswater

A592
To
Penrith

Ullswater
Hotel

Goldrill
Beck

To
Kirkstone Pass

Glenridding

Egress

P

A

Swarth Beck

Start

YHA

1

2

N

1 km

GLENRIDDING BECK

GLENRIDDING BECK

From :	Youth Hostel	366 174	**Grade :**	IV ,V
To :	Car Park	386 169	**Maps :** O.S. 90,	Explorer OL5
Distance :		2.25 km	**Stars :** ✷ ✷	**Scenery :** ❀ ❀ ❀

SUMMARY
An exciting, steep, hard bouldery run which needs plenty of water to bring it into condition. It contains two contrasting hard sections of rapids, the first of which is the steepest in the area on a section of open crag and has the feeling of falling off the edge of the world ! The second is in the woods and contains a couple of narrow chutes and awkward turns.

INDICATORS
An difficult run to get just at the right level for all the sections. The two harder sections get very serious when there is a good level for the rest of the run. However it is possible to run the whole section in moderate high water, when there must be a good flow covering all the rocks in the channel by the car park at the egress. Only experience and judgement can tell if you wish to run the top rapid at this level.

START
As you approach the youth hostel, on the road, the Edge of the World rapid is obvious on the left. Start just above or below this rocky fall. Do you feel lucky, punk ?
If there is enough water flowing then there may also be enough to start the run in the Youth Hostel Cat Park by putting into Swarth Beck which tumbles down the hillside from the right. Launch into the pool below the bridge and ricochet down the rocks hitting the occasional bit of water to join the main beck in one hundred metres

DESCRIPTION
A) IV (V)   The whole of this beck is fast, rocky and continuous with no part less than grade III and no flat water. However most of it can be run on sight except the two main rapids mentioned below.
1)   V   The Edge of the World. The run in to this rapid is very dramatic. A small mini gorge with vertical walls concentrates the mind as the fell sides drop away before being spat into the void. Close inspection reveals that this 20 m fall is actually made up of many small drops each with a tiny plunge pool. Stay left after the first drop and be ready to drop into a couple of the slots sideways.
2) IV   Underworld. As the beck enters the wood just after the footbridge there is a drop blocked by a boulder. There are narrow slots either side of the boulder and this should be inspected to make your choice. Shortly after another small drop leads to a rocky slide with a choice of lines.

EGRESS
Egress is made directly to the car park in the centre of Glenridding.

`Edge of the world`,
Glenridding Beck.
Stuart Miller

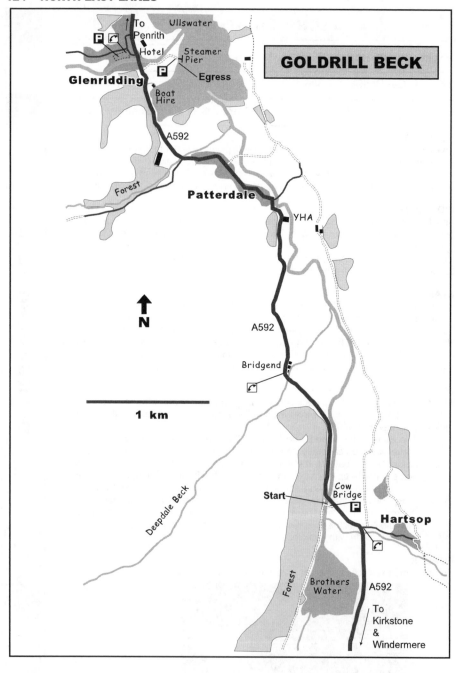

GOLDRILL BECK

To Penrith

Ullswater

Hotel

Steamer Pier

Egress

Glenridding

Boat Hire

A592

Forest

Patterdale

YHA

N

A592

Bridgend

1 km

Deepdale Beck

Start

Cow Bridge

Hartsop

Forest

Brothers Water

A592

To Kirkstone & Windermere

GOLDRILL BECK

From :	Cow Bridge	402 134	Grade :	I / II
To :	Steamer Pier	390 169	Maps : O.S. 90,	Explorer OL5
Distance :		4.5 km		Scenery : ❀ ❀

SUMMARY
This beck joins Brothers Water to Ullswater and flows slowly and calmly through beautiful scenery with occasional tree lined sections. There are no rapids but a few sections between wooded banks. The best bit about this river are the magnificent surroundings with the finish on Ullswater.

INDICATORS
The river can be viewed from the A592 as it runs alongside the road near the start at Cow Bridge. If it looks navigable here the rest will be OK.

START
The river can be accessed directly from the car park at Cow Bridge.

DESCRIPTION ???
A) I / II Nice place, nice scenery, gentle paddling.

EGRESS
It is best to finish on Ullswater and paddle across to the Glenridding Steamer pier where there is car parking .

Goldrill Beck   *Thomas Allom 1838*

GOLDRILL BECK

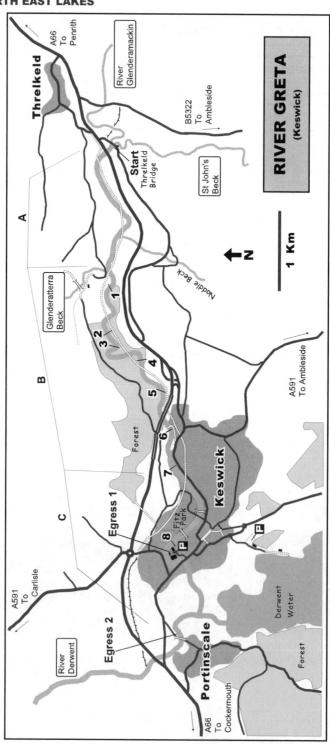

RIVER GRETA
(Keswick)

GRETA (Keswick)

From :	Threlkeld Bridge	314 247	Grade :	III
To :	Portinscale Bridge	253 237	Maps : O.S. 90, Explorer OL4 & 5	
Distance :	8 km		Stars : ✳✳✳ Scenery : ❀❀❀	

SUMMARY
An excellent river with no major hazards and several play spots make this an enjoyable outing amongst beautiful scenery. Formed by the confluence of St. John's Beck and the Glenderamakin the Greta flows through a beautiful wooded valley before calming down to pass through the centre of Keswick, joining the river Derwent just before Portinscale. For most of its length the river is followed by a footpath along the old disused railway line which crosses the river many times and gives good access for spectators.

INDICATORS
Much of the Greta's catchment is held back by Thirlmere Dam so the level rises and falls quite quickly after rain. The best place to judge the level is in Keswick where the river flows between the main road and Fitz Park.
If the shingle rapid by the footbridge into the park is navigable then the gorge nature of the upper river will be OK. 100 m above this footbridge there are some slate steps sticking out of the wall of the park bank. The bottom step should be covered to make a trip worthwhile. High water washes out many of the rapids producing large standing waves.

AGREEMENTS
A good and long standing access agreement is in place which gives me the confidence to publish it, and also in the hope that it may be an example for others. Nothing should be done to jeopardise this.

November 1st - - March 31st — No restrictions on canoeing.
April 1st - - - - - July 31st — No canoeing after 4.00 pm.
August 1st - - - - - October 31st — Closed. No canoeing

START
The usual start is at Threlkeld Bridge. This is found if approaching from Penrith on the A66 by taking a turn off to the left marked Youth Centre and Castlerigg Stone Circle, just after the second road on the right to Threlkeld village and just before the A66 crosses the river. Threlkeld Bridge is found 100 metres from the junction. Park on the side of the road by the bridge where a gate and path lead down to the river.

DESCRIPTION
A II A fairly gentle start with a few large boulders and trees which are easily negotiated and a couple of straightforward bouldery rapid.

B) III From here down to Keswick the river becomes slightly more channelled as it twists and turns in a narrow wooded valley giving fairly continuous and enjoyable grade III water with lots of minor rapids.
1) III Magnetic Rock. Glenderattera Beck enters from the right at the 4th railway bridge, 100 metres below this the river bends right and leads in to the rapid. Most of the water is channelled down a small drop on the right before flowing at a large smooth rock.
2) III Rock Hop. After the 5th bridge and a sharp left hand bend the river steepens as it twists and turns between boulders. Large standing waves in high water.

continued on next page ⇨

RIVER GRETA (Keswick)

⇨ continued from previous page

3) III The Wall. 100 metres below Rock Hop, after a couple of small steps, there is a sharp right hand bend where most of the water hits the vertical wall straight ahead forming a large eddy on the left. The strong currents often unseat beginners, but the wall can provide a good splat site for experts with a small surf wave below.

4) III 1st Weir. A bouldery rapid under another (6th) railway bridge leads to flat water above the weir. This is a large broken weir which apart from some protruding metal bolts at the top on river right is a quite safe and natural rapid giving good rough water down to the next bridge. A good fast surfing hole often forms halfway down.

5) III 2nd Weir. After passing a caravan site and holiday park the river splits around an island. To the left of the island the river flattens above a second weir but this is usually avoided by following the natural channel right of the Island through a section of small bouldery drops.

6) III Forge Bridge. After passing under the dual carriageway the river is constricted through an arched bridge with a small shelf below. This forms a grabby stopper on river right but can be avoided easily on the left. A convenient eddy immediately below the stopper river right gives good access for playing. Although bouncy and appearing retentive at times, this hole is usually fairly friendly and isn't known for holding bodies or boats once they have come separated. This is a great surfing wave in high water, but the eddy tends to wash out.

7) III A small island marks the end of the gorge and can be passed on either side but be aware of several metal bolts protruding from rocks at the start of the right hand channel.

C) II   The river calms down as it passes through Keswick and after a couple of minor rapids in the town it flows flat all the way to the confluence with the Derwent and Portinscale.

8) W A tiny weir is hidden just after the second footbridge in the town but usually poses no problems.

EGRESS
E1) A popular egress is to the climbing wall car park on the left at the end of the straight section past the park. A steep muddy bank amongst the trees just before the left hand bend leads to the car park. However it is much better to continue 30 metres just around the bend to where the bank is lower and there are no trees.

E2) It is possible to continue another 1.5 km on fairly flat water past the confluence with the Derwent to egress on the right bank before the suspension footbridge at Portinscale.

Magnetic Rock rapid, River Greta.   *Frank Cope*

Workington Weir, River Derwent.

Cowan Head, Upper Kent.

Stuart Miller

Quality time on Derwent Water.   *Stuart Miller*

Arnside Viaduct.   *Guy Austin*

Fairy Glen, Langstrath Beck.

Stuart Miller

Ashness Bridge & Derwentwater *Thomas Allom 1836*

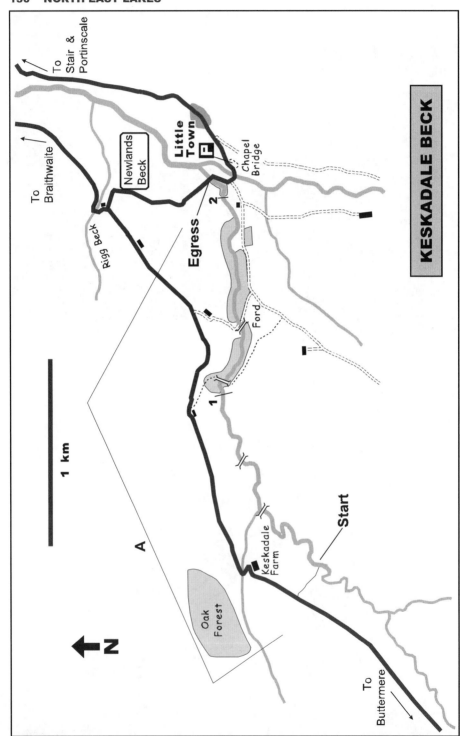

KESKADALE BECK

To Stair & Portinscale

Little Town

Chapel Bridge

To Braithwaite

Newlands Beck

Rigg Beck

Egress

2

Ford

1

1 km

A

N

Oak Forest

Keskadale Farm

Start

To Buttermere

KESKADALE BECK

From :	Intake Wall	210 189	Grade :	III / IV
To :	Chapel Bridge	231 195	Maps : O.S. 90, Explorer OL4	
Distance :	2.25 km		Stars : ✳	Scenery : ❀ ❀

SUMMARY
Starting high up near Newlands Hause a series of narrow switchbacks soon develops into a vicious tree lined ditch. In medium water this can provide an entertaining start to Newlands Beck. In high water it provides a scary `run the gauntlet` type experience with many of the branches trying to whack you on the head as well as grab you and drown you, particularly in the last hundred metres to the bridge. Only venture in here if you are trained, armed, and prepared for battle.

INDICATORS
There needs to have been plenty of rain to bring this up, and Newlands beck needs to be well above its low runable level. The best place to look is at the start where the beck is obviously runable or not, and at the end where the road runs along the beck for the last hundred metres before the bridge. Here one can view the trees blocking the channel and gauge the respective danger. However most of the beck above is not so tree infested and can be quite enjoyable if this section is portaged.

START
Drive up to the head of Newlands valley past Keskadale Farm until the road becomes unfenced. Park and carry down to the beck and portage the first fence before starting.

DESCRIPTION
A) III / IV There are several fences and the odd footbridge to negotiate before the beck steepens and enters the wood. Once in the wood there are continuous rapids and tree obstacles to the end with a brief respite in the middle at a footbridge and ford. The grade indicates the serious and continuous nature of the beck rather than any technical rapids.
1)   IV   Start of rapids.
2)   T   The most tree choked section begins.

EGRESS
It is possible to egress to the Bridge near to Chapel Bridge on Newlands Beck but if you have come this far its well worth continuing on down Newlands beck to Stair.

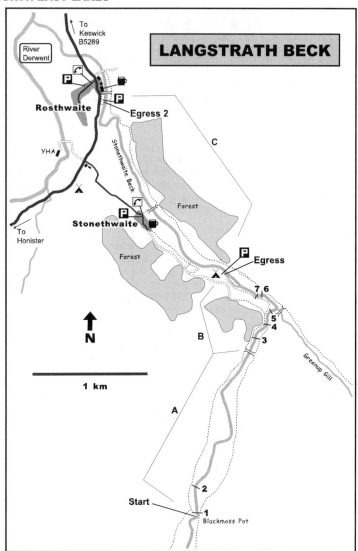

continued from opposite page ⇦

6) IV / V   Galleny Force. A bit of a hit or miss affair. Several boats have been dented here, but usually in low water. In high flows a horrible hole, tow back and boil, develop, but then in flood conditions a chicken chute on the right opens up.

7) IV   Final Fling. On the final corner there is a rocky ramp on the left or a bouldery hole on the right. At the exit from the pool below the fall beware of a small sump to the left of the large boulder, but this is usually well covered at normal levels.

EGRESS

A breeze back to the campsite and egress just below the island **(E1)**.

C) II / III   From the campsite onwards the river is known as Stonethwaite Beck and there are no rapids of note from here down to the junction with the River Derwent, but in high water it can be a fast way down to the pub at Rosthwaite, so a car could be left at the Scafell Inn **(E2)**.

LANGSTRATH BECK

From :	Black Moss Pot	267 113	Grade :	IV / V
To: Stonethwaite Campsite	258 133		Maps : O.S. 90, Explorer OL4	
Distance :	2.5 km		Stars : ✶ ✶ ✶ Scenery : ❀ ❀ ❀	

SUMMARY
A beautiful and popular Lakeland gem. Crystal clear water, smooth rocky gorges, technical falls and stunning scenery all above the farmland on open fell - so no access problems. The last section through what is known locally as the Fairy Glen contains four falls of note and is often paddled on its own. However its well worth the 30 minute walk up to Black Moss Pot for the full experience into the Pot and the long series of slabs that follow.

INDICATORS
This Lakeland beck obviously needs rain to bring it up. But maybe not as much as you would imagine as it has a large catchment area and the water is concentrated in the narrow gorges, especially through the Fairy Glen. Unfortunately the only way to check if the level suits your bravery on the day is to drive up to the campsite and walk up to inspect the glen. Ideally there should be water flowing around the left side of the island at the egress. The grade given is for when water is just starting to flow round this island. Higher water levels, obviously raise the grade. Some idea can be gained at Rosthwaite where the river can be viewed just above the Scafell Hotel . It needs to be flowing quite fast here but not necessarily across the whole width of the river bed.

START
Drive up to the campsite by following the track beyond the Langstrath Hotel and park at the top end of the campsite at the egress by an Island. Carry your boat up the river from here over the stile at the end of the campsite and follow the footpath up Langstrath. The lower section is usually started at the first footbridge by Johnny House. (GR 272 126) Otherwise carry on up the path for another 15 to 20 minutes to Black Moss Pot.

DESCRIPTION
A) IV / V   After the initial few drops there are a couple of minor rapids and shingle beds on the way back to Johnny House Bridge.
1) IV / V Black Moss Pot. This is a popular swimming hole in the summer, but changes character considerably with a bit of water flowing through it. Dropping into the narrow slot is an exciting start to the run and has unpredictable results. Even forward loops are not unknown, and watch those paddles as it would be a shame to break them in the first 2 metres !!
2)   IV   The Slabs. A series of slides down smooth slabs with a couple of stoppers to negotiate, these can make lining up for the bottom drop awkward. There is a sump in the bottom pool on the left, but it is usually well covered at the correct levels.

B) IV / V   The Fairy Glen. Although quite short this gives an excellent concentrated section of hard rapids often done in its own right. It has been run in all water levels, and given various grades varying from a grade III giggle at low levels to one large continuous grade V+ in flood levels.
3)   III   Johnny's Rock. The first rapid below the bridge winds left around a rock.
4)   IV   Slip and Slide.   A crafty drop into the pool on the left at the top before a quick cross back right.
5)   IV   The Fairy Hole. Rocks at the start make lining up awkward.

⇦ *continued on opposite page*

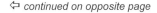

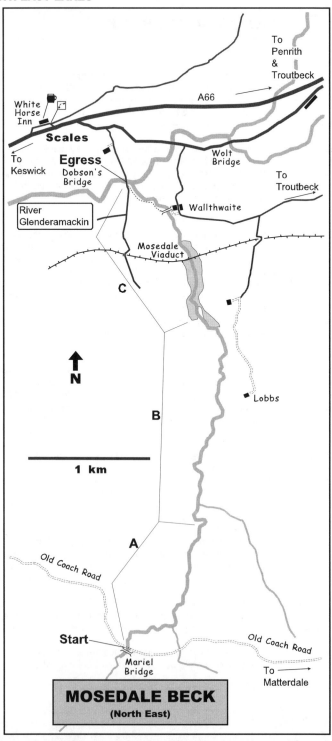

MOSEDALE BECK
(North East)

MOSEDALE BECK (North East)

From :	Mariel Bridge	350 227	Grade :	IV+ / V
To :	Dobson's Bridge	350 264	Maps : O.S. 90,	Explorer OL5
Distance :		5 km	Stars : ✷✷✷	Scenery : ❀❀

SUMMARY
Mosedale Beck drains the area at the back of Clough Head and Great Dodd, on the end of the Helvellyn range. It crosses Threlkeld common to give a brilliant and varied run which starts up on bleak moor land with narrow switchbacks, then drops into a kilometre and a half of continuous steep bouldery rapids before entering a small wooded valley and on into farmland. The middle kilometre drops some 100 m in height which provides an exhausting challenge for both mind and body and is probably the longest and most continuous rapid in the area. Despite its quality this is a difficult run to do for several reasons. First the start is 3.5 km from the road and either a four wheel drive or an hours walk are necessary to get there. Secondly the catchment is quite small and the level often goes up and down again within a couple of hours. Thirdly access on the bottom section of the beck is discouraged. However if all these problems are overcome and you find it at a good level, do it and enjoy!

INDICATORS
The only place the beck can be viewed conveniently is at the hamlet of Wallthwaite, where the beck passes under a bridge on a public footpath behind the cottages. It needs to be in spate with all the boulders covered and ideally it should be almost bank full. If it is flowing go quickly as it drops off again fast and if it is in flood beware, as it becomes a sustained and manic grade V.

START
Mariel Bridge is found halfway along the old Coach Road from St John's in the Vale to Matterdale. It is best approached from Matterdale by either four wheel drive or walking. The road end (GR 380 219) is found at a spot called Red Moss, which is reached by turning right off the Troutbeck to Ullswater road about a kilometre before Matterdale End. There is a car park at Red Moss and from here the Coach Road contours the fell fairly easily for 3.5 km to the bridge.

DESCRIPTION
A) II At first the beck is very narrow and winds its way back wards and forwards as it starts to sink deeper into the moor land forming its own narrow gorge.

B) IV+ / V Boulders start to appear in the beck and it obviously steepens at a bend back left. This is the `The Mad Mile`, a hectic continuous rapid with hardly any rests. The initial hundred metres probably contains the most awkward section with sharp rocks from the landslide on the left, but the remainder just keeps on coming and only starts to ease off at the approach to the woods below. There are no particular falls that stand out but the grade indicates the sustained nature of the section, the constant risk of pinning, and the painful result of rolling or swimming.

C) III / IV As you approach the wood the gorge opens out for a short section but watch out for a fence as the beck enters the wood. From here to the end there are numerous pleasant rapids and chutes but the hazard is mainly from trees and fences. Just after entering the wood there is a large tree blocking the whole beck, and there could well be more. There are several fences across the whole river and be warned that some of these contain barbed wire and may need portaging.

EGRESS
Egress to the road at Dobson's Bridge, soon after the confluence with the Glenderamackin.

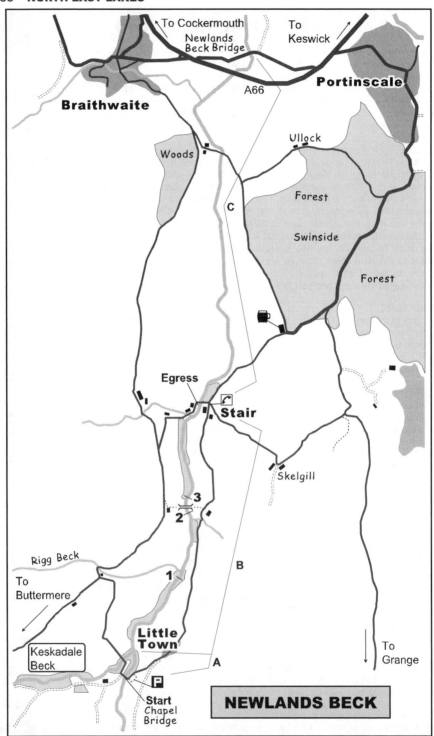

To Cockermouth

Newlands
Beck Bridge

To
Keswick

A66

Portinscale

Braithwaite

Woods

Ullock

C

Forest

Swinside

Forest

Egress

Stair

Skelgill

3

2

Rigg Beck

1

To
Buttermere

B

Little
Town

Keskadale
Beck

A

Start
Chapel
Bridge

To
Grange

NEWLANDS BECK

NEWLANDS BECK

From :	Chapel Bridge	231 294	Grade :	III (IV)
To :	Stair Bridge	236 212	Maps : O.S. 90, Explorer OL4	
Distance :		3 km	Stars : ✶ ✶ Scenery : ✿ ✿ ✿	

SUMMARY
A lovely short trip with continuous interest down a quiet wooded valley. When in flood Newlands belies its beck name and is more of a river with large standing waves.

INDICATORS
Needs heavy rain. If all the rocks just above Stair Bridge are covered then it will be a good run. There is a pipe covered in concrete sticking out of the base of the wall on the bank adjoining the Adventure Centre. This can be viewed from the road at the egress and needs to be covered to make a trip worthwhile.

START
The usual start is at Chapel Bridge where there is a car park.

DESCRIPTION
A) III Initially the beck is narrow and fast flowing with the banks lined with trees making breakouts awkward.

B) III (IV) After the confluence with Keskadale Beck the trees become less of a problem and the rapids are small but continuous all the way to Stair.
1) III After about a kilometre the river appears blocked by a large boulder. Follow the main flow down a narrow chute right of the boulder.
2) III The river appears to drop out of sight at the next obvious steepening. Although a fairly straight forward 1.5 m drop the chute is often blocked by trees and needs inspecting. This leads to a footbridge.
3) IV The footbridge indicates the approach to the final drop into a narrow boily gorge.

EGRESS
The normal egress is onto the left bank just before Stair Bridge.

C) I / II The beck can be followed for a further 2 km to near Braithwaite and an egress made at Newlands Beck Bridge (GR 240 237). However this lower part is channelled between man made bank for the whole of its length and is of no particular interest.

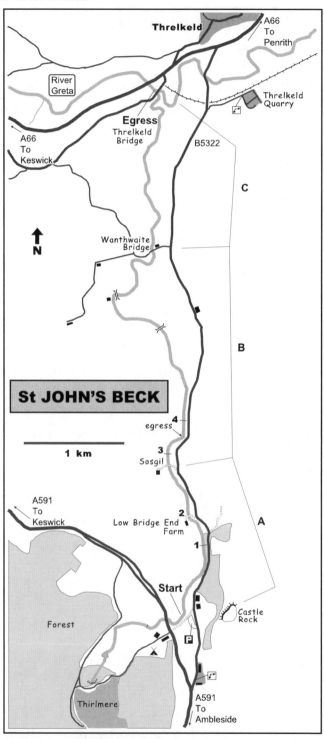

Threlkeld

A66
To
Penrith

River
Greta

Threlkeld
Quarry

Egress
Threlkeld
Bridge

B5322

A66
To
Keswick

C

↑
N

Wanthwaite
Bridge

B

St JOHN'S BECK

1 km

4
egress

3
Sosgil

A591
To
Keswick

2
Low Bridge End
Farm

A

1

Start

Castle
Rock

Forest

P

X

A591
To
Ambleside

Thirlmere

St JOHN'S BECK

From :	Picnic Site	317 196	Grade :	II

To :	Threlkeld Bridge	314 247	Maps : O.S. 90, Explorer OL5

Distance :	6.5 km	Scenery : ❀

SUMMARY
Despite starting at a lovely setting below Castle Rock of Triermain this river soon develops into a meander through farmland within canalised banks and occasional fences which spoil the run and can make it quite serious even though there are few rapids. When there is enough water flowing then the man made banks force the river, in places, into a narrow swift flowing channel which contains many small bushes and trees along its banks and some **sturdy fences** across the channel. Because of this it is not really a good place for beginners which may otherwise be attracted by its low technical grade. Better known as a feeder river for the mighty Greta than as a trip in its own right.

INDICATORS
Thirlmere Dam holds back most of the water from the valley and unless there is a prolonged wet spell with the reservoir brim full there is unlikely to be enough flow for this trip. Water needs to be escaping from the overflow of the dam for the river to run. If there is obviously a navigable flow covering the shingle rapids at the start then the more channelled sections below will be ok.

START
Park in the car park at the southern end of St John's in the Vale, below Castle Rock. At the head of the car park a gate leads across the old road to a picnic site beside the river. Launch from here.

DESCRIPTION
A) II The first kilometre is fairly fast flowing over shingle beds with trees on the bank. In high flows care is needed as these trees can be in the river.
1) F A wire fence strung between the trees. May need Portage.
2) F A wire mesh fence below the bridge at Low Bridge End Farm. Portage.

B) II After Sosgill Bridge and the first fence the river bends right and narrows as it enters the man made banks, these last for about a kilometre, making this section very serious as finding eddies and escape is difficult where it is needed.
3) F The first fence is just after Sosgill Bridge. Portage.
4) F A fence in a straight section of river with high banks making portage difficult but necessary. Get out at the sharp left bend before the straight run into the fence.

C) I / II The river now enters some woodland and is allowed to run a more natural course to its confluence with the Glenderamackin.

EGRESS
Egress on the left just under Threlkeld Bridge at the confluence with the Glenderamackin, where the two rivers form the start of the Greta.

.
.

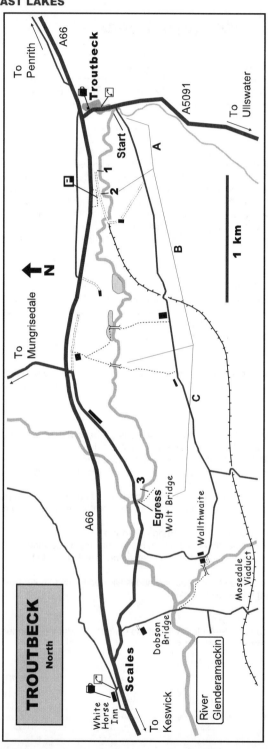

TROUTBECK (North)

From :	Troutbeck	389 269	Grade :	IV
To :	Wolt Bridge	358 267	Maps :	O.S. 90, Explorer OL5
Distance :	3.5 km		Stars : ✱	Scenery : ✿

IV

SUMMARY
A fast bouncy run with one large drop followed by a continuous kilometre of bouldery rapids falling at 50 m/km through a tunnel of trees. Great care is necessary due to the ever present possibility that trees or wire may block the beck.

INDICATORS
It needs heavy rain to bring it up and cover the boulders. Common sense will tell you if its running and navigable at either the start or finish. Beware: too much water will cause problems with the trees.

START
The start is found in Troutbeck Village by turning off the A66 onto the A5091 to Ullswater.
After 200 metres take the first right and park just after the bridge over the beck. There is a fence to portage at the put in.

DESCRIPTION
A) IV   This first section is fairly flat as it twists through fields, but a large boulder marks a small drop in a gorge and then the run in to Troutbeck Fall 200 m below.
1) III Entry drop. Just after the first large boulder
2) IV Troutbeck Fall. A large but straight forward 2.5 m drop into a deep pool. This lies hidden up against the right side of a small gorge next to a lay-by on the A66.

B) III / IV- From the pool below the falls the beck charges off for the next kilometre down a bouncy bobsleigh run under the viaduct and on through a tunnel of trees. This whole section is one long rapid falling at a steady gradient with few breakouts and the constant threat of being grabbed by tree branches. Despite this or perhaps due to it, this is an enjoyable blast and the grade indicates the serious and continuous nature of the beck rather than any technical rapids. Although clear at the time of writing, single strands of barbed wire have occasionally been found across this beck, particularly between the two foot bridges at the bottom of this section. Fallen trees are also a constant threat.

C) III Below the 2nd foot bridge the gradient eases although interest is maintained all the way to the finish.
3) B Care is required in the last 200 metres where there are a couple of low **wooden beams** across the beck at head height. It is usually possible to duck under these but in high water it may be prudent to walk up from Wolt Bridge to check them out before starting.

EGRESS
Egress onto the left bank and a public footpath just above Wolt Bridge.

TROUTBECK (North)

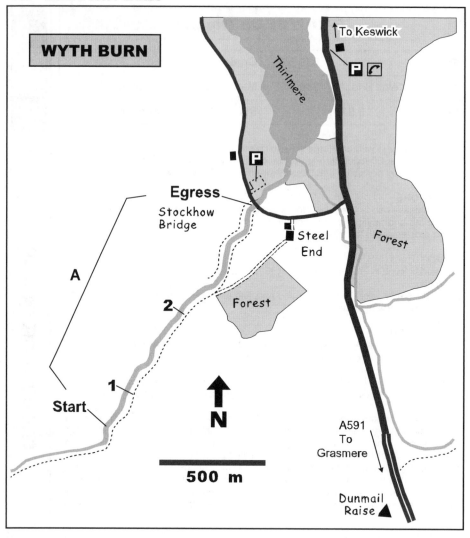

WYTH BURN

WYTH BURN

From :	Fence in Beck	313 118	Grade :	IV (V)
To :	Stockhow Bridge	321 129	Maps : O.S. 90, Explorer OL5	
Distance :	1 km		Scenery : ❀ ❀	

SUMMARY
A short typical Lakeland boulder bounce with a **nasty drop** into a narrow slot in the middle, and for some reason a Scottish name!!

INDICATORS
Common sense. If it is obviously flowing and navigable at Stockhow Bridge the more confined beck above will be ok.

START
Park in the car park at Stockhow Bridge and walk up the beck on the right bank. The upper reaches of the beck fall from the high fells through a steep narrow gorge which is unrunnable. Where it escapes this gorge the angle obviously eases and there is a small pool and fence across the beck. Start immediately below this fence.

DESCRIPTION
A) IV (V) Most of the section is down small bedrock falls.
1) F An obvious fence in the middle of a long rocky rapid can be swung up and held open from the bank.
2) V Wythburn Slot. This nasty 3 m angled slot has an awkward run in and a strong tow back. It is hidden at the end of a rocky section by some small trees on the right bank. Inspect and portage on the left bank.

EGRESS
It is best to get out just before the bridge on the left bank.

WYTH BURN

Castle Rock, St John's Vale. *Thomas Allom 1835*

SUMMARY TABLE

Name of Run	Page	Grade	WW Stars	Scenic Stars	Km	Water	Notes
Calder (Cumbria) / Section 1	147	4	★★	✿✿	4	High	mountain beck
Calder (Cumbria) / Section 2	149	3	★	✿✿✿	5	Med	rhododendron gorge
Cocker / Section 1	151	1(2)		✿✿	9	Med	
Cocker / Section 2	153	3	★	✿	3	Med	lake fed
Derwent (Lower) / Section 5	155	1(2)		✿✿✿	14	Low	beautiful intro run
Derwent (Lower) / Section 6	157	1(2)		✿	15	Low	play at wooky weir
Ehen / Section 1	159	2		✿	9	Med	
Ehen / Section 2	161	2			9	Med	
Ellen	334	2				High	
Gatesgarthdale Beck	163	4	★	✿✿✿	2	High	mountain scenery
Liza	165	4	★★	✿✿✿	7	High	A remote challenge
Marron	167	3			10	High	

Concrete Bridge Fall, River Liza   *Graham Watson*

RIVERS OF NORTH WEST LAKES

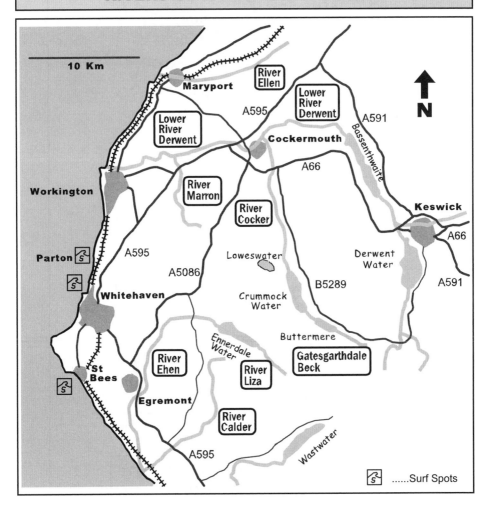

10 Km

Maryport

River Ellen

Lower River Derwent

A595

Lower River Derwent

A591

Cockermouth

N

River Marron

A66

Workington

River Cocker

Keswick

A66

Loweswater

Derwent Water

Parton

A595

A5086

B5289

A591

Whitehaven

Crummock Water

Buttermere

Ennerdale Water

River Ehen

River Liza

Gatesgarthdale Beck

St Bees

Egremont

River Calder

A595

Wastwater

[s] ......Surf Spots

Fox

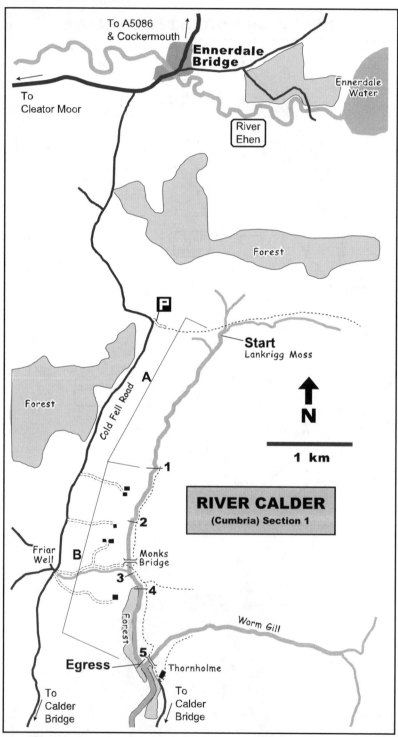

To A5086
& Cockermouth

**Ennerdale
Bridge**

Ennerdale
Water

To
Cleator Moor

River
Ehen

Forest

P

Start
Lankrigg Moss

N

1 km

A

Cold Fell Road

Forest

1

2

RIVER CALDER
(Cumbria) Section 1

Friar
Well

B

Monks
Bridge

3

4

Forest

Worm Gill

5

Egress

Thornholme

To
Calder
Bridge

To
Calder
Bridge

CALDER (Cumbria)

The best of the north west rivers, giving a little taste of everything with open moors, narrow gorges, steep boulder rapids, and bedrock falls in its upper half, then doubling in size to give an energetic valley river with shingle rapids, sculptured sandstone cliffs, and a unique avenue of Rhododendrons. The best kept secret of the west coast is now out of the bag ! The final bizarre twist is that it is possible, though not encouraged, to continue to the sea right through the middle of the Sellafield Nuclear Complex. The consequences of being taken for a terrorist or receiving a heavy dose of radiation are probably enough to discourage most from this finale.

SECTION 1

From :	Lankrigg Moss	075 128	Grade :	IV
To :	Worm Gill	066 090	Maps :	O.S. 89, Explorer OL4
Distance :		4 km	Stars : ✶ ✶	Scenery : ❀ ❀

SUMMARY
Starting high on the moors of the Cold Fell road The Calder emerges from Lankrigg Moss to quickly form a navigable channel. As this falls off the fells it cuts through some small gorges with boulders and bedrock falls to give a couple of kilometres of fairly continuous and interesting rapids.

INDICATORS
It needs quite a lot of rain to bring this up and it runs off fairly quickly so get out there while its raining. If you look over the bridge at Calder Bridge and the river is brown and swollen then the constricted nature of the upper gorges will probably be OK. The only place to actually view this section however involves a ¾ km walk. Park at Friar Well Junction (GR 055 101) on the Cold Fell road and walk east down the track to the river. This arrives at the river by a foot bridge halfway down the section of rapids. This is the widest and flattest part of this section and if most of the boulders are covered here with the river obviously navigable then the rest will be a good level.

START
Park at the highest point of the Cold Fell road between Calder Bridge and Ennerdale Bridge (GR 066 130). At this point the road has a right angle bend and a rough track heads off east on the bend. There is a metal bar across the track sometimes. Follow the track for about ¾ km ,which soon reduces into a grassy path as it descends towards the river.

DESCRIPTION
A)   III   For the first 1.5 km the river is a small beck cutting its way through the moor. For most off the way it is a fairly deep channel which should present no problems. The moor soon develops a small valley and the sides of the valley start to get closer and steeper until eventually they appear to meet with a sharp turn through a wall of rock, Trees can be seen beyond the rock on the right bank, and it is best to egress on the left bank just before the rock as this is the entrance to Gill Force.

B)   IV   The beck now steepens up and is continuously interesting for the 2.5 km down to Worm Gill.
1) IV   The first gorge is known as Gill Force, and although there are no nasty falls hidden in the 100 m gorge, it is quite committing, contains plenty of rough water, and ends with being thrown against the left wall overhung by a holly tree.

2) IV   A few small rapids lead down to the less serious second gorge which starts after a right angle bend and ends with a small fall under the old Monks Bridge.

continued on following page ⇨

⇨ *continued from previous page*

2) IV A few small rapids lead down to the less serious second gorge which starts after a right angle bend and ends with a small fall under the old Monks Bridge.

3) F Below Monks Bridge the beck ease in angle and widens for a short distance as it passes below a footbridge. At the first corner left below the footbridge there is a broken fence which can be passed at the time of writing.

4) IV After the fence the beck bends back right and starts to steepen up again through some large boulders. There are then several small bedrock falls and a more awkward two tier fall before the beck eases in gradient on its approach to the Worm Gill confluence.

5) F Just before the confluence with Worm Gill there is a fence which needs portaging.

EGRESS

Egress at the fence (5) to a footpath which crosses a footbridge over Worm Gill and on up to Thornholme (See start of next section), or continue to Calder Bridge.

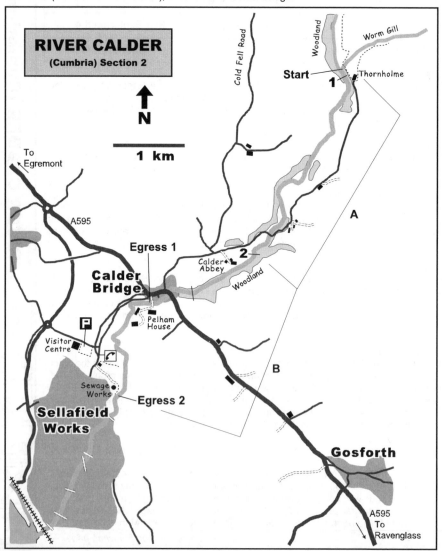

SECTION 2

From :	Worm Gill	066 090	Grade :	III
To :	Calder Bridge	035 058	Maps : O.S. 89,	Explorer OL6
Distance :	5 km		Stars : ✶	Scenery : ✿ ✿ ✿

SUMMARY
From its confluence with Worm Gill the Calder doubles in size and becomes a swift valley river with wooded banks and many shingle rapids maintaining its interest all the way. The last two kilometres are quite different as the bedrock changes to sandstone and rhododendrons line the banks.

START
Where the main Cold Fell road takes a sharp turn uphill a minor road carries straight on up the Calder valley. Follow this road crossing the river at Stakes Bridge (possible entry / egress for a shorter trip) right to its end at Thornholme. From here a public footpath runs down to the river at its confluence with Worm Gill.

DESCRIPTION
A) III   Immediately after the confluence there is a steep rapid with some large boulders, then the river settles into a series of meandering bends and shingle rapids, but keeps a fast flow with trees on the banks forming occasional hazards.

B) III   Soon after Stakes Bridge the river takes on a different character as the bedrock changes to sandstone.
1) III   The river curves left, with the remains of Calder Abbey seen directly ahead and then rushes down to a sharp turn right where the first signs of the sandstone intrude on the river and form some funny water around the corner. Rhododendron bushes line the banks for the next kilometre, making landing anywhere quite serious, and small steps in the bedrock form a few standing waves but other than the tree roots in the river there is nothing of note until the houses of Calder Bridge can be seen on the left bank.
2) III   As the river approaches the first houses it hits the left bank which is a massively undercut sandstone cliff at this point. In high water this could be a problem but usually the overhang is above head level. Be wary of several more overhanging cliffs in this final section.

EGRESS
E1 - Continue into an interesting sandstone gorge to egress at the 2nd bridge in the village. Egress onto the right bank just after bridge at the entrance to Pelham Hall where there is a shingle beach and a path climbs the bank to a stile. Parking is only available back in the centre of the village by the Church.

E2 - It is also possible to carry on through the sandstone gorges and more farmland for a further kilometre to egress by the sewage works at the entrance to Sellafield. A pipe across the river marks the spot and a sharp corner just below allows a large eddy to be gained. It is possible to park at the Sellafield Visitors centre close to the end of the track down to the sewage works.

RIVER CALDER (Cumbria) 2

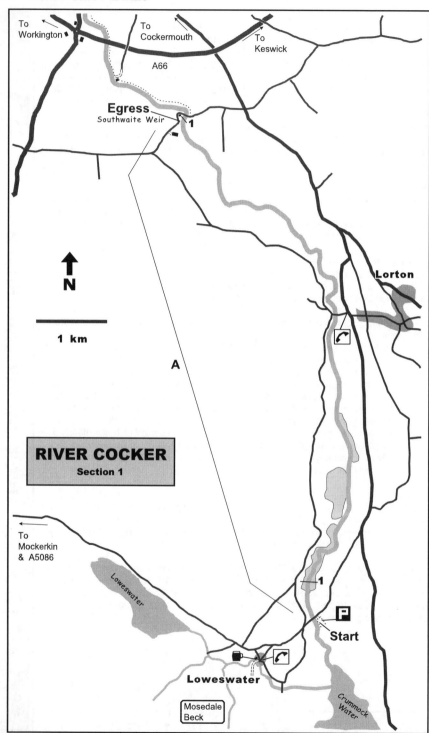

To
Workington

To
Cockermouth

To
Keswick

A66

Egress
Southwaite Weir

1

N

1 km

A

RIVER COCKER
Section 1

Lorton

To
Mockerkin
& A5086

Loweswater

1

P

Start

Loweswater

Mosedale
Beck

Crummock
Water

COCKER

The River Cocker flows out of Crummock Water to join the river Derwent at Cockermouth. It keeps it level well for a few days after rain as it is fed by Buttermere, Crummock Water and Loweswater. Most of the upper river is flat and flows through lazy farmland, it is not until just before Cockermouth that rapids start appearing and the main interest starts.

SECTION 1

From :	Scalehill Bridge	148 214	Grade :	I / II
To :	Southwaite Weir	130 282	**Maps :** O.S. 89, Explorer OL4	
Distance :	9 km		**Scenery :** ❀ ❀	

SUMMARY
The first kilometre contains the interest in this section as the river passes through woodland with some tight turns and the risk of trees blocking the channel. After this the long flat stretch down Lorton Vale becomes more a test of endurance than skill, with the possibility of fences spanning the river to wake you up. A good introductory trip for those wishing to avoid white water.

INDICATORS
Although the Cocker is lake fed and keeps flowing for several days after rain it does need a fair amount to make it worthwhile. At the start if the small weir is washed out then it will be a worthwhile level. At Southwaite Bridge the river is quite wide and most of the rocks need to be covered to give a navigable level.

START
Park in the parking area at Scalehill Bridge, which is found on the Lorton to Loweswater road. Access to the river can be made directly from the parking area by a small concrete weir.

DESCRIPTION
A) I / II No particular water hazards, but don't fall asleep as trees can block the river in the first kilometre and fences can appear from time to time in the lower part.
1) II Small rapids as the river runs through the woods.

EGRESS
It is best to egress to the left bank in the flat water just above Southwaite weir, where there is a small parking area by the trees on the road corner.

RIVER COCKER 1

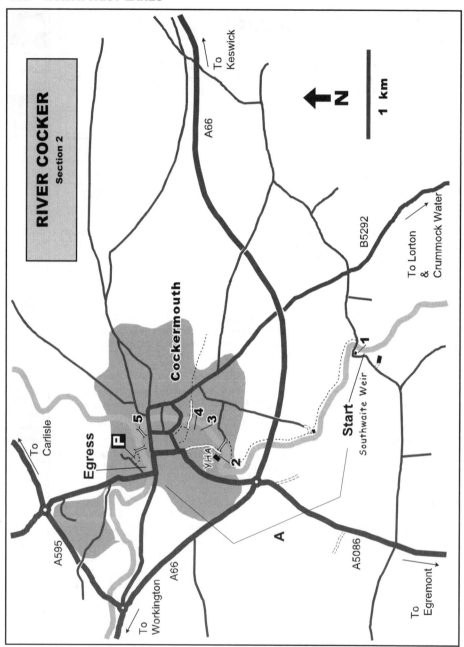

RIVER COCKER
Section 2

SECTION 2

From :	Southwaite Weir	130 282	**Grade :**	II / III
To :	Cockermouth	116 307	**Maps :** O.S. 89 , Explorer OL4	
Distance :	3 km		**Stars : ✶**	**Scenery :❀**

SUMMARY
The main interest of the Cocker lies in this section and it is a popular introductory run with a couple of kilometres of fast grade II as a warm up, before several short and fairly safe grade III rapids lead down through the town. Many local paddlers only put on at the Youth Hostel for the final section.

INDICATORS
It is best to view the level on this section from one of the bridges in Cockermouth. At low water many small rocks are visible which really need to be covered for a pleasant run.

START
It is best to park in the small lay by under the trees at the corner of the road by Southwaite weir. This is about 100 m from Southwaite bridge on the left bank of the river. Access is directly from the parking area to the flat water above the weir.

DESCRIPTION
A)   II /III   From the weir the river is fairly straightforward down to an Island after 1 km, which is usually passed on the left. The river then passes under the main road bridge and after another kilometre starts to steepen slightly looping back round to the right to the first rapid as it passes the Youth Hostel. A short flat section by a foot bridge then leads to a broken weir which marks the start of a more continuous set of rapids down through the town.

1) W   Southwaite Weir is small and easy angled and does not present any serious threat at normal levels. However, as the river rises it can produce small strong stoppers in places but soon washes out in high flows.

2) III   The Youth Hostel rapid. A straight forward bounce through standing waves and small stoppers.

3) III   The broken weir leads to a sharp corner which can produce some strong eddies and currents.

4) III   A corridor of standing waves, with a surf wave near the bottom.

5) W   A tiny concrete ledge under the last bridge can give an easy and fun introductory surf wave at certain levels. This however soon washes out in higher flows.

EGRESS
It is best to continue past the confluence with the river Derwent and egress at the next main road bridge. Get out upstream of the bridge on the right bank to parkland and a large car park.

RIVER COCKER 2

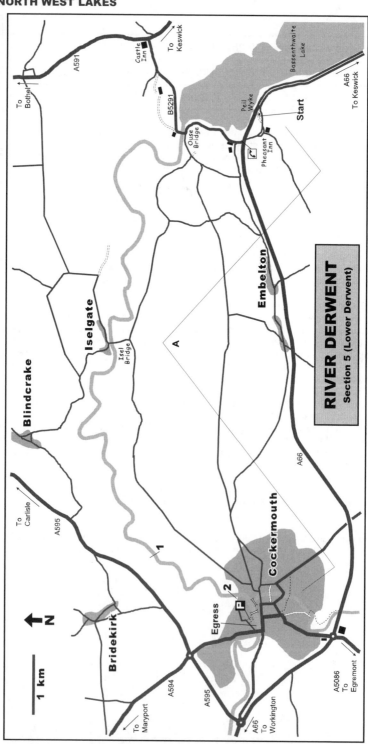

DERWENT (Lower Derwent)

The Derwent starts high in the central fells of the Lake District. The upper and middle sections are covered in the north east lakes section of this guide. After flowing some 30 kilometres and passing through two lakes the Derwent has by now grown to be a large valley river which keeps its volume for several days after heavy rain and is often navigable all year round.

SECTION 5   **Bassenthwaite to Cockermouth**

From :	Peil Wyke	203 308	Grade :	I / II
To :	Cockermouth	116 307	Maps : O.S. 90, Explorer OL4	
Distance :	14 km		Scenery : ❀ ❀ ❀	

SUMMARY
A beautiful section of river passing through quiet picturesque farmland. An excellent stretch of water for beginners, groups, touring and open boating.

INDICATORS
This large lake fed river is navigable at most water levels and can easily be inspected at Ouse Bridge where the river leaves Bassenthwaite. The Environment Agency give a recorded message of the levels of this river at Ouse Bridge on 09066 197733. The river needs to be at least 0.2 m above normal summer levels to be possible at a low level, while 0.3 above normal summer levels would give a good trip at a medium level.

START
The obvious place to start a trip on this section of river would be the car parks on the lake shore near Ouse Bridge on the B5291. However due to erosion control canoeists are asked not to use these car parks. The Lake District National Park management team have requested that access at Peil Wyke car park be used. This is found by turning off the main A66 at the end of the dual carriageway section coming from Keswick onto the old loop road for the Pheasant Inn. Peil Wyke is immediately on the right after turning onto the old road.

Please check with the B.C.U. local access officer.
Please note also that **Access to Bassenthwaite Lake is by permit only.**
(SEE LAKE ACCESS NOTES page 18).

DESCRIPTION
A) I / II Apart from the obvious hazards of moving water and banks lined with trees in many places there is nothing that warrants special attention on this lovely stretch of water. Isel Bridge at 6 km could be used as another start / egress point for a shorter trip. The River Cocker joins from the left just after entering Cockermouth.
1) I / II A few large boulders litter the river.
2) W A small weir just before entering Cockermouth.

EGRESS
The best egress is on the right bank just upstream from the road bridge in Cockermouth. This is onto parkland with a nearby car park.

RIVER DERWENT 5 (Lower Derwent)

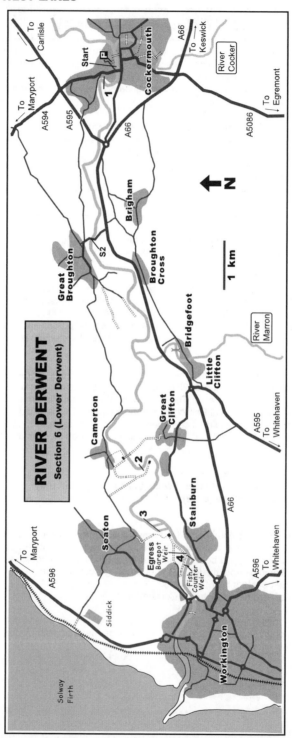

RIVER DERWENT

Section 6 (Lower Derwent)

To Carlisle

To Keswick

A66

Start

P

Cockermouth

River Cocker

1

To Maryport

To Egremont

A594

A595

A66

A5086

Brigham

N

Broughton Cross

S2

1 km

Great Broughton

Bridgefoot

River Marron

Little Clifton

Camerton

Great Clifton

Whitehaven

A595

To Whitehaven

2

Stainburn

A66

3

Seaton

Egress

Barepot Weir

4

Fish Counter Weir

To Maryport

A596

To Whitehaven

A596

Siddick

Workington

Solway Firth

SECTION 6   Cockermouth to Workington

From: Cockermouth Bridge 116 307 Broughton High Bridge 081 312	**Grade :** I / II
To : Barepot Weir 016 292	**Maps :** O.S. 89, Explorer OL4
Distance : 15 km	

SUMMARY
A gentle meander through flat farmland with one easy rapid and several weirs

INDICATORS
The Derwent is the longest river in the Lake District and being fed by some five lakes it remains at a paddleable level for most of the year. If there is enough water at Cockermouth Bridge to float then the rest of the river is navigable.

START .
It is best to start just upstream of Cockermouth Bridge (**S1**). From the town centre follow the Carlisle and Maryport road. Turn right at a mini roundabout and cross the bridge over the river. Take the first right over the bridge and there is a car park in 100 m with access to the river from the adjacent parkland.
Alternatively a slightly shorter trip can be started at Broughton Bridge (**S2**).

DESCRIPTION
A) I / II   Most of this section is grade I with one bouncy rapid of grade II. However, beware of the weir at Seaton which contains nasty spikes and is a **definite portage**.
1) I / II   Just round the corner after leaving Cockermouth Bridge are the old remains of a broken weir. A few boulders and wooden spikes are on the right but the left side is an unobstructed passage.
2) II   After passing the footbridge to Cameron the river bends left through 180` and steepens slightly to produce a few standing waves and rough water for 100 m.
3) X   Be careful on approaching Seaton Weir and get out in good time. The whole of the base of this weir is littered with metal spikes pointing upstream, making a portage at any water level mandatory.
4) W   Barepot Weir. This large weir is fairly bumpy in most places and has a certain amount of debris littering its base. It can be shot on the extreme right at most water levels. It is easiest to egress just above this weir to the track and large parking area on the right bank.

EGRESS
The best egress is to the track and parking area on the right bank just upstream of Barepot weir. This is approached by heading north out of Workington on the A596 and turning right at a roundabout just over the river onto the road to Seaton. Immediately turn right again to follow a small road along the river to Barepot. Just after crossing a small narrow bridge it is possible to turn right, opposite a post box, onto a rough track which follows the river bank past the fish counter weir to a parking area next to the large weir.

Fish Counter Weir - `Wooky Weir`
This weir is a popular play hole for local paddlers and access is not a problem outside the fishing season. It is 100 m below Barepot weir and consists of four chutes separated by concrete dividers. It has been requested that canoeists do not actually shoot the weir as it gives erroneous results to the counter readings. We should respect these wishes and put on below the weir itself if playing in the stoppers. There is a small amount of parking on the track beside the weir or further up by Barepot weir.
The right hand gate, nearest the road, contains a safe chute with an entertaining surf wave. The next chute is steeper and more retentive with a strong tow back although exiting is usually OK with a loop or capsize.

RIVER DERWENT 6 (Lower Derwent)

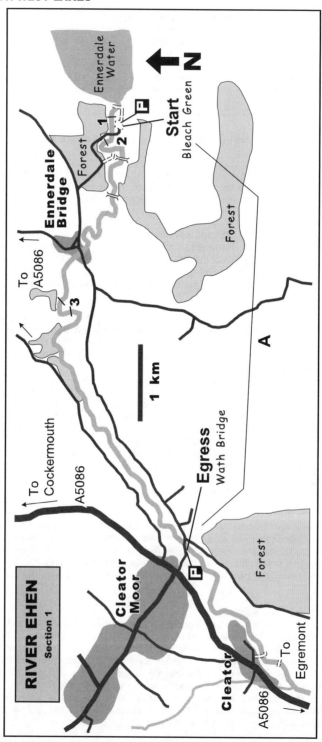

RIVER EHEN
Section 1

Start
Bleach Green

Ennerdale
Bridge

Ennerdale
Water

Forest

Egress
Wath Bridge

Cleator
Moor

Cleator

Forest

To
A5086

To
Cockermouth

A5086

To
Egremont

A5086

1 km

A

N

EHEN

One of the main west coast rivers, the Ehen is fed by Ennerdale Water and at first flows through idyllic Lakeland farmland in a low valley with a feeling of remoteness. It then skirts past Cleator Moor and Egremont via a pleasant little valley that belies its west coast geography before it becomes flat and uninteresting eventually ending up flowing along the edge of the coast and the Sellafield Nuclear complex where it joins the Calder as they both spill into the Irish Sea.
Because of this rather flat and unpleasant final part only the higher sections are described.

SECTION 1

From :	Bleach Green	085 153	Grade :	II / III
To :	Wath Bridge	031 144	**Maps :** O.S. 89, Explorer OL4 / 303	
Distance :	9 km		**Scenery :** ✿	

SUMMARY
A pleasant outing through the fringes of the Lake District with no great technical difficulty, but a feeling of quiet isolation as the river twists and loops around away from the road.

INDICATORS
Quite a small river which needs a fair amount of rain to bring it up. Ennerdale Water helps it hold its level once up. A good place to see if its flowing is at Wath Bridge. The shingle bed just below the bridge should be covered to a navigable depth to avoid scraping.

START
Start from the car park at Bleach Green Cottages, a few hundred yards below where the river flows out of the Lake. There are two small weirs at the start which can be usually shot easily.

DESCRIPTION
A) II From the two small weirs at the start the river flows under the road bridge to soon arrive at a larger weir. The river then flows gently, twisting back and forth down to Ennerdale Bridge but with a big problem from trees and their branches, which must be fought through. After Ennerdale Bridge the trees thin out a bit as open fields are reached and some pleasant easy rapids lead to a couple of small weirs made from boulders. The paddling continues easily to Wath Bridge.
1) W Two small weirs at the start.
2) W A large sloping weir which can usually be shot easily down the centre or sides channels.
3) W Small boulder weirs.

EGRESS
At Wath Bridge, it is possible to egress to a small picnic area and lay-by on the right bank just after the bridge.

RIVER EHEN 1

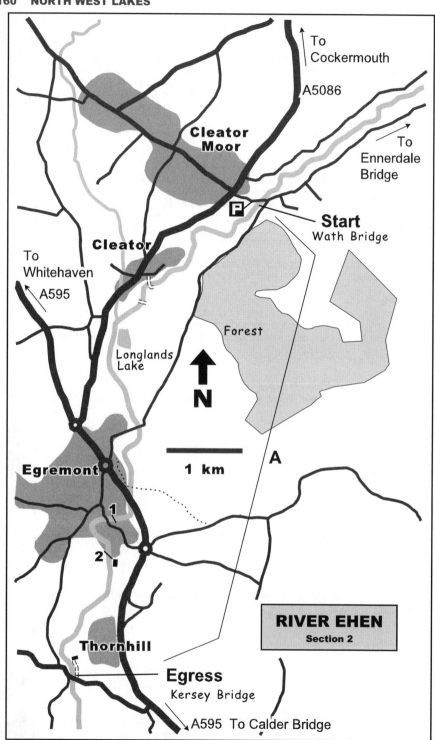

To
Cockermouth

A5086

Cleator
Moor

To
Ennerdale
Bridge

Start
Wath Bridge

Cleator

To
Whitehaven

A595

Forest

N

Longlands
Lake

1 km

A

Egremont

1

2

Thornhill

RIVER EHEN
Section 2

Egress
Kersey Bridge

A595 To Calder Bridge

SECTION 2

From :	Wath Bridge	031 144	Grade :	II
To :	Kersey Bridge	007 083	Maps :	O.S. 89, Explorer 303
Distance :	9 km			

SUMMARY
A little more barren now, the river leaves the Lake District and passes factories, mines, mills and the town of Egremont in its rush to escape the dark clutches of the west coast.

INDICATORS
If the river is obviously flowing after rain and the bed is well covered at Egremont then its on. At Wath Bridge the shallow shingle rapid at the put in should be navigable without scraping.

START
At Wath Bridge, it is possible to access the river from a small picnic area and lay-by on the right bank just below the bridge.

DESCRIPTION
A)   II   From Wath Bridge the river flows through a small open valley past Cleator and Egremont with occasional small rapids. There are a couple of weirs after the main road bridge at Egremont.
1)   W   After passing under the A595 road bridge at Egremont the river swings in a large bend right around the town to a weir just behind some houses on the left and before the next bridge. This is easy angled and should present no problems at normal levels.
2)   W   A second easy angled weir is found by the industrial estate on leaving the town.

EGRESS
At Kersey Bridge on Cop Lane (B5345). Egress is to the left bank just above the bridge.
.

RIVER EHEN 2

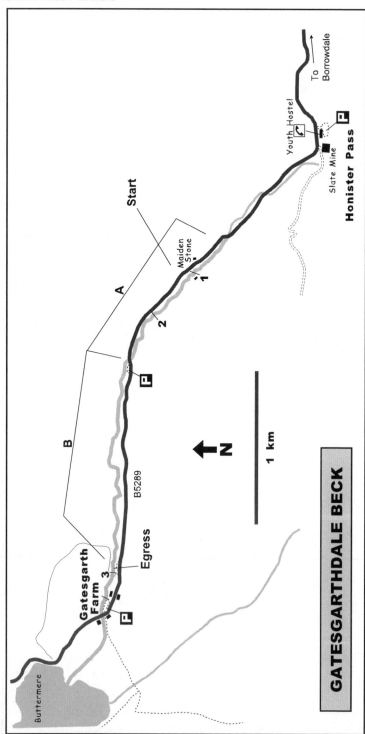

GATESGARTHDALE BECK

GATESGARTHDALE BECK

From :	Maiden Stone	216 144	Grade :	III, IV
To :	Intake Wall	197 149	Maps : O.S. 89, Explorer OL4	
Distance :	2 km		Scenery : ✿ ✿ ✿	

SUMMARY
This usually dry rocky stream bed is ideal for picnics most of the year, but is transformed into a fast twisty toboggan run by flood conditions. Save this for when everything else is too big and don't blink, in case you miss it. The beck starts at the top of Honister Pass and its gradient is like a parabolic curve, impossibly steep at the top and almost flat at the bottom, where it runs into Buttermere. The middle section however can give a short but fun run on open fell before becoming tangled amongst fields and fences at Gatesgarth, with the difficulty depending on how high up you start.

INDICATORS
Lots and lots of rain, and everything in flood conditions brings this beck up to cover the normally dry bed and large boulders. If you are up to this you will know the level you want as the whole beck runs along the side of the road.

START
Between Gatesgarth Farm and the top of Honister the road crosses the beck four times, and a starting point between the two central bridges would be usual. Put in as high as you dare, usually somewhere around the Maiden Stone, a large boulder beside the road between the bridges. By starting at the lower of the two bridges all the rocky rapids are avoided, whereas starting at the upper of the bridges will be very scary. Pick your spot.

DESCRIPTION
A) IV / V   Above the `Maiden Stone` the beck is extremely rocky and sustained. A solitary tree on a corner near the Maiden Stone will cause problems, and so will a constricted drop a few hundred metres lower where the beck comes close to the road. After the drop the beck starts to ease before shooting through the tunnels under the road.
1)   T   Tree
2)   IV   Constricted Drop

B) III   After the road the rocks disappear as the beck cuts and twists through the grass and topsoil, remaining fast flowing to the end
3)   F   The first fence at the intake wall, and best place to egress.

EGRESS
Egress above the first fence where the stream enters a walled enclosure. There is nothing below here except more fences and low bridges. The road is easily gained on the left, with several places to park.

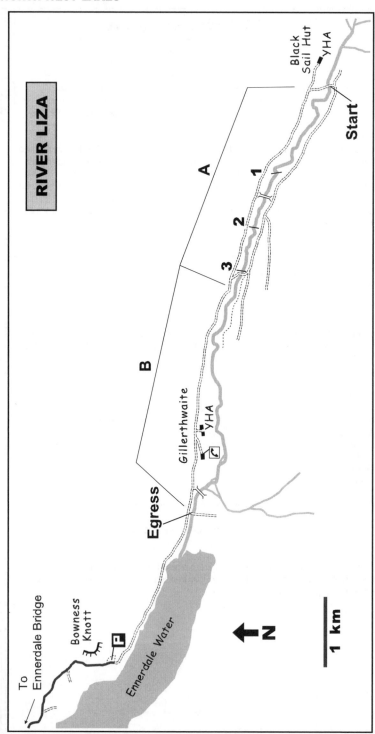

RIVER LIZA

Black
Sail Hut
YHA

Start

A

1

2

3

B

Gillerthwaite
YHA

Egress

To
Ennerdale Bridge

Bowness
Knott

P

Ennerdale Water

N

1 km

LIZA

From :	Ford	191 122	Grade :	II, III, IV
To :	Concrete Bridge	131 142	Maps : O.S. 89, Explorer OL4
Distance :	7 km		Stars : ✶✶	Scenery : ✿✿✿

SUMMARY
A brilliant river hidden in the forests of upper Ennerdale. The top section gives 3 km of lovely grade III / IV paddling on long bouldery rapids with some harder bedrock falls and short gorges more reminiscent of Scotland or the Alps then the Lake District. There is one big problem however unfortunately the restriction of vehicle access along the forestry roads makes the approach unfeasible for most, or a challenge to overcome for others.

INDICATORS
Heavy rain is needed to fill the bouldery bed. At the egress the whole bed of the river should be covered to at least 30 cm depth and this will be at least half way up the openings under the concrete bridge. This will give a good minimum level but the more the better, especially to sweep you down the long braided lower section.

START
From the car park at Bowness Knott follow the forestry roads up the valley for 9 km to a ford close to Black Sail Youth Hostel. Cars are not allowed beyond Bowness Knott, unless you are staying at Gillerthwaite Youth Hostel which reduces the journey to 5 km, but it is still a very long and tiresome walk.

DESCRIPTION
A) III / IV Continuous bouldery rapids start immediately, with three harder falls through short bedrock gorges. As this is a forest there is the usual potential hazard from fallen trees blocking the river in places
1) IV A sharp left bend signals the run in to the first fall where the river drops back immediately right over some large boulders into a pool. The fall is also marked by some old iron work sticking up from a rock at the top of the fall on the right. Beware of a large flake of rock on the right in the pool which has a small cave behind it. Inspect / portage on the left.
2) IV A great section of rapids around large boulders leads down from the footbridge this second fall. It can be awkward to stop immediately above it and most of the flow leads down a narrow chute left of the central rocks. Inspect / portage on the left.
3) IV A series of small steps leads down under the concrete bridge followed by another short but powerful drop left of a large boulder. Inspect / portage on the left, or best on the way up to the start.

B) II / III The river now eases considerably with the final two kilometres becoming wide shallow and braided.

EGRESS
Egress at the low concrete bridge 500 m before it runs into Ennerdale Water. This bridge is obvious on the way up the valley. If you have made the long trek from Bowness Knott then portage the bridge and continue down to the lake where the flat paddle into a prevailing headwind may be only slightly more preferable than walking along the track on the shore.

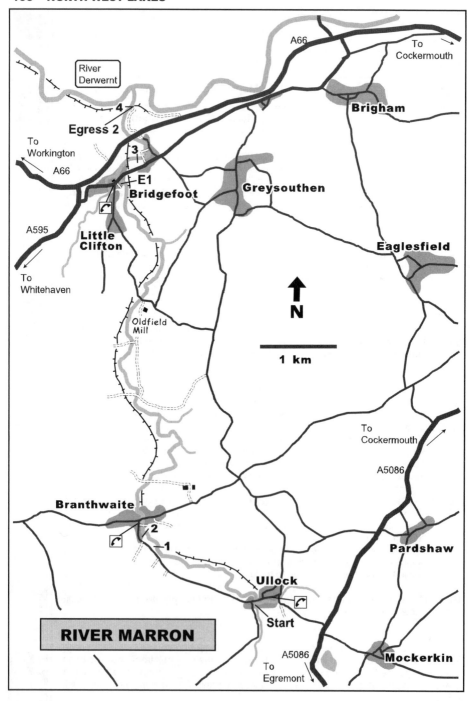

River Derwernt

4

Egress 2

To Workington

A66

3

E1

Bridgefoot

A595

Little Clifton

To Whitehaven

A66

Brigham

To Cockermouth

Greysouthen

Eaglesfield

N

1 km

Oldfield Mill

To Cockermouth

A5086

Branthwaite

2

1

Ullock

Start

Pardshaw

RIVER MARRON

A5086

To Egremont

Mockerkin

RIVER MARRON

From :	Ullock	073 238	Grade :	II / III
To :	Old Railway Bridge	058 301	Maps : O.S. 89,	Explorer OL4
Distance :	10 km			

SUMMARY
A small lowland river with a fairly gentle gradient, the Marron flows mainly through farmland with a few wooded vales and weirs.

INDICATORS
Several roads cross the river in its length and viewing from any of them should give a good indication if the river is up. It needs quite a lot of rain and should be brown and frothy. Look at the top and bottom because the river tends to get wider and shallower throughout its length and what may be navigable up at Ullock can spread out and be a scrape lower down.

START
As mentioned before several roads cross the river and the river may be accessed at Branthwaite or Oldfield Mill for a shorter trip. However the highest point of access is at Ullock where the road borders the beck.

DESCRIPTION
A) II / III The river twists around the valley through farmland and often lined by trees making both branches and fences a potential problem. Watch out for the weirs around Branthwaite, then there is nothing much to note until Bridgefoot where the river becomes more enclosed by a steep sided valley with trees and more weirs.
1) W   Weir.
2) W   Weir.
E1) B   Possible egress to left bank at Bridgefoot Bridge.
3) W   A set of three small weir steps lead down under a small bridge.
4) F   A fence is occasionally hung from the large beam at the egress.

EGRESS
E1) The easiest egress, to gain a road, is at the bridge in Bridgefoot. It is possible to park on the left bank by the bridge by turning into the entrance of the sewage works and turning again into an old road.
E2) There is another kilometre of river but it means walking out with your boat or carrying on down the River Derwent. After passing under the large A66 road bridge the river swings back right and enters between the remains of an old bridge. The remains of a 2nd and 3rd old bridge follow shortly and it is best to egress on the right bank just before the third set of bridge remains where there is a large beam across the river. This has had a fence hung on it in the past. From here it is possible to follow the route of the old railway line rightwards across the field to a track beside the river Derwent which leads to the A66. There is also a track which leads from the egress back up along the river to Bridgefoot.
Alternatively, carry on to join the Derwent and continue down to Workington, to egress at Barepot weir (see Lower Derwent).

SUMMARY TABLE

Name of Run	Page	Grade	WW Stars	Scenic Stars	Km	Water	Notes
Brathay	171	2(3,5)	✱	❀❀❀	4.5	Med	classic intro
Church Beck - Section 1	175	5	✱	❀❀❀	0.4	Med	narrow waterfalls
Church Beck - Section 2	177	4+	✱✱	❀❀	1	High	steep fast start
Crake	179	3	✱	❀❀	9.5	Med	classic intro
Cunsey Beck	183	3(4)		❀❀	2	High	
Force Beck.	185	4(5)	✱✱	❀❀	2	High	steep long rapid
Great Langdale Beck	187	3(4-)		❀❀❀	5	High	pretty + 1 fall
Kent - Section 1	189	4+	✱	❀❀❀	0.5	High	short & fast
Kent - Section 2	191	3(4)	✱	❀❀❀	6	High	
Kent - Section 3	193	2(4)	✱✱	❀❀	13	Med	weirs + 1 long rapid
Kent - Section 4	195	4	✱✱✱	❀❀❀	4.5	Low	classic pool drop
Leven	199	3(4,5)	✱✱✱	❀❀❀	4	Low	classic quality water
Little Langdale Beck	201	3(6)	✱	❀❀❀	2	Med	1 big fall portage
Mint - Section 1	203	3(4)		❀	5	Med	
Mint - Section 2	205	3+(4)	✱✱	❀	7.5	Med	
Oxendale Beck	207	5	✱	❀❀❀	2.5	High	mountain scenery
Rothay	209	2(3-)	✱	❀❀❀	7	Med	classic intro
Scandale Beck (Ambleside)	211	6	✱✱	❀❀	2	Med	intense & trees
Sprint - Section 1	213	5	✱✱	❀❀	0.6	Med	steep rocky beck
Sprint - Section 2	215	4	✱✱✱	❀❀❀	8	Med	classic pool drop
Stock Ghyll	219	5	✱✱✱	❀❀❀	1	High	sustained gorge
Torver Beck - Section 1	221	6	✱	❀❀	1	High	unusually extreme
Torver Beck - Section 2	223	4	✱✱	❀❀	1	High	spate pool drop
Trout Beck (South)	225	4	✱✱✱	❀❀	3	Med	continuous classic
Yewdale Beck - Section 1	227	6	✱	❀	0.7	High	extreme boulders
Yewdale Beck - Section 2	229	3(4)	✱✱	❀❀❀	4	High	good intro beck

RIVERS OF SOUTH EAST LAKES

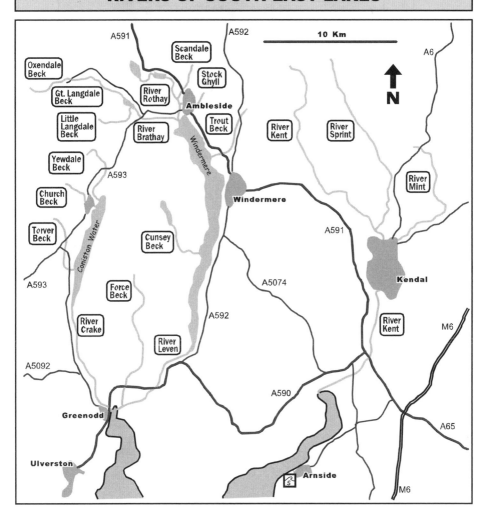

A591
A592
A6
10 Km

Scandale
Beck

Oxendale
Beck

Gt. Langdale
Beck

Stock
Ghyll

River
Rothay

N

Ambleside

Little
Langdale
Beck

River
Brathay

Trout
Beck

River
Kent

River
Sprint

Yewdale
Beck

A593

River
Mint

Church
Beck

Windermere

Torver
Beck

Coniston Water

Windermere

Cunsey
Beck

A591

A593

Force
Beck

A5074

Kendal

A592

River
Crake

River
Kent

M6

River
Leven

A5092

A590

Greenodd

A65

Ulverston

Arnside

M6

Badger

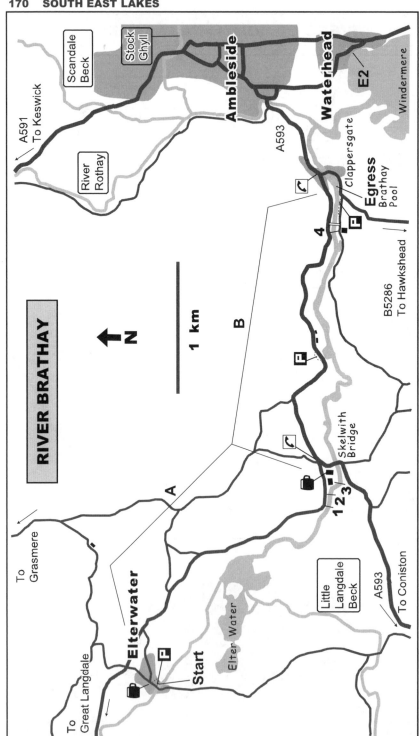

RIVER BRATHAY

N

1 km

To Keswick
A591

Scandale
Beck

Stock
Ghyll

Ambleside

Waterhead

E2

To Windermere

River
Rothay

A593

Clappersgate

Egress
Brathay
Pool

P

4

B5286
To Hawkshead

B

P

Skelwith
Bridge

P

A

1 2 3

To
Grasmere

Elterwater

Little
Langdale
Beck

A593

To Coniston

To
Great Langdale

P

Elter Water

Start

BRATHAY

From :	Elterwater	328 047	Grade :	II / III (V)
To :	Brathay Pool	366 033	Maps : O.S. 90,	Explorer OL7
Distance :	4.5 km		Stars : ✱	Scenery : ❀❀❀

SUMMARY
Ease of access, ease of technical difficulty, beautiful scenery, and positioned in the centre of the most popular part of the Lake District add up to give the area's most paddled river. Many Outdoor centres and groups use the lower half of this run regularly as an introduction to white water. However the Brathay also has a special surprise for more expert paddlers with Skelwith Force and the Looping Pool. Skelwith Force has achieved a somewhat legendary status due to several fatalities and its high public profile. While the main fall certainly demands respect, it is now regularly canoed and regarded as a straightforward grade V fall. (If there is such a thing). The looping pool has been a local park and play spot for many years, and should nowadays maybe be renamed the cartwheel pool.

INDICATORS
Most of the water for the Brathay comes from the central fells down Great Langdale Beck, which runs off quickly. However it is topped up a little more from Little Langdale Beck and held back and stored a short while where they meet in Elterwater. Much of the river is flat, deep and slow flowing and can be navigated at almost any level, therefore it is best to view the rapids you intend to paddle themselves and judge if the rocks are sufficiently covered. The first grade III rapid is the most braided and widest with many rocks and can be viewed by looking upstream from Skelwith Bridge. The main rapid in the lower section is the run from the Brathay foot bridge down to Brathay Pool. This can be viewed from the road on either side of the river.

START
The start for this whole section is actually onto the last bit of Great Langdale Beck from the car park in Elterwater. If the paddle across Elterwater and Skelwith Force wish to be avoided then another possible access point is a lay by beside the river (GR 352 035) on the A 593, 1.5 km above the Brathay road bridge.

DESCRIPTION
A) II (V)   An easy but fast stretch soon leads down to Elterwater. Cross the lake and seek out the exit amongst the reeds. The Brathay now starts as it flows out of the lake. Stay alert as you start this stretch from the lake as Skelwith Force lurks about 500 m below and although the river is flat it can pick up speed quite quickly and lure the unwary on to a place they most definitely do not want to be. So, after a twisting flat section, watch out for a sign on the left side warning of the **waterfall**, and get out immediately to portage on the left bank.

1) V   Skelwith Force. A large shelf in the bedrock has produced this intimidating 3.5 m fall, which has become a major tourist attraction. For many years this was regarded as the hardest fall in the area only done by "a few loopy enthusiasts", and then only in high flows when a line over the left hand rocks could be taken. However, over the years the raising of standards has seen descents of this fall now become fairly commonplace, although a high degree of respect, careful consideration and bank support should be present. In low flows the water disappears into an ugly, rocky slot which is certainly a portage, but at medium to high flows the slot is filled and the rocks become covered to form an almost circular tube which gives a unique meltdown experience from which most return giggling. The alternative is a strong boof on the right.
   In high flows; then the scary run over the left hand rocks should avoid the stopper. ↪

continued on next page ↪

⇨ continued from previous page

2) Play `The Looping Pool` There are two narrowings at the exit from the pool below the main fall, and strong currents form a couple of play spots. The lower chute which has the best eddies and the strongest flow is the more popular. For years paddlers have been coming here to loop their boats and rip their bows on the sharp rocks hidden in the channel. However, the advent of short play boats has meant less knocking on the bottom and more wheelies. Go enjoy.

B) II / III   After portaging the falls by the tourist path on the left it is possible to launch back into the flat water below the Looping Pool. A more rocky section from here down to Skelwith Bridge is probably the crux of the river for most and awkward to inspect. Below the bridge the river calms down again and flows through broad flats which often flood. The lay by access point is passed on the left bank somewhere in these flats. Eventually the river narrows again a picks up pace as the banks are lined by thick bushes. A big eddy pool on the right provides a place to gather and rest before the final rush down under the footbridge and the last rapid into Brathay pool.

3) III   Skelwith Bridge rapid. In low water this can be a scrape and best avoided. At normal levels there are many tree and rock obstacles to avoid.

4) II / III   Brathay Falls. This last small rapid down to Brathay Pool is normally a bouncy grade II and it seems a bit of a misnomer to call it them `falls` but it can seem grade III in flood conditions, and forms a fast surfing wave.

EGRESS
Most will egress at Brathay Pool to the parking area on the right bank.
It is however possible to add another kilometre of easy river down to Windermere and then paddle across to the Waterhead boat landings.

Surfing the Brathay Wave   *Ian Wilson collection*

Skelwith Force, River Brathay.   *Stuart Miller*

CHURCH BECK

YHA

Coppermines Valley

Section 1

A

A593
To
Ambleside

N

Start — 1
2
Miners
Bridge
3 4
8 9
10
Start / Egress

Coniston

Sun Inn

Section 2

B

Egress
Bannock Stone
Bridge

P

500 m

A593
To Torver

Coniston
Lake

CHURCH BECK

A small beck falling out of the copper mines valley down to Coniston with two distinct halves. The top section is a short, hard, steep, low volume waterfall run which will involve several portages, awkward climbing, abseiling and possibly jumping for a complete descent, and will only appeal to those with a penchant for stunts rather than paddling. The lower section however, while also being short, gives a fast and entertaining high water ride back to the town over several rocky shelves and chutes.

SECTION 1 The Waterfalls

From :	Top Waterfall	293 981	Grade :	V (X)
To :	Weir	297 978	Maps : O.S. 96, Explorer OL6	
Distance :	400 m		Stars : ✶ Scenery : ❀❀	

SUMMARY
The falls on this section start amongst lovely open scenery at the bottom of the Copper Mines valley, however things change abruptly and the beck soon drops into a dark and foreboding tree lined gorge containing several large falls, these can be either entertaining or frightening depending on water level, skill and frame of mind. An Indiana Jones sense of exploration will be of great benefit.

INDICATORS
A low to medium level trip which needs some flow to fill the gaps between the boulders. Different falls will become possible or not at different levels, so its up to you. At medium flows it may be possible to combine both sections of the beck for a run back to the town.

START
There is a fall higher up in the Copper Mines valley, near the Youth Hostel and mine buildings which has been run, but in anything other than flood conditions the kilometre back to the main gorge will be too dry to paddle.
It is best to drive up the Youth hostel road from Coniston town centre until the gorge can be seen on the left. Park considerately where the road starts to steepen or continue further to where the road starts to flatten out again. The first fall is found about 100 m above the packhorse bridge where the flat upper valley ends. Where to start ? You make your own mind up in this territory.

DESCRIPTION
A) V It would be advisable for anyone contemplating a descent of this beck to scramble up the gorge from the bottom in dry conditions to get an idea of what is entailed as only the first few drops are visible from the road and escape would be difficult once started.

1) V The top fall is a tight, twisty gorge in the bedrock with four small drops followed by an undercut constriction.

2) X Beware not to be swept into this next 3 m fall which follows immediately and drops onto boulders, and is currently also blocked by a tree.

3) X The fall just after the Miners Bridge may look inviting but has a nasty projecting rock half way down and a small, very shallow plunge pool.

4) V+ The first fall in the gorge proper is a clean drop, but lands in a narrow frothy undercut defile from which paddling, rolling, or rescue would be a problem.

5) IV The next small drop is more straight forward and you have no choice but to run it after running the first one, but beware of a rock in the pool very close to the bottom of the fall. A bit of speed or a boof usually clears it.

6) V+ The third fall requires a difficult line to get on the rock slide formed by a large chock stone. Beware of underwater ledges on both sides of the narrow pool.

continued on next page ⇨

Top Falls, Church Beck.   *Ian Wilson collection*

⇨ *continued from previous page*

7) V   The 4th fall is L shaped and normally can be taken right of centre, Check for trees.

8) X   The last big fall must be portaged. Usually by climbing out of the gorge or by sliding / abseiling down hard river right.

EGRESS
Climb out of the gorge on the right above the portage and follow the path back to Coniston or continue the lower section if water levels allow.

SECTION 2   The Town Run

From :	Weir	297 978	Grade :	IV+
To : Bannock Stone Bridge 305 973			Maps : O.S. 97, Explorer OL6	
Distance :	1 km		Stars : ✶ ✶ Scenery : ❀ ❀	

SUMMARY
A short but entertaining high water run over several rapids and shelves, with some grabby stoppers. Towards the village the beck runs through enclosed man made banks.

INDICATORS
Plenty of rain is needed to get the best of this section in high to flood conditions. A look over the bridge in the centre of Coniston will show if its running with the bed and all the boulders covered .

START
Park in the village and carry up a footpath, from behind the Sun Inn to meet the beck at a footbridge. Carry on up the left bank to the weir which is found about 150 m above the bridge at the top of a difficult looking multi-tiered fall. Choose your own start depending on water level, tree blockages, and adrenaline levels with the rapids getting steadily easier the lower you get.

DESCRIPTION
B) **IV+** Slide in and hang on for a fast ride back to Coniston.

9) **IV+** The first multi tiered fall from the right side of the weir is the most difficult and ends in an enclosed hole that produces a monster stopper in high water

10) **IV** Steep slides and small drops lead down and under the footbridge. Be beware of tree blockages.

11) **III** The beck remains fast flowing but is only grade III from the footbridge.

EGRESS
Continue through the town to egress easily below the second road bridge to the left bank.

CHURCH BECK 2

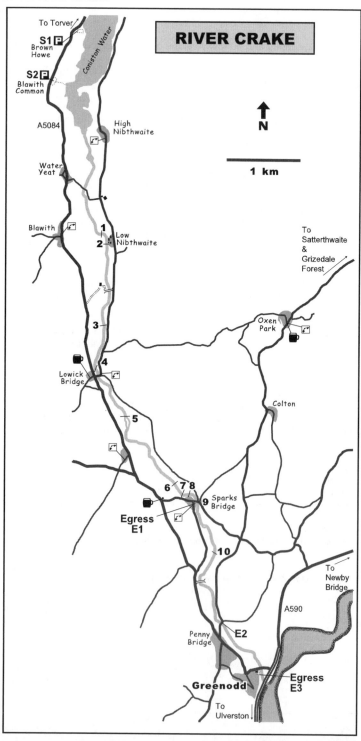

CRAKE

From :	Blawith Common	287 903	Grade :	III
To :	Greenodd	315 825	Maps : O.S. 96 , Explorer OL6 & 7	
Distance :	9.5 km		Stars : *	Scenery : ※ ※

SUMMARY

The Crake is a fairly long flat river interspersed with some seven weirs and only two real rapids. Although starting with the beautiful scenery of Coniston Water the views soon disappear as you enter the mouth of the river and a corridor of trees and bushes line the banks for most of the way. However it does keep its level well and can be paddled for several days after rain . Beginners will be kept on their toes as even though much of the river is easy the tree lined banks can make breakouts and rescue awkward, and although most of the weirs are fairly safe and easy to run, the apprehension of their presence will add to the excitement. Reputed to be an exciting high water run with the flat water changing to fast currents flowing through the trees, the eddies disappearing and the very low bridges may need rolling under.

INDICATORS

Fed by Coniston Water it holds its level well, with only the Leven possibly holding its water for longer. It is also possible in a wide variety of water levels without really any change in grade, other than the associated problems with tree branches in high water, and lack of headroom under the bridges. Sparks Bridge is the best point to look and judge the level. If there is about 1.5 m clearance under the bridge then it is a low navigable level. Anything less than 1m and get ready to rock and roll.

START

It is possible to start from either car park on the west side of Coniston Water with access to the lake.
Brown Howe (**S1**)(GR 291 111) is on the lake shore and probably the most popular starting point, but requires a paddle down the lake for 1.5 km to the mouth of the river.
Blawith Common (**S2**)(GR 287 903) is slightly more southerly with about 0.5 km to paddle to the mouth of the river, but the parking area is next to the road and boats need to be carried about 200 m over a small hill from the car park to the lake.

DESCRIPTION

A) II / III   The end of Coniston Water is lined with reeds and there is little increase in the flow for the first few hundred metres down to the widening of Allan Tarn. The river then picks up pace and is lined with bushes and trees as far as Sparks Bridge, needing care when finding breakouts, especially in higher flows.
1) III   Nibthwaite. This first grade III rapid is found about 600 m below Bouthrey Bridge at a sharp left bend. It can be inspected from the right bank, and starts with a weir, which can be shot anywhere. The main flow then twists between rocks.
2) W   A small weir follows almost immediately.
3) W   About 600 m after a footbridge a low easy angled weir.
4) W   A small weir angled across the river on the approach to Lowick Bridge, and with trees blocking parts in the middle. Best shot far left or far right .
5) II   The flow quickens after the bridge and two islands are passed. The main flow goes right of the Islands, but take care as this can lead to problems with trees and a low beam, the narrower left channel will be better.
6) W   Another weir on the approach to Spark Bridge. With a slate wall and houses on the right this has a drop of just over a metre and contains some sharp rocks.
So take care, stay upright and it is normally shot just right of the middle.

continued on next page ⇨

⇨ *continued from previous page*

7) W 100 m further on the river takes a sharp left turn and a large sloping weir marks the start of the Bobbin Mill Rapid. Normally run on the left easier angled side.

8) III Bobbin Mill Rapid. This immediately follows the weir and is quite a long section of rough water from the footbridge through some small stoppers by the slate wall and around the corner to the right. Beware of tree branches on the corner in high water.

9) B Sparks Bridge. The river bends back right and soon flows under this bridge which can have very limited headroom in high flows. Many groups egress here.

B) I / II From Sparks Bridge the river becomes more open in its final meanderings to the sea. Then from below Penny Bridge the river becomes flat and tidal which may make the last kilometre hard going if the tide is on the flood.

10) W A few hundred metres after passing an island on the left a weir made of boulders is found, this can be negotiated in several places.

EGRESS

(E1) Sparks Bridge (GR 306 849). Get out on the right bank just after the bridge. Please park and change considerately so as to not upset the villagers.

(E2) Penny Bridge (GR 833 310). Useful if hit by an incoming tide to avoid the last Kilometre.

(E3) Greenodd (GR 315 825). Egress to the right bank between Greenodd bridge and the dual carriageway. Ask permission at the garage for access and they can be very helpful.

Coniston   *T. Aspland 1850*

C1 on the Crake

Ian Wilson

Arnside parking.

Guy Austin

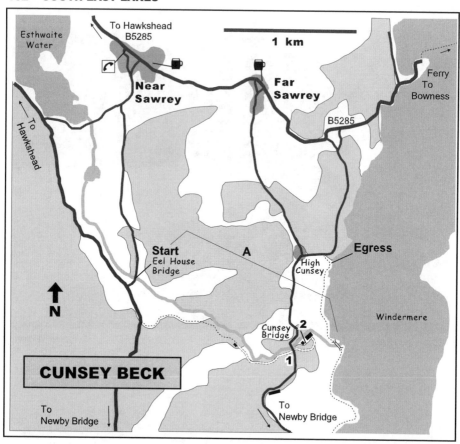

Esthwaite
Water

To Hawkshead
B5285

1 km

Near
Sawrey

Far
Sawrey

Ferry
To
Bowness

To Hawkshead

B5285

Start
Eel House
Bridge

A

Egress

High
Cunsey

N

Cunsey
Bridge

2

1

Windermere

CUNSEY BECK

To
Newby Bridge

To
Newby Bridge

CUNSEY BECK

From : Eel House Bridge 369 941	Grade : III (IV)
To : Windermere 384 942	Maps : O.S. 96 , Explorer OL7
Distance : 2 km	Scenery : ✿✿

SUMMARY
A short trip of mostly fast grade II / III water through the forest, saving its only notable rapid for the last hundred metres as it rushes down a narrow gorge past the old mill below Cunsey Bridge. Although lake fed from Esthwaite Water, it really needs to be in flood conditions to warrant the short sharp blast. Beware of trees often blocking the last fall or immediately below it, and there have been reports of fences also appearing sometimes on this section.

INDICATORS
It actually needs a lot of rain to bring Esthwaite Water up enough to produce high water in the beck. If the beck is bank full and perhaps flooding the fields at the end of Esthwaite Water then it is on.

START
Starting at Eel House Bridge avoids the flat water in the first half of the beck. The bridge is found just off the Hawkshead to Newby Bridge road, 4 km from Hawkshead where there is a turn off back to Near Sawrey.

DESCRIPTION
A) III (IV) After about 400 m the beck enters the forest and speeds up to give fairly straight forward paddling down to Cunsey Bridge with only a few minor points of interest and tree branches to watch out for. An awkward move through the bridge leads to the top of the main rapid. The rapid past the old mill quickly eases off again and soon leads to the lake.

1) B Cunsey Bridge is **very low** and has a weir just above it. This makes it awkward to get the correct line on the left, and it will need portaging in high water. Inspect or portage on the right over the road.

2) IV Mill Force. This follows the bridge almost immediately with a fast powerful flow which rushes and twists down a small v shaped gorge for 100 m. Check for trees.

EGRESS
It is necessary to paddle north up the lake for 600 m to egress by large larch tree on the lake shore. A public footpath leads to the road at a corner overlooking the lake near High Cunsey.

CUNSEY BECK

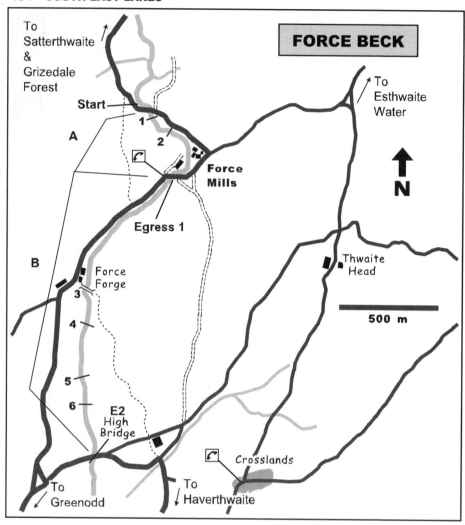

FORCE BECK

To
Satterthwaite
&
Grizedale
Forest

Start

1

A

2

Force
Mills

To
Esthwaite
Water

N

Egress 1

B

Force
Forge

3

Thwaite
Head

4

500 m

5

6

E2
High
Bridge

Crosslands

To
Greenodd

To
Haverthwaite

FORCE BECK

From :	Bridge	337 913	Grade :	III, IV, (V)
To :	Force Mill Bridge	339 909	Maps :	O.S. 96, Explorer OL7
	High Bridge	335 306		
Distance :	2 km		Stars : ✷ ✷ Scenery : ✿ ✿	

SUMMARY
A short very steep run where Grizedale Beck escapes from Grizedale valley to form Force Beck. It gives a superb 500 m blast in high water, but a bony, crunchy, bouncy hell in lower conditions. Often regarded as a one-off hard rapid, but the following run down to Rusland gives a pleasant and worthwhile continuation.

INDICATORS
Lots of rain needed to cushion the rocks on the main rapid. As this is right next to the road at Force Mills. Look and see if its your cup of tea.

START
Follow the road up the hill from Force Mills towards Saterthwaite, past the falls, to put in just above the bridge at the top.

DESCRIPTION
A)   V   A short gorge leads to a strange rock band at the top of the falls, Then the madness starts.
1)   IV   From the bridge the beck immediately shoots through a short gorge.
2)   V   Force Falls. 150 m of confused slides which in high water merge into one very steep and rough rapid with trees blocking some of the lines. The gradient steadily eases to grade III again by the bridge at Force Mills.

B)   IV   From Force Mills down to Rusland the beck follows the road for a short way before passing Force Forge and dropping into the forest over some small rocky shelves. It then eases off again but remains entertaining down to High Bridge.
3)   IV   Force Forge. The beck narrows under the footbridge and a sharp turn left leads over several rocky steps.
4)   III   A small rock bluff with low fallen trees to dodge. May need a portage in high water.
5)   F   An obvious large fence has a fallen tree at water level just above it. Portage.
6)   T   200 m beyond the fence a major tree dam needs portaging.

EGRESS
Many will treat the falls as a one off and get out just after the first bridge at Force Mills **(E1)**. The lower egress is to the right bank just below High Bridge **(E2)**. There is room to park one car by the bridge.

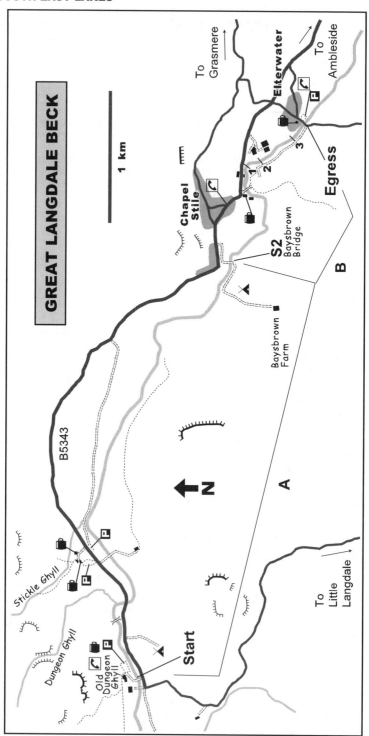

GREAT LANGDALE BECK

1 km

To Grasmere

Elterwater

To Ambleside

Chapel Stile

3

2

1

Egress

S2
Baysbrown
Bridge

B

Baysbrown
Farm

A

N

B5343

Stickle Ghyll

Dungeon Ghyll

Old
Dungeon
Ghyll

Start

To
Little
Langdale

GREAT LANGDALE BECK

From : Old Dungeon Ghyll 286 060	Grade : II, III, (IV-)
To : Elterwater Village 328 047	Maps : O.S. 90, Explorer OL6 & 7
Distance : 5 km	Scenery : ❀ ❀ ❀

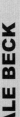

SUMMARY
The first half of this run is canalised between man made walls giving a fast and straightforward ride to the lower section with the main interest being the fantastic views of the fells in this central Lakeland valley. From Baysbrown Bridge the river starts to pick up interest for the last kilometre and a half, climaxing with `Pillar Falls` and a short rocky gorge.
Worthy of note are the two excellent pubs at the start and finish of this river.

INDICATORS
Water needs to be streaming off the fells for the many small becks to fill the river up. Looking upstream from the bridge in Elterwater at the egress will give a good indication if the river is up and the rocks in the final gorge covered.
Alternatively at the start if there is enough water to paddle under the bridge at the put in by the Old Dungeon Ghyll then the rest will be ok.

START
It is usual to start at the bridge at the entrance to the Old Dungeon Ghyll Inn, where there is a National Trust car park and a gate giving access to the river.
A much shorter trip on the final section can be started at Baysbrown Bridge **(S2)** (GR 317 053), which is found by following the track to the campsite at the west end of Chapel Stile along the Cumbrian Way.

DESCRIPTION
A) II   The first three kilometres are a fast and easy ride between man made walls, but with few eddies.
.
B) III (IV)   From Baysbrown Bridge the river picks up slightly with a few rocks in the river and a couple of sharp corners to add interest. An entertaining section then leads down past a footbridge and some large boulders in the river to a large flat pool above the weir in Chapel Stile. It may be best to inspect or portage **Pillar Falls** from here on the right bank, as once over the weir the falls follow quite soon. If portaging it is possible to regain the river just below the falls for the final rush through a rocky gorge to the bridge and egress.
1) W   Chapel Stile Weir. A large sloping weir at the exit from the large flat pool close
        to the Wainwright's Bar. This can be can be run fairly safely anywhere.
2) IV- Pillar Falls. Back in the days of long, pointy, fibreglass missiles this fall gained
        a serious reputation due to the unfortunate pinning and subsequent rescue of a
        canoeist being captured on video. So beware there are jagged rocks and
        potholes in there somewhere, but a line close to the right bank has seen most
        paddlers since shoot through wondering what all the fuss was about.

EGRESS
Egress is on the left bank just below the bridge to the car park in Elterwater Village.

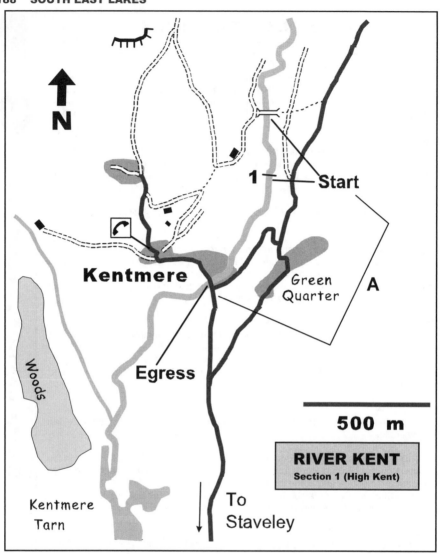

N

1

Start

A

Kentmere

Green Quarter

Woods

Egress

500 m

RIVER KENT
Section 1 (High Kent)

Kentmere Tarn

To Staveley

KENT

Starting high in the small and pretty south Lakeland valley of Kentmere, the Kent is one of the Lake District's longer rivers. It collects the water from the Sprint and the Mint on its way to the coast, so holding its level quite well in the lower reaches. There are four distinct sections giving a wide range of paddling experiences from a narrow tree lined ditch, through a flat reed infested tarn, a meandering section sprinkled with weirs before slipping through Kendal to the final undercut gorges with spectacular falls. It is this last section where the falls and water levels are at their largest that the most action is concentrated.

SECTION 1

From :	Footbridge	460 046	Grade :	IV+
To :	Kentmere	458 040	Maps :	O.S. 90, Explorer OL7
Distance :	0.5 km		Stars : ✷	Scenery : ❀❀

SUMMARY
A short steep yet fun start to the river which attracts the odd descent. Only really worth it if you start below the portage and plan to carry on down the next section. The portage at Force Jump spoils what would otherwise be an excellent run. Do not be tempted by this fall, as the pool is totally blocked by a boulder which is hidden at otherwise runnable levels, or you could be the next Mad Yaker to break their leg here!

INDICATORS
High water or flood levels needed to bring this run into condition. Take a look at the egress where the river flows under the bridge at Kentmere Village. A good flow is needed with all the rocks upstream covered.

START
It is best to park at the village and walk up to the start. Follow the road from the bridge up the left bank of the river. It climbs a steep hill, then turn left at a sharp junction and go 200 metres further to where a bridleway leads off towards the river (possible parking for one car on right just before path). Shortly a path then leads left down to the put in at a footbridge. However, as it is **extremely difficult to stop above Force Jump** without bank support it is more usual to start the river on the ramp from the pool half way down the fall.

DESCRIPTION
A) IV+ Make sure you know where to, and are able to, get out above Force Jump. As from the start the river is quite fast, rocky and tree lined with the run into the fall sucking you in without much warning. Portage the fall on the left and regain the river at the exit from the plunge pool where a 4 m ramp shoots off into continuous tight rapids which however soon ease towards the bridge
1) X Force Jump. Mandatory Portage due to large rock completely blocking the landing.

EGRESS
Egress at the Bridge in Kentmere. Or continue the next section.

KENT 1 (High Kent)

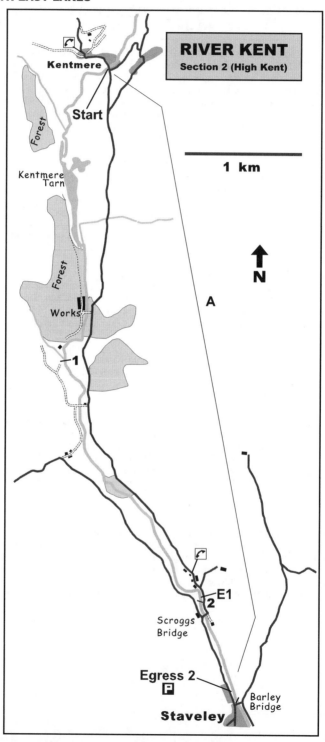

RIVER KENT
Section 2 (High Kent)

1 km

N

Kentmere

Start

Forest

Kentmere
Tarn

Forest

Works

A

1

E1
2

Scroggs
Bridge

Egress 2
P

Barley
Bridge

Staveley

SECTION 2	Kentmere to Staveley		
From : Kentmere 458 040	**Grade :** II / III (IV)		
To : Scroggs Bridge 467 994 Barley Bridge Weir 470 987	**Maps :** O.S. 97, Explorer OL7		
Distance : 5 or 6 km	**Stars : ✶** **Scenery : ❀❀❀**		

SUMMARY
A pleasant trip on mainly straight forward but never placid water, except for the lake. While trying to find the mouth of the river on Kentmere Tarn reeds can make navigation a problem.

INDICATORS
High water is needed for this trip, At Scroggs Bridge there should be navigable lines down both sides of the island above the bridge and most of the rocks covered.

START
Start at the bridge at the entrance to Kentmere Village.

DESCRIPTION
A) II / III (IV)   From the bridge a series of tiny weirs will not usually be noticed on the run down to the lake. Head straight down the lake and hope to find the river at the end on the left. Once found, the river leads down a canalised section past some works buildings. From the end of this straight section the river meanders through pleasant countryside with one long grade III rapid before easing off until the obvious falls just above Scroggs Bridge. However be aware of trees which can block the whole river. Either get out above the fall or try your luck.

1) III   As the river passes a cottage on the right bank it picks up a bit for the start of a long grade III rapid.

2) IV   Scroggs Bridge Fall. This rapid is a long grade IV with sections above and below the bridge which can provides an exciting finish to the trip. The river splits round two islands. Which side to run? Various lines depend on different water levels and tree blockages, so make your own choice (as always).

EGRESS
Egress to the road on the left bank above the falls at Scroggs Bridge **(E1)**, This should be inspected before you start as it can be hard to spot from the river. It is steep, covered in trees, and awkward to make in high water.

If you run the fall its best to carry on for 600 m and egress to the right bank at the pool above the next weir where there is a small car park **(E2)**.

KENT 2 (High Kent)

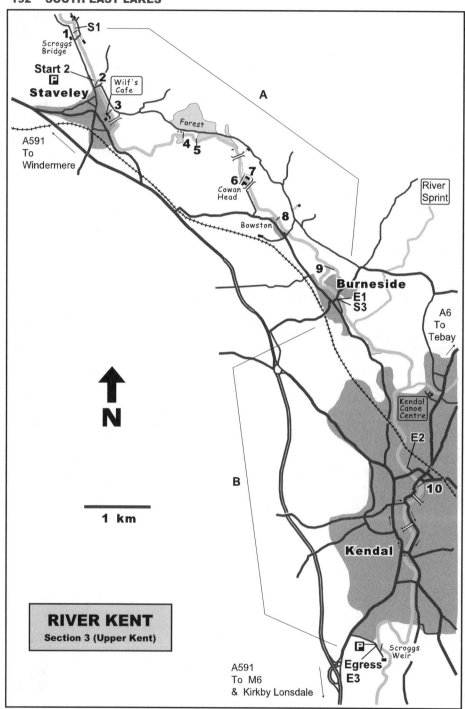

S1

1 Scroggs Bridge

Start 2

P

Staveley

2

Wilf's Cafe

3

A

Forest

4 5

A591 To Windermere

6 7

Cowan Head

8

Bowston

9

River Sprint

Burneside

E1 S3

A6 To Tebay

Kendal Canoe Centre

E2

B

10

Kendal

N

1 km

RIVER KENT

Section 3 (Upper Kent)

P

Scroggs Weir

Egress E3

A591 To M6 & Kirkby Lonsdale

SECTION 3		Staveley to Kendal	
From :	Scroggs Bridge 467 994 Barley Bridge Weir 470 987	**Grade :**	II / III (IV)
To :	Scroggs Weir 512 906	**Maps :** O.S. 97, Explorer OL7	
Distance :	12 or 13 km	**Stars : ✶✶**	**Scenery : ✿✿**

SUMMARY
A long and mostly easy section of river which flows amongst some pleasant countryside before the final flat three kilometres through Kendal Town centre. The difficulty is mostly only grade II except for two grade IV falls. One of these can be avoided right at the start and the other easily portaged. It is however the incredible number of weirs which festoon this section which make it fairly serious and not a good choice as a grade II option, unless accompanied by more experienced paddlers. Because of these contrasts this section is often ignored by both beginner and expert alike, but it makes an interesting and pleasant trip with the right combination of water levels and camaraderie for a mixed ability group.

INDICATORS
A fairly decent amount of water is needed for the upper part of this section and the levels should be checked at the start and in Staveley village. The initial rapid should be runable without hitting too many rocks and there should be enough water to float comfortably through the village. A couple of small streams join after the village and for the lower half the Sprint and Mint both add to the volume. The second weir can be inspected from the balcony of Wilf's Cafe in Staveley, found behind the Mountain Bike Centre.

START
Scroggs Bridge is found by following the road to Kentmere from Staveley for a kilometre to where it crosses the river. Start from the left bank just above the bridge **(S1)** and go straight into the first difficult fall. If you wish to start below the fall it is probably best to go back down the road to a car park **(S2)** on the right bank above the first weir, at Barley Bridge, which is found just on the edge of Staveley Village. A much shorter and easier trip can be made by starting at Burneside **(S3)**.

DESCRIPTION
A) II (IV) Scroggs Bridge Fall, Barley Bridge weir, and Wilf's Cafe weir all set this trip off with a bang. Things soon settle down after the village however as the river flows through fields with small rapids for a few kilometres, and only a few overhanging bushes to avoid. On seeing a bridge wake up as in a few hundred metres there is another weir on a left bend followed immediately by the second hard rapid. In the next two kilometres through Bowston and Burneside there are **two nasty weirs** which need inspection and probable portage. After Burneside the Sprint soon enters from the left followed shortly by the Mint on the outskirts of Kendal. Go under the railway bridge and the first road bridge and then stop to inspect the **first weir** in the town.

1) IV Scroggs Bridge Fall. The entrance exam for the bolder guys. Different lines at different levels.
2) W Barley Bridge Weir. A 3 m steeply angled weir with a shallow landing.
3) W Wilf's Cafe Weir. Inspecting this weir before you start gives a good excuse for a coffee in one of the area's best cafes. Once on the river however, inspect and portage left. A limbo under the metal bar on the right avoids the main central stopper. Keep away from the left side as a metal stake protrudes.
4) F A chain fence by the sewage works can be at an awkward height at low levels.
5) F Following soon after the chain is nasty strand of barbed wire on a left bend which can be a problem at certain levels, but it is usually covered in high water.
6) W Cowan Head Weir. This complicated weir leads straight into the next rapid and is best inspected and portaged by a path on the left bank.

continued on next page ⇨

⇨ *continued from previous page*

7) IV Cowan Head Rapid. This once had the distinction of being underneath a factory and was only paddled in the darkness by the very brave. Now the factory has gone to leave a holiday flat development and an entertaining rapid over several rocky steps before it narrows down beneath the bridge.

8) W Bowston Weir. Found at the entrance to the village where the river goes flat and appears to disappear. A large nasty vertical weir full of debris and with concrete ledges as landings. Inspect and portage on the left bank, although a ramp far left may allow passage.

9) W Burneside Mill Weir. Found just above a large right bend before the village, where water is directed into the mill complex. It has several large fish steps which should be avoided and it must be treated with great caution. Inspect and portage on the right bank.

B) II Many finish the trip at Burneside **(E1)**, soon after which the river joins the Sprint where it becomes broad and flat for the next seven kilometres through Kendal. Once past the **dangerous Town Weir** the banks become canalised and there are many tiny man made shelves and weirs creating small waves and stoppers which should not be any problem. Eventually the river takes a sharp swing right then back left around a large `S` bend, becoming flat and sluggish on the approach to Scroggs Weir and the egress.

10) W Kendal Town Weir. This is the first weir in the town just after the second road bridge and can have a strong tow back in high water. After passing under the railway bridge and the first road bridge stop on the right bank to inspect before going under the second road bridge as the banks beyond are canalised. Possibly even best to inspect before starting the trip if in any doubt. Portage by egressing right then crossing the bridge and putting back in on the left bank in the park.

EGRESS

E1 It is possible to access / egress just below the bridge in Burneside to the right bank onto the Millennium Green in the village centre, this avoids the long flat section down to Kendal.

E2 It is possible to egress to the left bank just before the first road bridge in Kendal where parking can sometimes be found, and this avoids portaging the weir.

E3 Just above Scroggs Weir where there is easy access and some parking on the right bank. Description to find this is in start of section 4.

Barley Bridge Weir, River Kent.   *Stuart Miller*

SECTION 4		Kendal to Park Head			
From :	Scroggs Weir Hawes Bridge	512 906 512 892	**Grade :**	IV	
To :	Park Head	507 864	**Maps :** O.S 97, Explorer OL7		
Distance :		4.5 km	**Stars : ★★★**		**Scenery : ❀❀❀**

SUMMARY
A great section of river which although fairly short flows through two committing, narrow and undercut gorges and several exciting falls. It is paddled at most levels and at low to medium flows the pool drop nature of the falls are often an intermediate paddlers introduction to grade IV and can seem a soft touch, but as one might expect in flood conditions it becomes extremely serious without any escape in the gorges and large river wide stoppers increasing the grade to a big water grade V.

INDICATORS
A large catchment area including the Sprint and the Mint gives the Kent enough water to be paddleable at most times of the year. If it is possible to shoot Scroggs weir at the start without too much of a scrape then the river will be fine. If it is flowing well over the weir with a small but playable stopper at the bottom then waves and currents in the gorges will be quite powerful, however if a scrape on the weir looks likely then starting at Hawes Bridge avoids most of the shallows by dropping straight into the first gorge.

START
Scroggs Weir **(S1)** is found by leaving Kendal on the A6. Where the houses finish on the left there is a Filling Station with a small road beside it leading down through Scroggs Wood to the weir, and a small parking area.
Whereas Hawes Bridge **(S2)** which has been known locally for many years as Prizet Bridge, is found by taking the small road to Naitland 1 km south of the A591 / A6 junction. There is only room for parking one car on this narrow road.

DESCRIPTION
A) II Easy water leads through fields to Hawes Bridge.
1) W Scroggs Weir. A shallow easy angled weir with no particular problems.

B) IV- The first gorge. The fall under the bridge drops into a narrow but flat undercut gorge which can have unsettling boils and currents in higher flows. Some easy rapids then lead to a longer multi tiered rapid with a cliff on the left bank.
2) III The entry drop below Hawes Bridge.
3) IV- An old broken down weir usually forces the main current into a S shaped wiggle before crashing through a large hole next to the cliff on the left bank. In high flows a couple of play and surfing waves form in the gorge below.

C) II The river opens out and flat water leads to a weir at Wilson Place, it then remains straightforward to a left hand bend which signals the run in to Sedgwick Bridge
4) W Wilson Place Weir. The centre chute is and best avoided, while the rest of the weir should always be treated with respect and portaged on the right bank if necessary. A very strong tow back develops in high flows.

D) IV The lower gorge again starts with a drop through the bedrock into an undercut channel beneath the bridge. Immediately after the bridge is a small but **serious L shaped drop** followed by an island with an easy angled weir either side of it and the final run in to Force falls.
5) III The drop into the lower gorge is straightforward, but commits one to the serious drop which follows, and rescue of a swimmer in the undercut gorge would be a problem. It is usually possible to land onto slabs on the right bank to inspect before committing to this first rapid.

continued on next page

KENT 4 (Lower Kent)

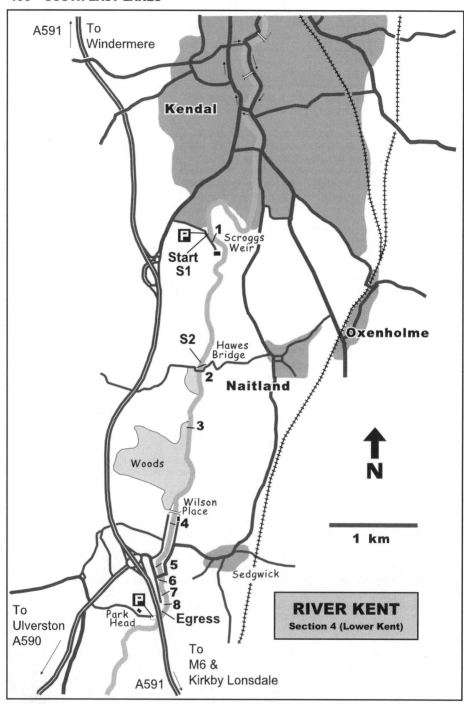

A591 To Windermere

Kendal

P
1 Scroggs Weir
Start S1

S2 Hawes Bridge
2 Naitland

3

Woods

Wilson Place
4

5
6
7
8

Sedgwick

P Park Head
Egress

To Ulverston A590

N

1 km

RIVER KENT
Section 4 (Lower Kent)

Oxenholme

To M6 & Kirkby Lonsdale

A591

⇨ *continued from previous page*

6) IV- Sedgwick Bridge Fall. This L shaped fall forms a serious stopper in high water and it can be awkward to avoid the main current flowing into the corner of the L. In low to medium flows a sneak line on the left over shallow slabs avoids most problems.

7) W   The easy angled weir either side of the island usually presents no problems, but the left side gives a more straightforward run into Force Falls.

8) IV- Force Falls. At first acquaintance this can be an intimidating drop but at anything except extremely low or extremely high water conditions it is usually nothing more than an exhilarating crash through the large wave at the bottom into the collecting pool with plenty of room to recover. In low water the main flow is channelled down a rocky shoot on the right which tends to bang the front end while in very high water be careful of the steel ladder on the left bank !!! Please avoid the fish pass at all times and avoid climbing back up the rocks for a second go. Access is always delicate and under review at this popular spot.

EGRESS

Egress to the concrete of the bridge foundations just at the exit from the Force Falls collecting pool on the right bank. This avoids disturbing fish spawning beds which apparently lie amongst the first rapids below the bridge. A path leads below the bridge to a small car park at the end of a lane at Park Head. This lane is found by taking the first turning left off the A590 to Ulverston from the Sedgwick roundabout on the A591.

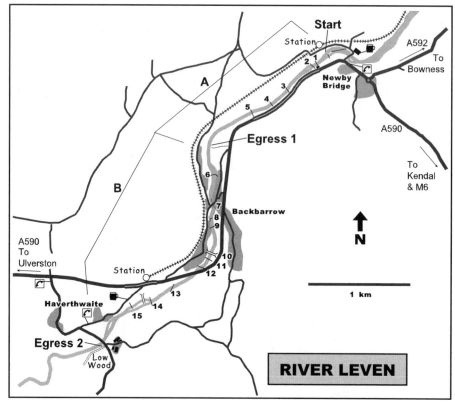

RIVER LEVEN

continued from opposite page ⇐

B) IV The complete run down to Haverthwaite is a classic with continuous interest.

6) W   Water Close Weir. A large weir which is both vertical and shallow across most of the river. An easy ramped section near the right bank gives safe passage.

7) IV   Backbarrow Bridge. The river is constricted to about a quarter of its width and drops some 6 m in a short distance to the final hole under the bridge. A very intimidating fall due to the difficulty of inspection and rescue. However, it usually flushes through except in very high water. Best to inspect it before starting or to pick out a landing for a portage. Rescues must be performed quickly and competently to avoid being swept into the narly weir which follows.

8) X   Backbarrow Weir. A large, complicated and **nasty weir** which is a portage for most. Various lines have been run by the brave and competent at grade V+. Portage on the left bank.

9) W   Following almost immediately below the eddy is a second weir which has a very strong stopper on the right, a tongue left of centre and smaller hole on the left.

10) B   A low footbridge with a pipe underneath it may need rolling under or portage in high water.

11) W   A small island with a weir either side. Left is a smooth enclosed shoot with a strong tow back in high water, while the right is a bouncy ramp with rocks.

12) III   An entertaining rapid with some big waves leads down under the A590 road bridge.

13) W   Fish Steps Weir. This large weir is nicely angled and can be shot almost anywhere. The last stopper at the base of the fish ladder can form a play hole.

14) IV   Fisherman's Island. The left channel is a grade easier in normal flows and the best way in high water. The right channel leads round a blind bend into a narrow rocky chute containing the remnants of an old footbridge which can be a problem in high water.

15) W   A series of small shelves form playful stoppers in the right channel.

EGRESS 2
Egress is to the left bank just below the B5278 bridge between Haverthwaite and Low Wood **(E2)**.

LEVEN

From :	Newby Bridge 367 864	Grade :	III, IV, (V)
To :	Test Course Field 356 855 Haverthwaite Bridge 345 836	Maps :	O.S. 97, Explorer OL7
Distance :	1.25 km or 4 km	Stars : ★ ★ ★	Scenery : ❀ ❀ ❀

SUMMARY

Despite it's close proximity to roads on both sides of the river, several weirs and the village of Backbarrow, paddling the Leven is always an absorbing and entertaining experience with the mind focused on the water features rather than the intrusion of man into this otherwise beautiful valley. It is fitting that this most southerly of Lakeland's rivers drains the largest collection of lakes in the area, with the waters of Grasmere, Rydal Water, Elterwater, Esthwaite Water and Windermere combining to keep it flowing most of the year round. Unfortunately the classic status of this run is not matched by mans generosity to let us enjoy it, and access agreements are at present harsh or non existent. The short test course section is the only part accessible at the time of writing and then only on a few weekends a year. The complete description is included in the hope that this unsatisfactory situation will change.

INDICATORS

As mentioned above the huge catchment area keeps the Leven flowing most of the year and long after rain. Although possible with a scrape in low water it improves greatly once the water is flowing over the sides of the Brick Chute weir.
If the flood gates are open in the weir above the start then a good high water level can be expected. If contemplating the whole river a quick peek at Backbarrow Bridge before starting will give a good idea of levels, line needed, and if you want to run it.

START

It is possible to start on the bottom end of Windermere with a kilometre of flat water, but this is discouraged due to fish spawning beds being apparently directly below the low header dam at Newby Bridge. It is best to access below these beds from the small road by Newby Bridge Station on the Lakeside to Haverthwaite Railway. Access from the road as far down as possible where it leaves the river bank to avoid the spawning beds. On open days a field is available for parking and access.

DESCRIPTION

A) III Beginning with the Brick Chute weir and followed almost immediately by Mill Force the river then soon enters a continuous technical Graveyard section with plenty of small drops, stoppers, standing waves, rocks and boils to play amongst.

1) W The Brick Chute Weir. Normally taken through the central channel. A popular play spot although narrow. The stoppers either side of the brick chute can be very retentive in high water and best avoided.
2) III Mill Force. The river splits around a rocky island with the normal route on the far left leading through a big wave while a rocky chicken shoot far right leads through a playful stopper.
3) III The Graveyard. Starts with a 1 m drop or a large wave (depending on levels).
4) III A large two tier rapid with several rocks to avoid.
5) III The third significant drop with standing waves on the right. Boulders and small stoppers then lead down to the Test Course Egress .

EGRESS 1

As the Graveyard section gradually calms down the river begins a large bend to the left and egress should be made to the field on the left **(E1)**. Or continue the full run.

↩ continued on opposite page

RIVER LEVEN A

LITTLE LANGDALE BECK

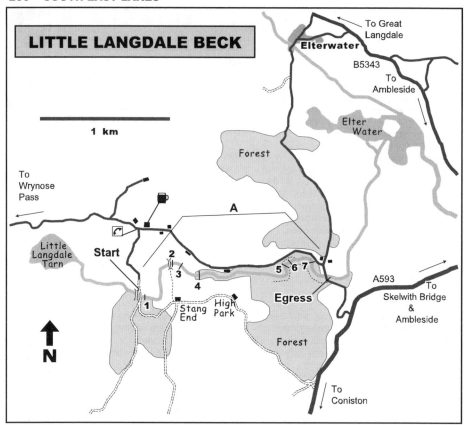

To Great
Langdale

Elterwater

B5343

To
Ambleside

Elter
Water

Forest

1 km

To
Wrynose
Pass

A

Little
Langdale
Tarn

Start

2

3

4

5 6 7

A593

Egress

To
Skelwith Bridge
&
Ambleside

1

Stang
End

High
Park

N

Forest

To
Coniston

LITTLE LANGDALE BECK

From :	Ford	306 028	Grade :	II, III (VI)
To :	Bridge	330 030	Maps : O.S. 90, Explorer OL7	
Distance :		2 km	Stars : ✱	Scenery : ⚘ ⚘ ⚘

SUMMARY
Once past the initial fence obstacles, this short but pleasant little river leads through a wooded gorge with a mighty waterfall to portage and wonder at. Waterfall freaks may well just walk up from the egress on the right bank to inspect the fall. Some may run it, but most will settle for the inspection alone. A longer trip can be made by continuing down to Elterwater but it is flat from just below the egress described.

INDICATORS
Although the beck is fed by a small tarn it needs heavy rain to bring it up. Probably best to look over the bridge at the egress and see if it is flowing nicely with all the rocks covered. If attempting Colwith Force you will probably want a different water level to that required for the rest of the river, but then that will be obvious to those contemplating this sort of thing.

START
The ford is found on a small track joining the hamlet of Little Langdale to Tilberthwaite and Hodge Close quarries. Parking is awkward and limited at the Little Langdale side, and boats need to be carried down the track to the ford, so an approach from the A593 to Coniston road via High Park and Stang End may be better (However, no trailers or mini buses please).

DESCRIPTION
A) III   From the ford a wire fence and two sheep fences have to be passed before the river improves. A wooded gorge with small falls and rapids lead down to a sharp left bend and a pool above a small weir, which marks **Colwith Force**. From the base of the falls a short gorge leads in two hundred metres to the bridge.
1) F   Wire fence . Portage on right.
2) F   Sheep fence.
3) F   Sheep fence.
4) III   Soon after the fences the river leads into a pleasant woody gorge with continuous small rapids and a couple of larger bedrock steps.
5) W   A sharp bend left with a large tree growing out over the river from a rock on the right leads to flat water at the top of a shallow weir. This indicates that Colwith Force follows immediately, and should be portaged from here.

6) X   Colwith Force. At water levels needed to run the rest of the river this should be avoided. Descents are usually only done as a low level stunt when it is more of a bounce down rocks and probably only a bold grade IV. However it soon gets very serious at normal levels becoming a dangerous grade VI, offering a vicious sequence with an awkward entry, followed by a horrible pinning spot and then a sharp right turn to avoid the direct line which is blocked by rocks in the bottom pool. Portage via either bank. The left bank leads past some huts and down slippery wooden steps to enter at the base of the falls, whereas the right bank as a good footpath past the fall from which it is possible to regain the river for the final gorge.

7) III   A large rock which partially blocks the river should be passed on the right.

EGRESS
Egress to the road on the right bank after the bridge.

LITTLE LANGDALE BECK

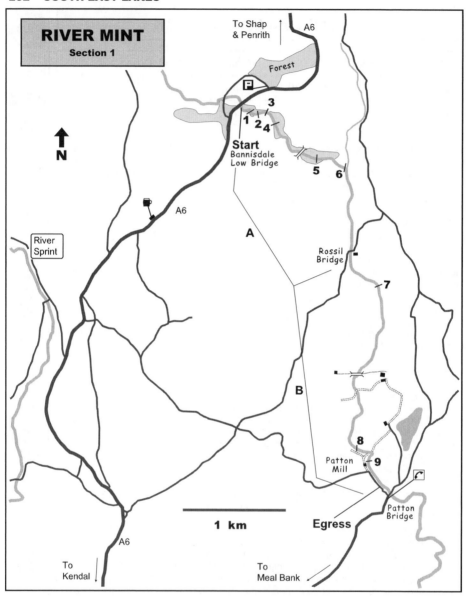

RIVER MINT
Section 1

To Shap & Penrith
A6

Forest

Start
Bannisdale Low Bridge

N

River Sprint

A6

A

Rossil Bridge

B

Patton Mill

8

9

Egress

Patton Bridge

1 km

A6

To Kendal

To Meal Bank

MINT

Rarely paddled in its entirety due to a scrappy start. The lower section however has a couple of interesting rapids and is a popular run , although this is probably due more for its ease of access and proximity to Kendal than its scenic beauty. Not exactly in Mint condition! rubbish rather than wildlife is to be more likely found along the river banks.

SECTION 1

From :	Bannisdale Bridge	542 011	Grade :	II, III, (IV)
	Rossil Bridge	553 997		
To :	Patton Bridge	557 974	Maps : O.S. 90 / 97, Explorer OL7	
Distance :		5 km	Scenery : ❁	

SUMMARY
No more than a small steep beck when it exits from Bannisdale the Mint is frustrating to start, with several portages around falls and fences, before settling down to give a mostly grade II run between trees and bushes. A weir and small rapid liven things up again just above Patton Bridge. In flood low trees and branches cause problems.

INDICATORS
This upper section needs recent heavy rain to bring it up. It is best judged at the start where there needs to be a good flow under Bannisdale Bridge with the whole bed covered looking upstream.

START
Park in a lay by found on a minor loop road off the A6 200 m north of Bannisdale Low Bridge. Carry back to the bridge and down a steep slope to the right bank of the river. Start below the narrow slot under the bridge for a very short section to the first portage.

DESCRIPTION
A) III (IV) After a **large unrunnable fall** and a short gorge several fences interrupt the first kilometre down to the confluence with Ashstead Beck.
1) X   This large 10 m fall is found after only 80 m of paddling. Get out in an eddy on the left at a right hand bend as just below nasty rocks and a tree blockage guard the fall. A potential line on the right, on the main drop, leads into a very restricted plunge pool of unknown depth so portage on the left bank.
2) IV   Immediately below the fall is a narrow twisty gorge. Easily portaged if need be.
3) F   A mesh fence at the end of the gorge can give problems in high water. Followed in 50 m by a second fence.
4) III   A 2 m fall starts a more continuous rapid.
5) F   Beware of a single strand of wire soon after a footbridge.
6) F   At the confluence with Ashstead Beck another fence blocks the river, followed by 200 m of low trees.

B) II (III) From Rossil Bridge, which can be used as an alternative access point, there are about 2 kilometres of tree lined banks before the weir and rapid at Patton Mill.
7) F   A fence may need portaging.
8) W   This weir has some wooden stakes in it but can be run through a broken section on the right.
9) III   Fish Steps rapid. Soon after the weir, a ford and sharp right bend lead to the top of this bouncy rapid formed by natural angled drops in the bedrock. There is a footpath on the right bank.

EGRESS
At Patton Bridge access to the road is easy as it runs alongside the right bank for 300 m.

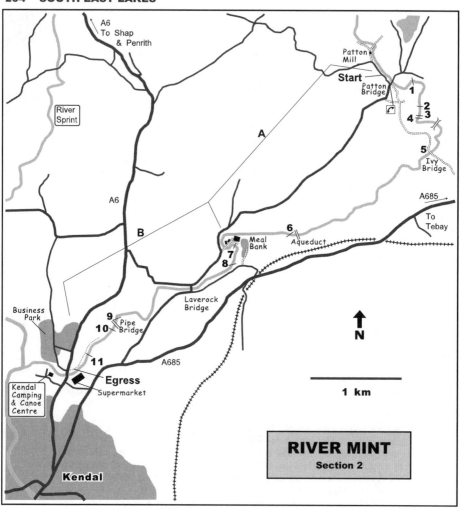

A6
To Shap
& Penrith

Patton
Mill

Start

Patton
Bridge

1

2
3
4

River
Sprint

5
Ivy
Bridge

A6

A685

To
Tebay

A

B

6
Meal
Bank

Aqueduct

7
8

Laverock
Bridge

Business
Park

9 Pipe
10 Bridge

N

11

A685

Egress

Supermarket

1 km

Kendal
Camping
& Canoe
Centre

Kendal

RIVER MINT
Section 2

SECTION 2

From :	Patton Bridge	557 974	Grade :	III / IV
To :	Mint Bridge	522 943	Maps :	O.S. 97, Explorer OL7
Distance :		7.5 km	Stars : ✶✶ Scenery : ✿	

IV

SUMMARY
Although not very pretty, with the main rapid at Meal bank being amongst the concrete banks of an industrial site, this is an interesting and popular run with some exciting rapids and several weirs. The two main rapids are awkward to protect or portage, giving a sense of seriousness and commitment to this otherwise medium grade run. High water levels can also affect the grade considerably.

INDICATORS
With only very small tributaries adding to the flow this lower section still needs heavy rain and is really only a spate run. Check the level at Laverock Bridge (GR 535 951) and if it is possible to canoe under the bridge then it will be OK, but the more the better.

START
Start just above Patton Bridge where the road runs along the right bank for several hundred metres.

DESCRIPTION
A) III   Mainly grade II with a couple of nice rapids, however watch out for the weirs and wire fences.
1) III   Below the bridge a left bend brings you to a pool which leads to a couple of short rapids over bedrock steps.
2) F   A single strand of barbed wire has been reported here, close to a 1 m high square man made structure.
3) W   A broken weir.
4) III   A good long rapid follows the weir, with some low tree branches in places.
5) F   At Ivy Bridge there is a fence which needs portaging in high water.
6) W   Garlic Weir. This **nasty weir** is shortly after passing below the aqueduct and while it can be shot on the left in low water it should always be inspected and possibly portaged.

B) III / IV   The gorge narrows and twists through Meal Bank before opening into much prettier countryside for the final run into the outskirts of Kendal.
7) III+   Meal Bank Rapid. The river goes around a large U bend to the left and under a bridge. A breakout just under the bridge on the right then allows inspection of the main rapid. However it is more easily inspected before starting the river from the works depot as the first stopper which is quite grabby lurks close to the left bank. Although it looks natural this rapid contains concrete steps and a few **metal rods** which would make a swim unpleasant.
8) III   Rocks and a small drop towards the end of the gorge can produce a stopper across the whole river in high water. Soon Laverock Bridge **(E1)** is reached.
9) W   Around a left hand bend, and just above a bridge made of pipes, there is an angled weir which should not pose any problems.
10) IV   Below the pipe bridge the river narrows and steepens for a good long rapid with several small steps. Inspect or portage on the left bank.
11) W   The final normally easy weir. However high water can create a strong stopper between the closed concrete sides.

EGRESS
Egress to the right bank and a footpath just above Mint Bridge **(E2)**. The supermarket car park is nearby and convenient.
A shorter trip can be ended at Laverock Bridge **(E1)** GR 535 951.

RIVER MINT 2

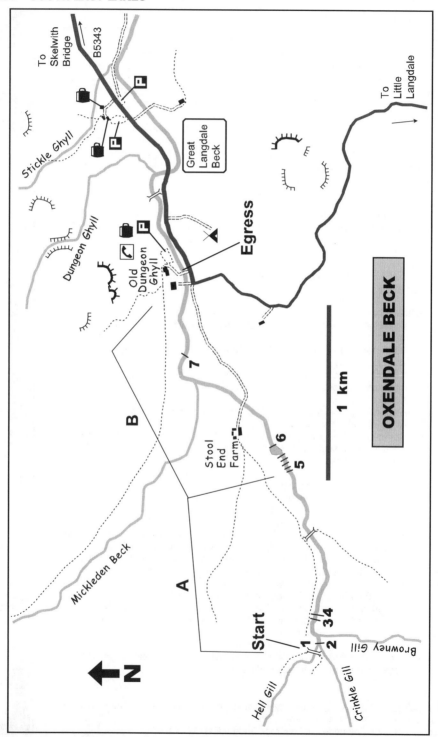

OXENDALE BECK

OXENDALE BECK

From :	Footbridge	263 052	**Grade :**	III, IV, V+

| **To :** Old Dungeon Ghyll | 286 060 | **Maps :** O.S. 90, | Explorer OL6 |

| **Distance :** | 2.5 km | **Stars : ✷** | **Scenery : ❀ ❀ ❀** |

SUMMARY
A long walk for a short but very intense section. High mountain beck paddling amongst steep boulder rapids and then a short confined gorge followed by more open boulder bashing and a canalised section through the lower fields.

INDICATORS
Flood level is required with a good flow filling the river bed at the egress. When everything else is too big a walk up here with a boat could be the answer.

START
Park at the Old Dungeon Ghyll Inn, where there is a National Trust Car Park, and walk up the valley through Stool End Farm. Once through the farm take the left path after the gate and walk up to the confluence with Crinkle Gill. Start here or 100 m further up Hell Gill, just above the footbridge.

DESCRIPTION
A) V+ Start straight into the nice but difficult slabby falls below the bridge followed by steep boulder strewn rapids down to another difficult fall. Below this powerful water confined in a gorge quickly leads down to the easier section and another footbridge.
1) V+ The fall under the bridge has three slides with constricted pools.
2) V   Very steep boulder strewn rapids and rocky slides lead past the confluence of Crinkle Gill and a short section of larger boulders at the confluence with Browney Gill.
3) V+ The main fall is at the entrance to the gorge and drops onto a nasty rock which will need portaging at most levels.
4) IV   The gorge contains another small drop with a rocky landing.

B) III Several weirs, to stop flood surges, lead to a small reservoir pool before the beck is canalised through the fields, with occasional sheep fences.
5) W   Small weirs
6) W   Large weir at exit from reservoir pool.
7) F / W After junction with Mickleden Beck a bend leads to another large pool with a fence blocking the exit over a ford and sloping weir.

EGRESS
Egress to the left bank below the second of the two bridges by the car park.
Or continue down Great Langdale Beck.

OXENDALE BECK

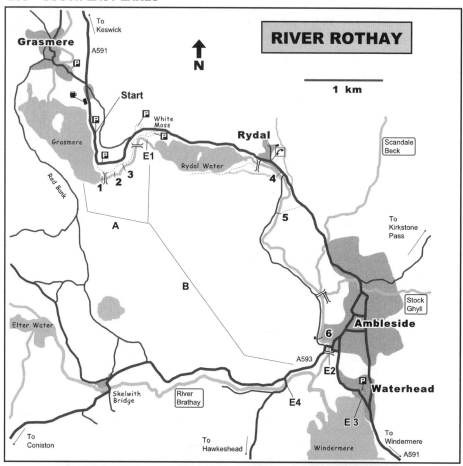

Deep in Scandale Beck, A steep Rothay tributary.　*Stuart Miller*

ROTHAY

From :	Grasmere Lay-by	352 065	Grade :	II / III
To :	Waterhead Beach	376 032	Maps : O.S. 90, Explorer OL7	
Distance :	7 km		Stars : ✶	Scenery : ✿✿✿

SUMMARY
A pleasant introduction to white water amongst the beautiful scenery of central Lakeland. With the road never far away and possible at a wide variety of water levels this is a popular run with beginners and groups. In particular the first kilometre between Grasmere and Rydal offers a short section with good access and parking at White Moss.

INDICATORS
Although not possible during a long dry spell the river holds water for a while after rain as it is fed by Grasmere and Rydal Water. A good idea of the level can be gained at Pelter Bridge (GR 366 059) just south of Rydal village. Looking upstream from the bridge the short rocky rapid needs to be navigable between the rocks at low level. If all the rocks are covered then it is a good medium level, and in spate it will be bank full.

START
At weekends and busy times parking can be awkward along the side of Grasmere but the most convenient is a small lay by 400 m south of Wordsworth's Dove Cottage on the opposite side of the A591 to the lake. Crossing the road with a boat can be the most hazardous part of the trip before climbing over the wall to access the lake.

DESCRIPTION
A) II A small weir starts a series of easy rapids down under a footbridge to Rydal water. Tree branches can often be a threat to beginners in the middle of this section.
1) W   The outlet weir can be taken safely anywhere.
2) II   The first rapid is about 100 m and contains many small boulders leading to a corner with sharp and confusing eddy lines which can catch beginners.
3) II   Three small rapids follow each other with short flat sections in between.
E1   Access / Egress to White Moss car park .

B) II / III A pleasant paddle across Rydal Water leads to a short grade III rapid down to Pelter Bridge. Below this the river winds through open fields giving good practise gaining the many eddies and avoiding tree branches before canalised banks lead past the outskirts of Ambleside to the confluence with the Brathay and on to Windermere. Most of this section is grade II but the short harder rapid should be considered mandatory as portaging is not welcome in this area.
4) III-   The short rapid down to the bridge can be rocky but is usually straightforward. Inspection and portaging is not possible as this rapid is in a private garden, which extends until below Pelter Bridge.
5) SS   Stepping Stones. In flood these are covered but at medium levels you will have to tilt your boat and possibly portage at low level.
6) W   Rothay weir. This safe sloping weir has eddies at either side and is a popular place to play and get possibly that first stopper experience. However it should be noted that the car park alongside is for hotel guests only, not paddlers!

EGRESS
It is possible to egress to a footpath and the road at a footbridge **(E2)** 50 m below Rothay Bridge which is soon after the weir. But there is no convenient parking and it may be best to carry on to the lake and turn left to the boat landings at Waterhead **(E3)**. It is also possible to turn right up the last flat section of the river Brathay to egress at the bridge by Brathay Pool **(E4)**.

RIVER ROTHAY

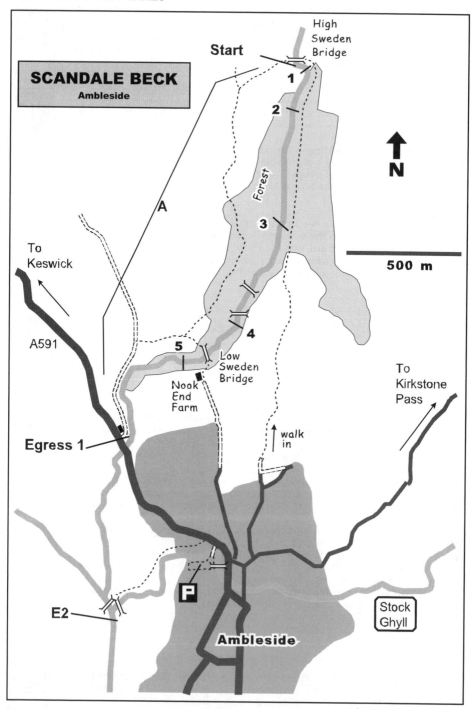

SCANDALE BECK
Ambleside

Start

High
Sweden
Bridge

1

2

Forest

3

N

500 m

To
Keswick

A

A591

To
Kirkstone
Pass

4

5

Low
Sweden
Bridge

Nook
End
Farm

Egress 1

walk
in

E2

P

Stock
Ghyll

Ambleside

SCANDALE BECK (Ambleside)

From : High Sweden Bridge 379 067	Grade :	VI
To : Scandale Bridge 372 051	Maps : O.S. 96, Explorer OL7	
Distance : 2 km	Stars : ✶✶ Scenery : ❀❀	

SUMMARY
This is a seriously steep beck with continuous falls and rapids through tree lined banks. Several of the falls are blocked by awkward rocks and many others will contain fallen trees, making this a dangerous undertaking. In moderate water it may be possible to eddy hop some of the way but the continually falling horizon line disappearing around blind bends that may contain nasty surprises and the distinct lack of eddies when needed will usually provoke continuous bank support and inspection. For a brief period the Guinness "Kayak World Speed Altitude Descent" record was held on the lower part of this beck.

INDICATORS
A good spell of rain is needed and the level goes up and down very quickly. Inspect the flow just above the bridge at the egress. If the bed of the canalised channel is flowing with the rocks just covered then a descent is possible. Any more and the ride will very quickly become out of control. This does not need as much water as one might think.

START
It is best to park in the main car park in Ambleside, by Stock Ghyll, but first it is easier to drive up to the high point on the road to drop boats off. Go up the Kirkstone Pass road past the Golden Rule Pub, just above the pub the road swings left and in another 50 m there is a smaller road leading left again. Take this left turn signposted to Sweden Bridge and keep going up this road until it becomes a footpath which eventually leads in 2 km to High Sweden Bridge. The beck has been started in the pool below the narrow fall at the bridge, but there is another awkward fall after only 50 m and many will start below this. The lower part of the beck from Low Sweden Bridge is more often paddled on its own, for the larger falls, and this can be done by parking in the small lay-by on the main road bridge and carrying up a path on the right bank.

DESCRIPTION
A) VI Continuous falls and rapids for the whole 2 kilometres make a full description pointless. If you are in this territory you know the score, inspect it all. However the following notes may be of interest.

1) V 50 m after the start there is a fairly unpleasant fall which drops against the left wall.
2) VI Soon after start the beck drops into a steep sided gorge. Inspect and find the first drop into this gorge on the walk up as it drops around a large boulder with a very narrow landing, a rock at the base and a tree branch in the fall. It is difficult to stop immediately above this and the portage is equally unpleasant.

3) VI The beck eases off for a short while but then starts its very steep descent to the first bridge. The first twisting fall around a rocky outcrop contains a nasty rock in the channel, more madness follows.

4) VI Between the pipe bridge and low Sweden Bridge there are many trees blocking the continuous series of chutes and drops.
5) V Below Low Sweden Bridge there are several larger falls of 3 m and 4 m, but still with continuous small ramps chutes and trees between them.

EGRESS
Egress to the right bank and a footpath just above Scandale Bridge **(E1)** where the beck flows under the A591. There is a small lay-by just over the bridge. Otherwise continue to join the Rothay and egress at the Stock Ghyll confluence **(E2)** to walk back across the park to the town and car park.

SCANDALE BECK (Ambleside)

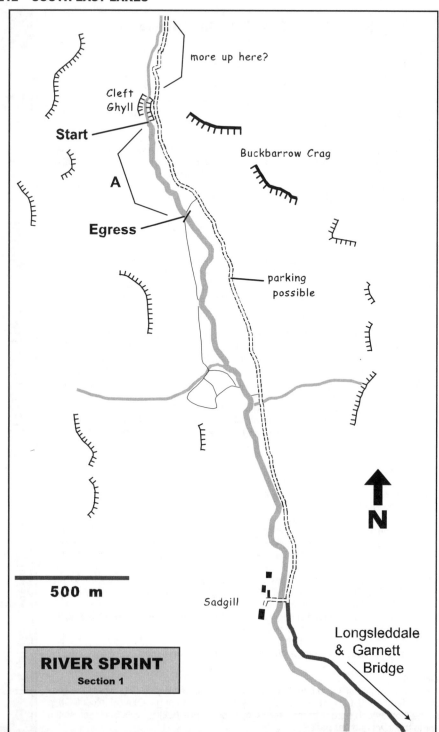

more up here?

Cleft
Ghyll

Start

Buckbarrow Crag

A

Egress

parking
possible

500 m

Sadgill

N

Longsleddale
& Garnett
Bridge

RIVER SPRINT
Section 1

SPRINT

One the area's best rivers with a short section of brilliant steep, hard, rocky, narrow falls at its head high up in Longsleddale and a long section of continuous and testing middle grade rapids as it falls out of the valley to join the Kent at Burneside. Beware however that zealous guarding of the water and limited parking can often make actually getting on the river the hardest part of a trip.

SECTION 1   The Upper Falls

From :	Cleft Ghyll	477 077	Grade :	V	
To :	Spot height 231	480 072	Maps : O.S. 90,	Explorer OL7	
Distance :		600 m	Stars : ✴ ✴	Scenery : ❀ ❀	

SUMMARY
Open fell, no crowds, no parking problems, clear water, clean smooth rocks, hard technical falls. This is short boat country, and full face helmet and elbow pads would come in handy. Sheer beauty, but a bit small and just too damn short !

INDICATORS
If the main river is starting to flowing at a low but possible level then this section will be just right. Higher water levels would make this section dangerous.

START
Drive to the head of Longsleddale, where at Sadgill the road becomes a rough track. With care it is possible to drive another kilometre and a half to where the track begins to climb (this is close to spot height marked 231 on the Outdoor Leisure map). Walk up the track until it is possible to cross through a field on the left to follow up the side of the beck and look at all the falls. The usual put in is in a small gorge where the beck comes out of the narrow defile of Cleft Ghyll. It has been reported that it is possible to carry up a further kilometre beyond Cleft Ghyll for even more narrow falls but with more portages.

DESCRIPTION
A) V   In only 600 metres this section loses 60 m in height down what is really just one rapid of continuous small falls. Amazingly there are no necessary portages and all the pools appear free of unpleasant rocks. The open banks allow easy inspection, rescue and photographic opportunities in a lovely mountain setting. At the base of the steep section there is a fence to be wary of at the egress

EGRESS
Egress at the base of the steep section back to your car.
Lack of technical interest, a need for higher water levels and access problems make continuing not a worthwhile option.

RIVER SPRINT 1 (Upper Sprint)

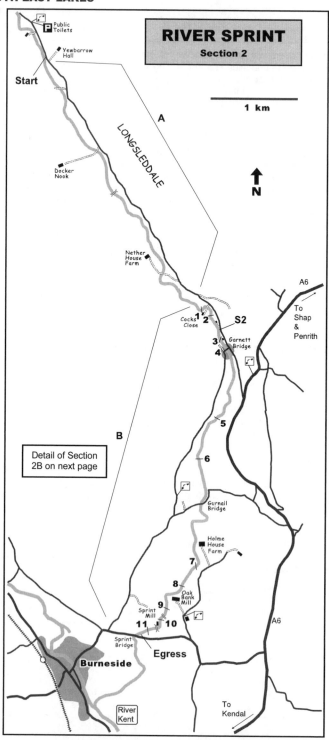

RIVER SPRINT
Section 2

1 km

Start

Public
Toilets

Yewbarrow
Hall

LONGSLEDDALE

A

N

Docker
Nook

Nether
House
Farm

Cocks
Close

1
2
S2
3 Garnett
Bridge
4

A6

To
Shap
&
Penrith

5

B

6

Detail of Section
2B on next page

Gurnall
Bridge

Holme
House
Farm

7

8

Oak
Bank
Mill

9

Sprint
Mill

11   10

A6

Sprint
Bridge

Egress

Burneside

River
Kent

To
Kendal

SECTION 2		The Main River	
From :	Public Toilet 501 029	**Grade :**	IV
To :	Sprint Bridge 513 960	**Maps :** O.S. 90 / 97, Explorer OL7	
Distance :	8 km	**Stars : ✶✶✶ Scenery : ❀❀❀**	

SUMMARY
A great trip with several difficult rapids and continuous interest in between. While not the hardest grade IV rapids around, confidence and competence are needed to run this river as the first three rapids are hard to inspect and protect and not convenient to portage. This is because the proximity of houses and private land on the banks by the rapids make paddlers very unpopular if they start tramping around where they shouldn't. Also inconsiderate parking has caused confrontation within the narrow confines of Longsleddale. Access is needed at all times to the head of the valley for large farm vehicles and the emergency services. Do not park at the side of the road in the valley but find a place off the road. Once on the river and below Garnett Bridge relax as the river twists and turns in a more isolated wooded valley setting with lots of action hidden round each bend.

INDICATORS
Longsleddale has quite a small catchment and fairly heavy rain is needed to bring it into condition. At Sprint Bridge if all the shingle is covered on the bend below the bridge and the water touching the banks then a trip will be worthwhile. 100 m upstream of the bridge is a weir with a gauge on the right bank. 0.6 on the gauge is a low level while 2 would be good. Another place to judge the level is Garnett Bridge where inspection of the rapid needs to be done before getting on the river and if looks possible without a scrape over the central rock then the river is up.

START
Access to the river without crossing private land, and with ample parking, can be found about 4 km above Garnett Bridge where the road runs alongside the river without a fence **(S2)**. There is a car park and public toilets by the church two hundred metres further on. Use the car park and walk back to get on the river.
It is also possible to gain the river just above Garnett Bridge by starting **below** the `S` Bends where the road meets the river by a gate to a water works building **(S2)** (GR 522 995). There is a very limited amount of parking here about 150 m beyond the access point close to the entrance to Cocks Close. The temptation to start from the Cocks Close Bridge and run the `S` Bends rapid should be resisted if using this start (as this is in a private garden) and walk back to where the road meets the river.

DESCRIPTION
A) II The gentle 3.5 km of swift flowing grade II back to the first rapid passes fairly quickly at a level worth doing the river and gives a good warm up.

B) IV The first few rapids come in quick succession in the run down to Garnett Bridge. After that they are more spread out and easier to inspect although interest is maintained all the way.
1) III Cocks Close. As the river bends left with a house on the right bank this rapid leads down to a bridge. The `S` bends follow immediately below the bridge so if possible get out onto the rocks on the left bank just below the bridge to inspect.
2) IV The S Bends. A difficult rapid which surprises many with its speed as they try to make the line. In low water beware of pinning in the narrow exit pool.
3) W Garnett Weir. Usually OK and shot on the right it can however develop a strong hold in high water.

continued on next page ⇨

RIVER SPRINT 2

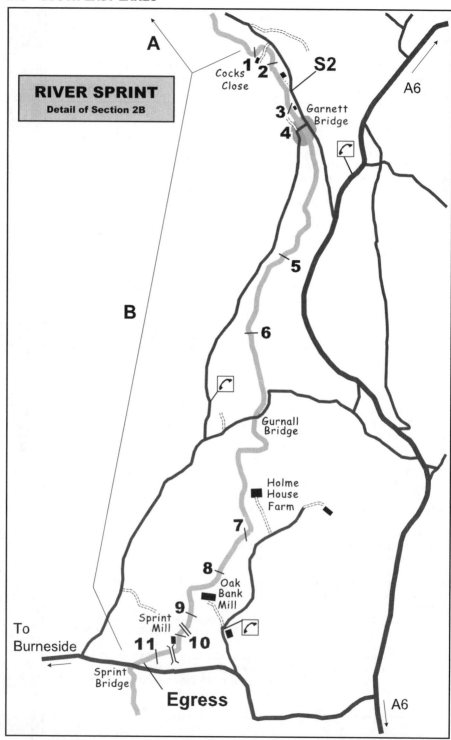

RIVER SPRINT
Detail of Section 2B

A

B

Cocks
Close

1 2

S2

A6

3
Garnett
Bridge
4

5

6

Gurnall
Bridge

Holme
House
Farm

7

8

Oak
Bank
Mill

9

Sprint
Mill

11 10

To
Burneside

Sprint
Bridge

Egress

A6

⇨ *continued from previous page*

4) IV Garnett Bridge. The main flow usually carries you down the line here and squirts you through the narrow gap under the bridge, over the central rock. No inspection or portage here, so look from the bridge before you start.

5) III+ Slot and drop. A narrow chute through the bedrock falls 3 m through a large hole into a deep pool. More bottle than skill but keep straight as there are some potholes in the chute which could pin. Inspect or portage on the left.

6) IV- Rock and Roll. A longer more complicated fall with a large curling wave halfway down. Quick recovery from this is needed to negotiate the narrow gaps either side of a large central boulder below.

7) W After passing Holme House Farm on the left bank a right hand bend signals the approach of a broken weir. This contains some old iron stakes, but these do not usually present a problem for those upright in their boats if a route on the right is followed.

8) III Oak Bank. A nice rapid over small shelves leads down to Oak Bank Mill.

9) IV Sprint Mill Falls. A complicated and difficult rapid needing inspection or portage from the left bank. The river falls over a series of shelves before narrowing between a rocky outcrop.

10) III A diagonal stopper under the pipe bridge can get quite big in high water.

11) III Cottage Falls. After the pipe bridge the river turns left and twists down a long rapid with the cottages on the right bank. At the bottom it turns right under a footbridge with some low branches overhanging the river.

12) W The small weir just above the egress can give fun surfing at certain levels.

EGRESS
Egress to the left bank just above Sprint Bridge.
Alternatively carry on to join the Kent.

Sprint Mill Falls, River Sprint.   *Mark Leicester*

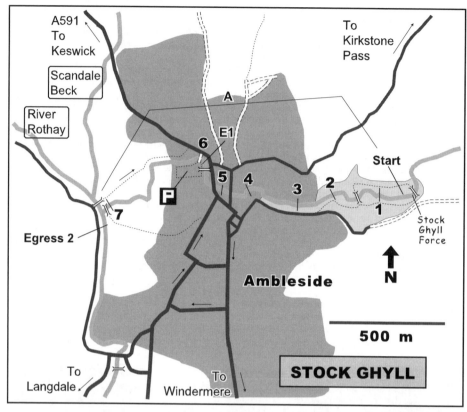

continued from opposite page ⇦

6)   B   Low bridge. Check headroom before starting.
7)   IV   Final fall. No chance to inspect this as the banks are enclosed all the way, but its a
         straight run and dumps immediately into the Rothay.

EGRESS

It is best to egress onto a small bank with trees **(E1)** on the left just after the footbridge into the
main car park, and just above the low bridge, this gives access direct to the car park. Check this
before starting as if this bank is covered then it may be also too high to get under the bridge which
follows.

If continuing to the Rothay, egress is onto the left bank 100 m after the confluence **(E2)**, and walk
back up to the bridge to gain the road, or back through the park to gain the Penrith road near the
Police Station and main car park entrance.

STOCK GHYLL

From : Base of Main Fall 382 045	Grade : IV / V
To : Rothay Confluence 371 045	Maps : O.S. 90, Explorer OL7
Distance : 1 km	Stars : ✱ ✱ ✱ Scenery : ❀ ❀ ❀

SUMMARY
A short but entertaining beck that gets very challenging in higher water levels. Starting below some large unrunnable falls, it is confined in narrow gorges before running through the centre of Ambleside with a low bridge to contend with. Due to the steepness and confined banks you are on your own in this one, with rescue being virtually impossible. Not a place to practise swimming, so as we say "Go with confidence and competence".

INDICATORS
This needs lots of rain and comes up and down very quickly. Looking upstream from the main road bridge in Ambleside there is a slate weir shelf topped with wooden sleepers, if this is possible without a scrape then the rest should be OK, but also check that there is room to get under the **low bridge** just below here, which is the entrance to the main car park, as in high water there may be no escape or possibility to portage once committed to the run through the town. It is also easy to inspect the beck from the road up to the start where it will be obvious if it has enough to be worthwhile. Once flowing the level can still change quite rapidly with the power and the grade varying quite dramatically.

START
From the centre of town take the first left after the Salutation Hotel, by Barclays Bank. Go left again behind the hotel marked `To the Waterfalls`. The road runs alongside the beck, where there is some parking, to a path on the left signposted to the waterfalls. The path soon leads to a large concrete weir. Many people start from below the weir, but the section above is also worthwhile. From the weir follow the track up to a footbridge and cross it to go up the right bank. Where a metal railing finishes it is possible to scramble down an extremely slippery old path to the base of the gorge. At the base of the main fall there is a jumble of large boulders before a narrow 3 m fall. This fall has been run but the landing is shallow so it is best to start below this. Beware this descent into the gorge is dangerous, and may be best protected by ropes.

DESCRIPTION
A) IV / V A bobsleigh ride in a narrow gorge down to a sharp bend. Then steep slabs lead to an easier section past the footbridge. Below the weir another narrow section leads to two larger falls. The beck then starts to twist round houses into a canalised section through the town and on alongside the park. A final fall spits you out into the River Rothay. The whole of the narrow sections should be checked for trees before you start, as once in there is no where to go and its rare to find it totally clear.
1) IV / V One particular twist in the first gorge could pin longer boats.
2) X A large concrete weir 100 m below the footbridge. A portage.
3) V The two larger falls. The first fall has a powerful stopper with some old iron spikes lurking on the left wall which can be threatening at certain levels. While the second creates some confusing water and is also potentially nasty. At medium levels it is possible to inspect and portage these two falls together from the right bank. Otherwise check them from the road before you start.
4) IV A small 1m drop into a pool on a sharp bend left by some buildings leads into the canalised section.
5) IV Slate and wood weir ledges.

⇦ continued on opposite page

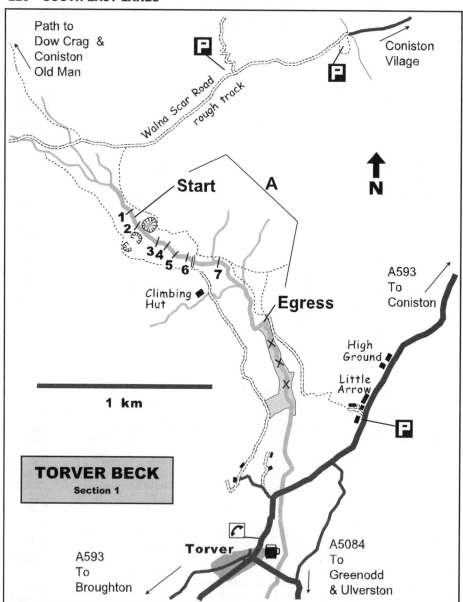

Path to
Dow Crag &
Coniston
Old Man

Walna Scar Road
rough track

Coniston
Vilage

Start   A

N

1
2
3 4
5 6
7

Climbing
Hut

Egress

A593
To
Coniston

High
Ground

Little
Arrow

1 km

TORVER BECK
Section 1

Torver

A593
To
Broughton

A5084
To
Greenodd
& Ulverston

TORVER BECK

The two short section of this beck give quite contrasting paddling. They are separated by an ugly series of portages and a canalised section with fences so it is not wise to try and connect them. The top section lies high on the fell with some very difficult falls amongst old slate quarry workings while the lower section is more moderate with several rocky shelves in a wooded gorge leading down to the lake.

SECTION 1   The Quarry Run

From :	Old Homestead	275 963	Grade	VI
To :	Sharp Bend	284 954	Maps : O.S. 96, Explorer OL6	
Distance :	1 km		Stars : ✷ Scenery : ❀ ❀	

SUMMARY
Hair-boating amongst bizarre slate quarries with a long carry in and out again. Only for the connoisseur. Its worth a walk up here on a dry day without your boat to check out if you really want to do the falls, as it is a pointless carry if you portage all the hard bits.

INDICATORS
Heavy rain needed to give almost flood conditions to cushion the rocks. It needs to be honking through the canalised section under the main road. Then go take a walk up and see if its your thing.

START
Park at Little Arrow (GR 290 949), which is 1 km north of Torver, and walk up through the cottages onto the footpath which makes its way up the fell for 2 km to the slate quarries. Above the quarries in the area of an old homestead is a narrow gully choked with holly and other trees. This is too narrow to paddle so start below it.
Slightly less masochistic, but needing a shuttle, is to drive up the Walna Scar road out of Coniston and drive along the track towards Dow Crag as far as your vehicle is able. It is then roughly a kilometre walk downhill to the same place. It is possible even to start a bit higher and portage the tree filled gully.

DESCRIPTION
A) V A continuous series of slides, falls and rapids varying from IV to VI. Each should be considered individually and judged by that old axiom of adventure boating "Dare I ?" One particular hole is essential to avoid. But which is it? Dare you ?
1) X   If starting higher on the fell make sure you get out before dropping into this little tree choked gully as it is only 30 cm wide in the middle!!
2) V   Roller Coaster. A scary ride along a ridge between two huge quarries!! Only a metre wide slab of slate separates you from the drop on the left. Beware the pool below the last small drop which has a gap in its left edge into oblivion.
3) X   A very low tree branch blocks a small fall.
4) VI   Big Meany. A steep 6 m slide with shallow pool and rocks encroaching on the left.
5) VI   Little Meany. A steep 4 m slide with no pool and pointed rocks on the right.
6) IV   Continuous rapids down under the footbridge.
7) F   Sheep fence.

EGRESS
Egress on a sharp corner where the path up joins the beck and before it enters a narrow tree lined valley as following shortly below are some impassable falls before the beck becomes canalised.

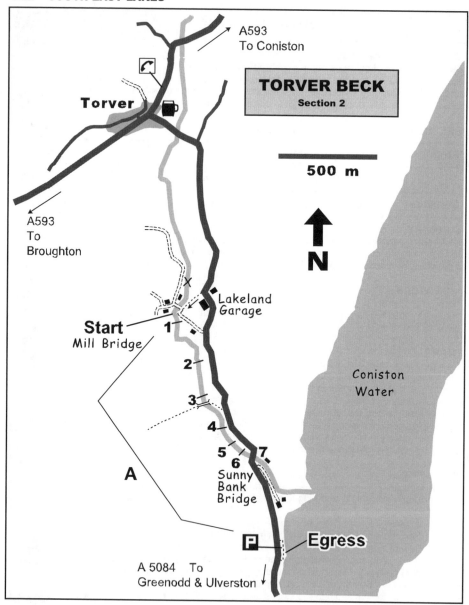

SECTION 1			The Lower Beck	
From :	Mill Bridge	285 932	**Grade :**	IV
To :	Coniston Water	291 920	**Maps :** O.S. 97, Explorer OL6	
Distance :	1 km		**Stars : ✶✶**	**Scenery : ✿✿**

SUMMARY
A short enjoyable spate run with several falls linked by continuous easier rapids.

INDICATORS
Although this beck carries more water than one would expect it requires fairly heavy rain to bring it up. But as rain comes in from the west this is often the first river in the central Lakes to rise. Look upstream from Sunny Bank Bridge on the A5084 and if the wide rocky fall is runable without scraping then the rest will be ok as it is mostly narrower.

START
There is parking opposite the Lakeland Garage on the main A5084 and a bridleway leads to Mill Bridge from the bend just north of the garage. Put in just below the bridge.

DESCRIPTION
A) IV Powerful water leads over several falls with continuous small rapids between.
1) III A small drop on the first bend should pose no problems.
2) IV The first large two tier fall becomes harder in high water and tree branches can cause problems lining up for the second step.
3) III A series of small steps lead down to a footbridge.
4) IV A 2 m chute which usually is straightforward, but can be a bit rocky in low water.
5) IV Small rapids lead to a sharp 1 m drop with a river wide stopper.
6) III The rocky river wide fall 50 m above the bridge.
7) IV An awkward stepped rapid under Sunny Bank Bridge partly obscured by trees.

EGRESS
Egress is possible to the road just above Sunny Bank Bridge, but this misses the last rapid and it is best to continue down to the lake. Turn right on hitting the lake and it is 200 m to land at a rocky outcrop by a lay by on the lake shore.

TORVER BECK 2 (Lower)

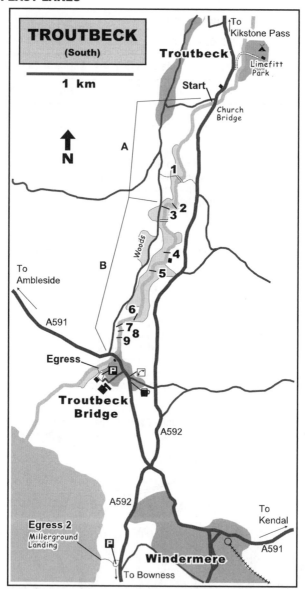

continued from opposite page ⇦

9) III / IV The river continues to drop steeply for the next 50 m over several rocky steps with accompanying stoppers, before easing on the final stretch to the bridge.

EGRESS

The best egress is 200 m beyond the bridge on the left bank where a short walk through a wood leads to Troutbeck Bridge swimming pool car park. If unfamiliar with the egress point it is best to park in the swimming pool car park, and then walk across the wooded area to check where to get out. Otherwise you can continue down to Windermere with a kilometre of grade II water followed by turning left and paddling another kilometre to Millerground Landings (GR 402 988). These landings are accessed by a short walk from a car park on the A592 Bowness road.

TROUTBECK (South)

From :	Church Bridge	412 027	Grade :	IV
To :	Troutbeck Bridge	403 003	Maps : O.S. 90, Explorer OL7	
Distance :	3 km		Stars : ★★★ Scenery : ❀❀	

SUMMARY
A great little river with exciting canoeing in a committing gorge. Not too hard by modern standards, but the continuous nature of the rapids, the difficulty of inspecting, portaging and rescue while on the river and the ever present danger from trees can make this a serious outing that should not be underestimated. The fact that the road is never very far away seems immaterial when you are engrossed in the depths of the valley.

It is often recommended that inspection of the first gorge is done from the Thickholme pipe bridge (GR 407 016) before you get on the water. While this can be reassuring for the second half of the gorge, do not assume the entry fall and first corners are clear as they are out of view from here and really need inspection from the bank, although this can be awkward.

INDICATORS
Quite a small catchment so it needs heavy rain and comes up and down very quickly. Its three main tributaries, however, all start in the high fells so when it does rain it often comes into condition. The best place to check the level is at Troutbeck Bridge where a look upstream will show if its flowing. If its obviously running with all the boulders covered then the more confined gorges upstream will be ok. Similarly, if it is possible to float at the put in without scraping on rocks then the rest will be paddleable. High water gives a brilliant although challenging and much harder ride.

START
Roads run up both sides of this narrow valley. But the most convenient to follow is the main A592 on the true left of the valley running from Windermere to Kirkstone Pass and Patterdale. This crosses the river at Church Bridge, 100 m south of Troutbeck Church. There is a small car park next to the river on a side road immediately north of the bridge.

DESCRIPTION
A) II / III The first kilometre of river is straightforward and a pleasant warm up while getting used to the power and speed of the water.
1) III   At a right hand bend there is a small island where the right side should be taken to avoid a very low bridge on the left.
2) Note   Gain an eddy on the left 200m after the island, just before the river turns sharply right and drops blindly into the gorge. From here a short scramble on the left bank allows a view into the gorge to see if its clear of trees.

B) IV Continuous rapids now lead through Thickholme Gorge and the wooded valley below to a final short section of weirs and drops between canalised banks.
3) IV   Thickholme or Pipe Bridge Gorge. A twisty start leads to a drop into the main gorge, which eventually eases below the pipe bridge.
4) III / IV   A long confused bouldery rapid down past a house.
5) III   Fallen trees are often a problem in this part of the valley.
6) W   This large angled weir is on a bend and usually does not present a problem.
7) W   The second weir should also not be a problem but signals the start of the canalised banks down to the egress.
8) IV   A powerful fast chute leads to a small drop with a diagonal stopper, which can be upsetting and quite grabby in high water.

↩ *continued on opposite page*

TROUTBECK (South)

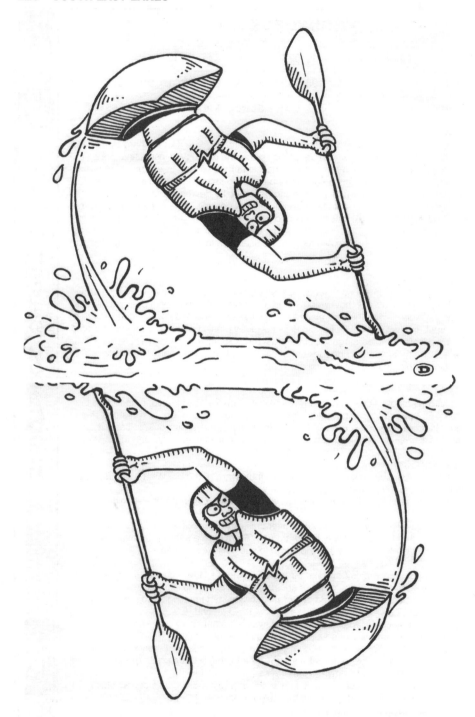

YEWDALE BECK

A fine beck in beautiful surroundings but unfortunately not often in condition and many fences interrupt an otherwise pleasant trip. Initially a steep hard flood run through sharp slate boulders, it eases considerably after a few hundred metres but a large fall, fences and trees hinder access down to Coniston Water.

SECTION 1   Tilberthwaite Gill

From : Tilberthwaite Gill 303 006	Grade : V / VI
To : Tilberthwaite Car Park 306 010	Maps : O.S. 90 / 97, Explorer OL7
Distance : 700 m	Stars : ✱ Scenery : ❀

SUMMARY
A short, steep, slate boulder field in an atmospheric gill, bounded by quarry spoil heaps (allegedly great fun!). Go well padded.

INDICATORS
The level you want and need to run this will vary for each individual, so the only way is to go take a look and you will soon know. Obviously it needs `shed` loads of water.

START
2 kilometres north of Coniston take the minor road signposted Tilberthwaite. Follow this up the right bank of the beck to a car park just before a bridge. Park here and carry up through the quarries to a footbridge which crosses the beck. It is possible to put on 100 m above the footbridge where it comes out of the narrow confines of the upper gill.

DESCRIPTION
A) V / VI A couple of bedrock falls break the otherwise continuous rapids. The grade very much depends on water levels and where you put on. Inspect well for trees as they can totally block the beck or lurk wedged between boulders in some of the steep drops.

EGRESS
Egress back out to the car park. or continue for the best of the lower section to the first portage.

YEWDALE BECK 1

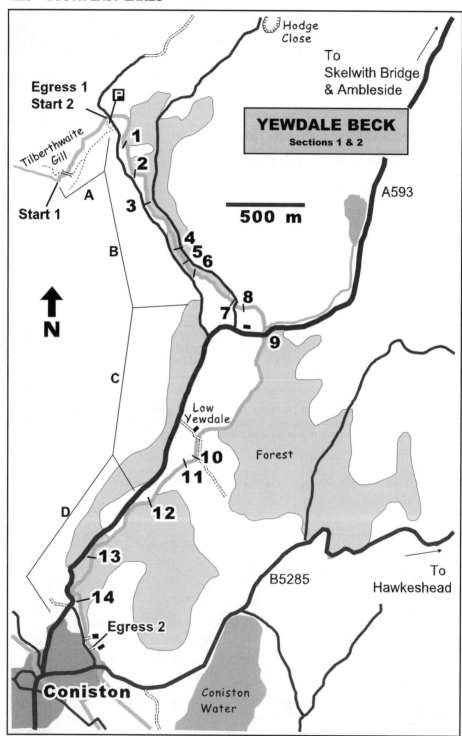

Hodge
Close

To
Skelwith Bridge
& Ambleside

Egress 1
Start 2

YEWDALE BECK
Sections 1 & 2

Tilberthwaite
Gill

A593

1

2

A

3

500 m

B

4
5
6

N

8
7

9

C

Low
Yewdale

Forest

10
11

12

D

13

14

B5285

To
Hawkeshead

Start 1

Egress 2

Coniston

Coniston
Water

SECTION 2	The Main Beck	
From: Tilberthwaite Car Park 306 010	**Grade :**	II, III (IV)
To : Bridge in Coniston 306 976	**Maps :** O.S. 90 / 97, Explorer OL7	
Distance : 4 km	**Stars :** ✷ ✷	**Scenery :** ❀ ❀ ❀

SUMMARY
A lovely river which deserves to be more popular despite having **10 fences** to portage. The initial section gives a good introduction to beck paddling with continuous rapids and fun little drops and chutes. An awkward portage then marks the start of a flatter and easier section with fences before another set of good rapids lead down into Coniston, all amongst superb scenery.

INDICATORS
Very heavy rain is needed to cover the bouldery bed of the beck, the top of which can be viewed easily from the road up to the start. At the put in it should be possible to run under the bridge without scraping on the concrete.

START
Park as for section one and start from the car park by shooting under the bridge.

DESCRIPTION
B) III (IV) The beck is open and pleasant for the first kilometre down to the portage.
1) III On a sharp bend left the bedrock narrows the flow for a short way.
2) III Small drops lead down around a corner to another narrows through the bedrock.
3) F A large sheep fence. Visible as you drive up where the beck comes close to the road by the first wall on the right bank.
4) IV Sheep Fence Slot. The beck gradually steepens from grade III to grade IV and finishes by dropping suddenly into a narrow slot **blocked** by a sheep fence. It is best to get out to inspect this where the beck first meets the road on the left bank before it steepens into the rapid. Many will either finish the trip here or portage the next 300 m by walking down the road to Shepherds bridge.
5) F The fence in the gorge. This can be pulled up out of the way by a bit of rope work on a handy tree to allow the rapid to be run.
6) X Egress 100 m beyond the fence before the beck turns sharply left over a large fall. Rocks at the base and a tree in the fall necessitate a **portage** on the left, by lowering boats down the steep bank into the gorge, then easy rapids lead down to Shepherds Bridge. Beware of tree blockages in this lower gorge.

C) II This central section flows gently through flat farmland with several fences.
7) F Shepherds Bridge has two fences just above it.
8) F 100 m below Shepherds bridge there is a wire fence which can be hard to spot.
9) F The A 593 road bridge has a fence under it.
10) F A double fence soon after Low Yewdale Bridge can be portaged on the left bank.
11) F Another fence.
12) F The last fence where the river bends right.

D) III The river steepens again as it leaves the fields and enters the woods for a nice set of rapids down to Coniston village. Be alert for tree blockages in the woods.
13) III Continuous rapids down to a collecting pool on a sharp left bend.
14) II Standing waves lead down to where the river is channelled between steep banks.

EGRESS
As you approach Coniston go under the first bridge by the school and egress to the left bank just above the second bridge made of iron girders and wood sleepers. There is a wire mesh fence blocking the river underneath this bridge which may be hard to see.

SUMMARY TABLE

Name of Run	Page	Grade	WW Stars	Scenic Stars	Km	Water	Notes
Appletreeworth Beck	257	5+		❋❋	0.5	High	steep trees !
Black Beck	233	4	✶	❋	2.5	High	narrow falls + trees
Bleng	235	5	✶	❋	2.5	High	2 fun falls
Crosby Gill	237	5(6)	✶✶	❋❋	2	High	intense big falls
Duddon - Section 1	239	3		❋❋	4	High	high spate run
Duddon - Section 2	241	4(5)	✶✶✶	❋❋❋	5	Med	continuous classic
Duddon - Section 3	243	3(4-)	✶✶✶	❋❋❋	3.5	Med	classic mid grade
Duddon - Section 4	245	3(4-)	✶✶	❋❋❋	6	Med	classic mid grade
Esk - Section 1	247	6	✶✶	❋❋❋	1	Med	rocky waterfalls
Esk - Section 2	249	4(5)	✶✶✶	❋❋❋	3	High	mountain pool drop
Esk - Section 3	251	3	✶	❋❋❋	7.5	Med	classic intro
Grassguards Gill	241	5	✶	❋	0.2	High	spate boulder field
Irt - Section 1	253	2		❋❋❋	9.5	Med	atmospheric start
Irt - Section 2	255	1(3)		❋❋	6.5	Med	awkward portage
Lickle	257	5	✶	❋❋	4.5	High	fun falls, bad trees
Lingmell Beck	259	3(4)	✶	❋❋❋	4	High	mountain spate run
Logan Beck	261	5+	✶✶✶	❋❋	1	High	sustained & steep
Mosedale Beck (SW)	263	5		❋❋	0.5	Med	too short
Nether Beck	265	4		❋❋	0.5	High	short spate run
Tarn Beck	267	5	✶	❋❋	1.5	High	main fall by road
Whillan Beck	269	5	✶✶	❋❋❋	1	Med	pool drop gorge

Troutal Gorge, Upper Duddon.   *Stuart Miller*

RIVERS OF SOUTH WEST LAKES

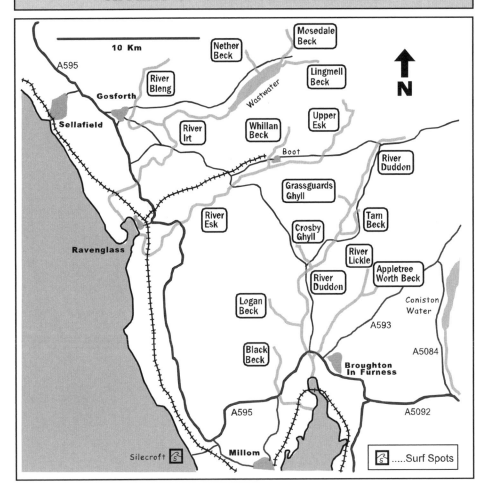

10 Km

A595

Nether Beck

Mosedale Beck

River Bleng

Lingmell Beck

Gosforth

Wastwater

N

Sellafield

River Irt

Whillan Beck

Upper Esk

Boot

River Duddon

Grassguards Ghyll

River Esk

Crosby Ghyll

Tarn Beck

Ravenglass

River Lickle

Appletree Worth Beck

River Duddon

Coniston Water

Logan Beck

A593

A5084

Black Beck

Broughton In Furness

A595

A5092

Silecroft ⑤

Millom

⑤ .....Surf Spots

Sandpiper

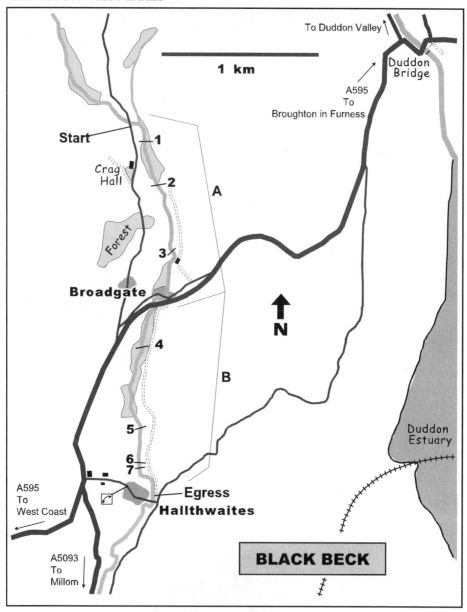

To Duddon Valley

Duddon Bridge

1 km

A595
To
Broughton in Furness

Start

1

Crag Hall

2

A

Forest

3

Broadgate

N

4

B

5

Duddon Estuary

6
7

A595
To
West Coast

Egress
Hallthwaites

A5093
To
Millom

BLACK BECK

BLACK BECK

From :	Bridge	180 877	Grade :	IV
To : Hallthwaites Bridge 182 853			Maps : O.S. 96, Explorer OL6	
Distance :	2.5 km			

SUMMARY
A beautiful little beck with a series of bedrock rapids flowing through two gorges either side of the A595 at Broadgate. Unfortunately the run is spoilt by some fences and trees, but worthwhile all the same.

INDICATORS
High water is needed to bring this up and common sense will tell you if its running by looking over the bridges where the A595 crosses the beck at Broadgate.

START
Turn north off the A595 at Broadgate and follow the fell road for 1.5 km to a bridge over the beck.

DESCRIPTION
A)   IV Below the bridge the beck enters the first gorge around the first right hand bend, and follows series of narrow bedrock falls. Watch out for **fallen trees**, and **fences**. Below the gorge the beck eases for a while with only one more fall of note before the Broadgate Bridge.
1) IV+ One of these rapids is notably harder than the rest requiring inspection and an inventive line.
2) F   A sheep fence at the end of the gorge.
3) F   A fence with no eddies to breakout, as you approach houses on the left bank.

B)   IV   Below the bridges the beck enters the second longer gorge which is more straight forward but quite committing.
4) T   Towards the end of the gorge however there is a low tree bridge which needs portaging. This is easily seen from above.
5) F   Barbed wire across the river at the end of the gorge
6) F   After the gorge there is a double fence which needs portaging.
7) W A small easy angled weir.

EGRESS
Egress to the left bank 50m above the next bridge, at the edge of Hallthwaites village. Find a spot before starting as undergrowth and walled banks can make landing a problem in high water.

BLACK BECK

RIVER BLENG

↑
N

1 km

Start

A

1

2

3

B

Blengdale

Bleng
Bridge

P

C

Egress 1

To
Wasdale

Egress 2

A595
To
Whitehaven

Wellington

Wellington
Bridge

River
Irt

Gosforth

A595
To
Ravenglass & Millom

To
Eskdale

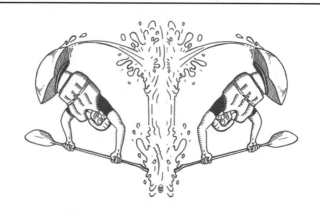

BLENG

From : Forestry Bridge 097 071	Grade : III, IV, V
To : Forestry Car Park 085 053	Maps : O.S. 90, Explorer OL5
Distance : 2.5 km	Stars : ✶ Scenery : ❀

SUMMARY
The first 500 m contains two interesting hard falls followed by another 500 m of boulder rapids before easing considerably, although it remains fast flowing back to the car park and has the ever present hazard of trees. A short but good blast.

INDICATORS
Quite heavy rain is needed to bring this into condition, as the large boulders in the top section need a good covering. The river is on your right as you drive up the forestry road out of Gosforth and it needs to have a good flow with most of the boulders in the bed covered.

START
Take the Wasdale road out of Gosforth and just before leaving the village at Wellington Bridge keep left and follow straight up the side of the river on the forestry road. Park in the small car park after a kilometre next to the river and well before the private houses at Bleng Bridge. From here access is up the forestry track over Bleng Bridge and straight up the hill. As the track reaches the top of the hill and starts to level off a bit it swings round left and splits. Take the left branch which contours round above the beck and then leads down to a bridge.

DESCRIPTION
A) IV / V The first steep section is continuously interesting and is worth inspecting before starting. Put in just upstream of the bridge for the first rapid. After the two main falls their are still some awkward bouldery rapids and tight turns before the gradient eases.
1) IV 100 metres below the bridge is the first big fall.
2) V The second set of falls follows in about 50 m and is a lot more complicated three tier affair.
3) IV Tight turns around a boulder and past a small cliff.

B) III The angle eases and the boulders get smaller but the flow is still fast as a footbridge is past, and then the river widens and gets shallower with less power in the current but still watch out for trees.

C) II / III Below the car park the river remains straight and swift with continuous but straightforward shingle rapids down to Wellington Bridge.

EGRESS
Get out back at the car park **(E1)** or continue down to Wellington Bridge **(E2)**. Below here the Bleng relaxes into meandering through fields to join the equally lazy River Irt in 2.5 km.

RIVER BLENG

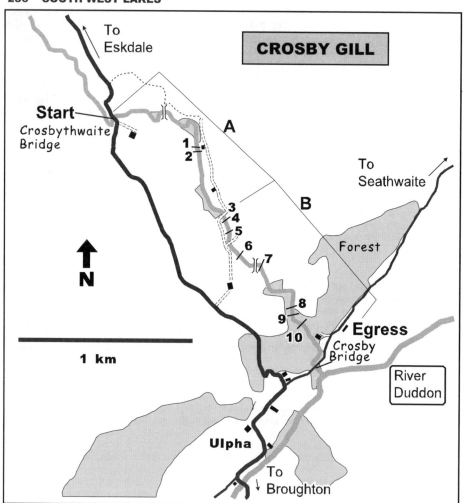

CROSBY GILL

To
Eskdale

Start
Crosbythwaite
Bridge

A

1
2

To
Seathwaite

3
4
5

B

6

7

Forest

N

8

9

10

Egress

Crosby
Bridge

River
Duddon

1 km

Ulpha

To
Broughton

CROSBY GILL

From: Crosbythwaite Bridge 189 951	Grade :	IV, V, VI
To: Crosby Bridge 201 937	Maps : O.S. 96, Explorer OL4	
Distance: 2 km	Stars : ✶✶ Scenery : ❀❀	

SUMMARY
A superb test of nerve and skill, or a nasty dangerous ditch. Go take a look, make your own decision, and be inspired or run away and cry. This beck is quite narrow and contains some big falls, with rocky landings in places. The falls have been described as pool drop style, yet the pools leave a lot to be desired. A local test piece and one of the infamous Duddon Ditches.

INDICATORS
This needs high water. The beck and the bottom of the last rapid can easily be seen from the road at the egress at Crosby Bridge. If you are up for this you will know the level you want!

START
Follow the road from Ulpha towards Eskdale Green for 2 km to Crosbythwaite Bridge where it crosses the beck near a farm. Put in here.

DESCRIPTION
A) III (IV) The beck starts easy enough with grade III water and one larger fall.
1)   T   A very low tree branch guards the top of the first fall and will need portaging. This is found level with an old barn on the left bank
2)   IV   The fall itself is fairly straight forward.

B) V (VI) Things steepen up now, with constant rapids and hard falls to the end.
3)   F   At the first bridge (In this section) there is a fence which may need a portage but it can some times be sneaked through. Take the opportunity to inspect the next couple of drops.
4)   V   A 3 m fall.
5)   IV   An easier fall leads to the second bridge.
6)   T   Low tree branches obstruct the beck in places down to the third bridge.
7)   VI   Mega Rapid X. Stop above the third bridge as this nasty beast lurks below. First a 5 m twisting ramp leading to a 5 m fall, then a 2 m fall into a narrowing 3 m drop, which lands **dangerously onto rocks**. Finally a boulder choke leads to another 4 m fall.
8)   X   Grade IV water leads down through woods to the top of the next fall which starts with a portage around an very narrow constriction.
9)   V   Mega Rapid Y. It is tempting to portage this fall while you are already out of your boat for the constriction. But for those who dare, put in immediately after the constriction where a ramp shoots you down over a small fall and then straight over the large 6 m drop via a scary slot in the middle.
10) V   Mega Rapid Z. This starts immediately below and is easier but more continuous. A brilliant rapid in flood conditions. 200 m of ramps, small drops and boulders lead down to the road.

EGRESS
Egress at Crosby Bridge, which is found only a few hundred metres out of Ulpha on the road up the valley just after the turn off to Eskdale Green.

CROSBY GILL

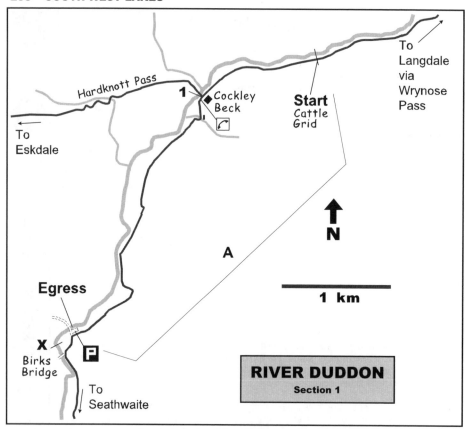

To
Langdale
via
Wrynose
Pass

Hardknott Pass

1 ◆ Cockley
Beck

Start
Cattle
Grid

To
Eskdale

↑
N

A

—— 1 km ——

Egress

X
Birks
Bridge

P

To
Seathwaite

RIVER DUDDON
Section 1

Playing on the Duddon.   *Paul Hill*

DUDDON

III

The Duddon is a personal favourite and must rate as the best river in the Lake District, as it not only lies in one of the most beautiful and unspoilt valleys, but is host to a great variety of excellent rapids with a range of grades and sections to suit many different groups. It also has some of the district's most testing becks tumbling into it from the valley sides making it a hard boater's mecca, home of the great Duddon Ditches.
When in flood the mighty Wallabarrow Gorge demands great respect and has been likened to the great rivers of Nepal, being christened the` Dhuddon Kosi` by the locals.
The full trip is some 18 km but it is rarely done in its entirety. It splits conveniently into 4 sections. Starting high in the central fells by Wrynose Pass the first section is a fast boulder rush only possible in flood. The second section is a beautiful trip through the upper Duddon Valley and includes the hard rapids of Troutal and Wallabarrow Gorges. The third section is a bit tamer as the river enters gentler farmland but there are still several bedrock falls to liven things up. The last section down to the sea is a lot easier proposition since the weir in the fall above Duddon Hall Bridge fell apart but it is still a continuously interesting grade III.

SECTION 1 The High Duddon

From : Wrynose Bottom 257 020	Grade : III
To : Birks Bridge Car Park 235 995	Maps : O.S. 89, Explorer OL6
Distance : 4 km	Scenery : ❀❀

SUMMARY
A high water run in the upper valley with only one fall of note under Cockley Beck Bridge.

INDICATORS
Water needs to be streaming off the fells during heavy rain. The road runs along the side of this section most of the way and it is obvious when it is possible. A good fast run when everything else is maybe too big.

START
The best place to start is at the cattle grid half way along the upper valley known as Wrynose Bottom. It would be possible to start a little higher but there are some nasty narrow twisting falls to be wary of, and then the hassle of portaging the fence beside the cattle grid.

DESCRIPTION
A) III From the start the beck is continuously fast and shallow over small boulders, until Cockley Beck Bridge. At the bridge the water from Mosedale Beck and Hardknott Gill can double the volume before shooting over the small fall hidden under the bridge. After the bridge there is nothing of note until the egress.
1) III Cockley Beck Bridge Fall.

EGRESS
The car park and picnic site, 200 m north of Birks Bridge is the best place to park and egress. There is a bridge over the river here, leading to forestry tracks, and it is best to get out above this bridge to make sure you go nowhere near the falls that lurk below at Birks Bridge.

RIVER DUDDON 1 (High Duddon)

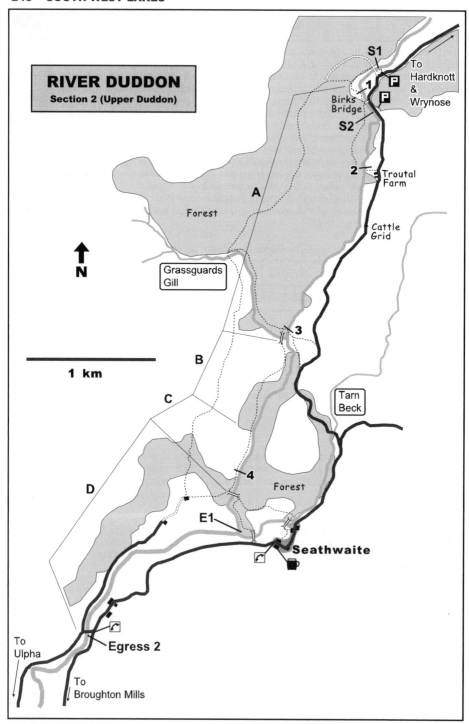

RIVER DUDDON
Section 2 (Upper Duddon)

S1

To Hardknott & Wrynose

1

Birks Bridge

S2

2 — Troutal Farm

A

Forest

Cattle Grid

N

Grassguards Gill

3

1 km

B

C

Tarn Beck

4

D

Forest

E1

Seathwaite

Egress 2

To Ulpha

To Broughton Mills

SECTION 2			The Upper Duddon
From :	Birks Bridge	234 993	Grade : IV (V)
To :	Hall Bridge	213 953	Maps : O.S. 89, Explorer OL 6
Distance :		5 km	Stars : ✷✷✷ Scenery : ✤✤✤

SUMMARY
The main meat of the Duddon, and a test piece for aspiring hard paddlers, usually referred to as the Upper Duddon. Set amidst stunning scenery it includes some of the most exciting and entertaining rapids in the area. Depending on the water level it can offer everything from a chilled IV- (portaging the hard rapids) to a full on V+. Birks Bridge, Troutal and Wallabarrow Gorges all contain serious **undercuts** and **siphons** which are dangerous at all water levels. It is important to know the egress points to inspect and portage these rapids as it would be all to easy to be swept upon them unwittingly.

INDICATORS
Just below the pool at Birks Bridge the river is at it widest and shallowest. If most of the boulders are covered here and it is possible to launch without scraping then the lower gorges below will be ok. The harder falls need a good deal more flow, however.

START
The extremely narrow slot just above Birks Bridge (V+) has been run but can not be recommended due to severe undercuts and siphons making it highly dangerous. Therefore a start from the car park and picnic site (**S1**) necessitates a portage almost immediately on the first bend, so the most usual put in is just below Birks Bridge by either a seal launch into the end of the gorge or opposite a small parking area 50 m below (**S2**).

DESCRIPTION
A) IV (V)   Below the narrows of Birks Bridge the river starts off again with some pleasant warm up rapids as it bends away from the road, then back left. Soon a series of small drops between crags signals the start of Troutal Gorge, and be prepared to egress on the left immediately after the first bend left as Troutal Farm Falls follows only 10 m below. Beyond the falls the gorge is continuous and interesting, but well supplied with eddies down to where it widens slightly and there are some stepping stones with a wire handrail.

1) V+ The Birks Bridge slot. A very narrow gorge with little room to manoeuvre or paddle. There are several nasty undercuts and siphons making this a serious undertaking.

2) V+ Troutal Farm Falls. This is a fairly nasty fall containing a horribly narrow and overhung gash on the right and a boat gobbling siphon on the left. Enough water for a central line is essential. Portage on the left. Prior inspection from the road is the only way to be sure of identifying the landing to portage the fall, and it can be found immediately behind Troutal Farm (GR235 988) by following a footpath on the right of the farmhouse.

3) F   Beware of the wire handrail over the stepping stones in high water. Just below the stepping stones **GRASSGUARDS GILL** joins the river from the right. In high water this can be an interesting diversion giving 200 m of grade IV / V paddling by walking up to below a large waterfall and bouncing back to the confluence.

B) IV The river then splits round a couple of small island as it drops into an s-bend and the woods of Wallabarrow Gorge. At first the gorge is fairly easy, but the rapids get progressively harder until you are faced with a huge boulder sticking out into the flow from the right bank. Be wary of this as water sumps underneath this and it acts as a log trap. Land just after this boulder to inspect the rest of the gorge.

C) V Wallabarrow Gorge. The main gorge is 200 m of difficult water which needs careful scrutiny as the correct route weaves between blind alleys, large boulders and

continued on next page ⇨

⇨ *continued from previous page*

sumps and then ends with a 2 m fall containing both a pinning spot and a sump. Both of which appear to be more of a problem at lower water levels. This whole section can be easily inspected and portaged on the right by a footpath. Smaller but entertaining falls then lead down to an arched footbridge and the end of the difficulties. The footpath to this bridge starts from Seathwaite and is often used for prior inspection.

4)   V   The main 2 m fall. In low water it is easy to pin on the right while the large boulder on the left in the plunge pool is undercut and contains a sump.

D) III Immediately after the bridge the gradient eases and soon Tarn Beck joins the river from the left. It is possible to land at the confluence (E1) and follow the footpath back to Seathwaite, but with the extra volume of water the river soon rushes down to Hall Bridge over a couple of easy bedrock rapids and gives time for reflection as the adrenalin is absorbed back into your bloodstream.

EGRESS
The usual egress (E2) is to land just after Hall Bridge on the left where a short track leads onto the road by a telephone box.

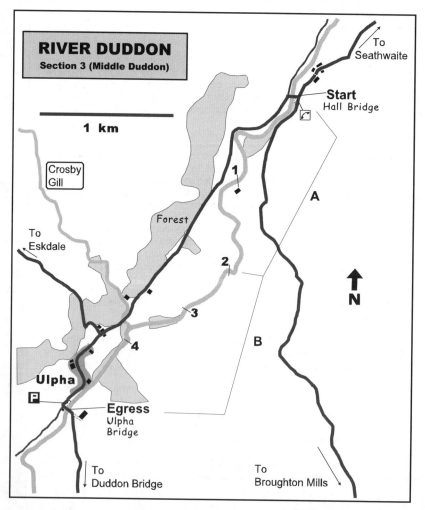

SECTION 3	The Middle Duddon			
From :	Hall Bridge 213 953	**Grade :**	III (IV-)	
To :	Ulpha Bridge 196 930	**Maps :** O.S. 89, Explorer OL6		
Distance :	3.5 km	**Stars :** ✶✶✶ **Scenery :** ⊛⊛⊛		

SUMMARY
A short but enjoyable part of the river, usually combined with either the section above or below to give a longer outing. As it flows through farmland it keeps a fairly steady gradient and is continuously interesting with several graveyard runs around large boulders, a couple of harder bedrock falls, and a vigorous little playhole.

INDICATORS
If the river is flowing with the shingle beds fully covered without a scrape at Hall Bridge then the more constricted parts below will be fine.

START
Park beside the telephone box at Hall Bridge and follow the short track down to the left bank of the river below the bridge.

DESCRIPTION
A) III   The first two kilometres are straight forward with only the water works weir to look out for.
1) W   The water works weir is roughly a kilometre after the start and is easily identified by a footbridge and concrete banks. The usual route is on the right.

B) III (IV-) The last part of this section is fairly continuous with boulder rapids split by a couple of bedrock falls.
2) IV-   Jill's Folly. Some larger boulders appear in the river on the approach to a wider, flatter section where the river bends sharply right. At the bend there is an island which hides a small obstructed drop. The main flow leads right of the island and bends back sharply left into a narrow slot with an awkwardly placed rock.
3) IV-   Funnel Steps. Below Jill's Folly the river flows between rocky banks and after 400 m it suddenly falls over four small steps into a mini gorge.
4) III   After the gorge the river settles for a short while as Crosby Gill enters from the right. then some boulders produce a short rapid on a right hand bend ending in a stopper. This can form an entertaining play hole at certain levels. From here down to Ulpha bridge large boulders form a fairly continuous graveyard section.

EGRESS
It is possible to egress upstream of the bridge, river right to the small car park, or more easily just downstream of the bridge, river left.

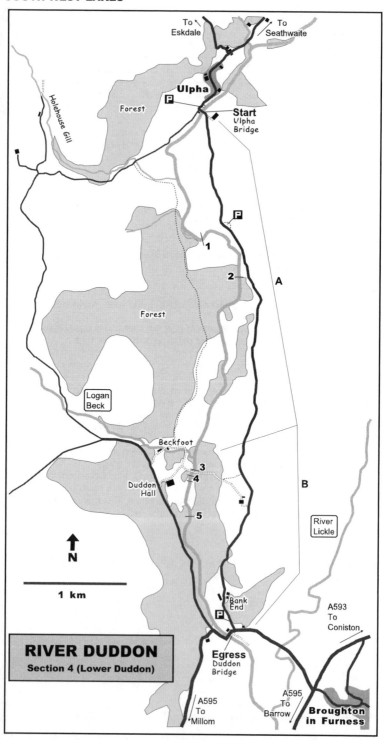

To
Eskdale

To
Seathwaite

Ulpha
P
Start
Ulpha
Bridge

Forest

Holehouse Gill

P

1

2

A

Forest

Logan
Beck

Beckfoot

3
4

Duddon
Hall

5

B

River
Lickle

N

1 km

A593
To
Coniston

Bank
End
P

RIVER DUDDON
Section 4 (Lower Duddon)

Egress
Duddon
Bridge

A595
To
Millom

A595
To
Barrow

**Broughton
in Furness**

SECTION 4			The Lower Duddon	
From :	Ulpha Bridge	196 930	Grade :	III / IV-
To :	Duddon Bridge	199 881	Maps :	O.S. 89, Explorer OL6
Distance :		6 km	Stars : ✳✳	Scenery : ✿✿✿

SUMMARY
The river now becomes slightly wider and gentler with fewer rapids but can still be a powerful high volume run when in spate. After a few loops through open fields it flows over large boulders to enter dense woodland for the last few kilometres. Duddon Hall Falls are the crux of this section. However since the collapse of the wall which channelled the water through Rawfold Bridge the excitement and aura of anticipation has somewhat lessened but the **two weirs** lurking immediately below means that caution should still be maintained for those of less confidence.

INDICATORS
At Ulpha a good run will be had if most of the boulders are covered at the put in, while at Duddon Bridge the level can be judged to be ok if the concrete platforms at the base of the bridge pillars are covered.

START
At Ulpha Bridge it is easy to put in upstream of the bridge river right, or downstream of the bridge, river left. This section is often combined with the Middle Duddon to give a longer trip.

DESCRIPTION
A) III Soon after Ulpha Bridge the river leaves the road as it flows fairly gently through flat farmland passing a couple of islands. But as the river swings back towards the road on the left it starts to steepen again and a fairly long section of boulder rapids lead down eventually into the woods and a narrowing through the bedrock before easing off again for a while.
1) III   Bouldery rapids begin.
2) III   Bedrock constriction.

B) III / IV- After about 2 km into the woods look out for Logan Beck entering from the right just above an island. Land at the confluence with Logan Beck on the right hand bank to inspect Duddon Hall Falls which drop through Rawfold Bridge. Beyond the bridge their are two weirs and then there is one final interesting rapid before the egress.
3) III / IV- Duddon Hall Falls. These used to be a daunting prospect down the right and twisting channel but since the collapse of the retaining wall on river left, a much more direct and straightforward line can be taken down the centre to a powerful eddy under the bridge.
4) W   Two weirs follow the bridge almost immediately. The first is easy angled and usually not a problem however the second should be treated with caution and possibly portaged as it can develop a strong tow back in high water.
5) III   The final rapid is a few hundred metres after the weirs. As the river bends back right the main channel flows down the right hand side of some islands with large boulders and a slight narrowing of the bedrock at the end.

EGRESS
Egress immediately below Duddon Bridge on the left. A low rocky weir just below this can provide a final little play but makes egress to the bank awkward.
Parking is possible in a lay by 100 m up the minor road towards Ulpha, straight across the main road from the egress.

RIVER DUDDON 4 (Lower Duddon)

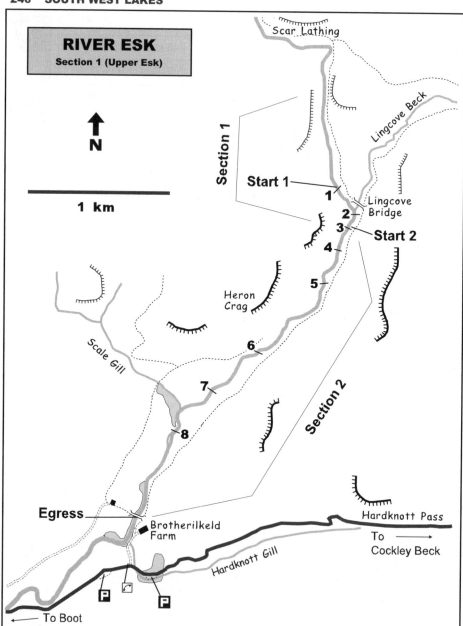

RIVER ESK
Section 1 (Upper Esk)

N

1 km

Scar Lathing

Lingcove Beck

Section 1

Start 1

1

Lingcove
Bridge

2

3

Start 2

4

Heron
Crag

5

Scale Gill

6

7

Section 2

8

Egress

Brotherilkeld
Farm

Hardknott Pass

To
Cockley Beck

Hardknott Gill

P

P

To Boot

ESK

The Esk is a river of three very contrasting sections, With its source amongst the highest of the central fells, the water collects in Great Moss before literally tumbling out of the mountains down the Esk Gorge in a series of steep cascades dropping some 150 m in less than half a kilometre. It then rushes down the upper valley over several interesting bedrock falls and mini gorges before easing off at Brotherilkeld and becoming a straightforward, but still swift and powerful, valley river. Each section of this river is a classic of its type and all give excellent paddling, in beautiful surroundings, with crystal clear water .

SECTION 1   The Esk Gorge Waterfalls

From :	Scar Lathing	225 047	Grade :	V / VI
To :	Tongue Pot	227 035	Maps : O.S. 96, Explorer OL6	
Distance :	1 km		Stars : ✶ ✶ ✶ Scenery : ❀ ❀ ❀	

SUMMARY
These impressive granite falls provide some of the best waterfall paddling in the Lakes and an excellent Ghyll scramble in the summer when the falls can be inspected at your leisure. The full gorge needs a long steep carry to its top where the beck starts to steepen and fall below the crag of Scar Lathing but unfortunately the top section involves as many portages as paddleable drops and it is usually only the bottom few drops which are attempted .

INDICATORS
Difficult to catch at the right level. It obviously needs to have been raining and quite a lot of water is needed to paddle section 2 back to Brotherilkeld but a high level for section 2 would probably be too much for the falls in the gorge. Only an intimate relationship with this area, its waterfalls and water levels will allow this wild ride to be successful.

START
Park at the grassy lay by at the bottom of the Hardknott Pass (GR 211 011) close to the phone box and track to Brotherilkeld Farm. Walk up the valley past the farm, and keep to the main path on the left bank of the river to Lingcove Bridge. Cross the bridge and carry up the falls as high as you dare, normally just above the seventh fall **(S1).**

DESCRIPTION
A) V / VI The bottom seven drops are all possible, although one section is hard (VI). Skid, slide, splash, fall, crash, whack, plop down to the confluence with Lingcove Beck. Just below the confluence is another hard fall before the narrow flat pool of Tongue Pot gives the first eddy of the run and a quiet moment for reflection.
1) V / VI The start of the last seven drops.
2) VI   Vicar Swa waterfall. A very difficult fall which drops in two tiers with two right angle turns to make, and a base guarded with rocks in places before being pushed onto the wall.

EGRESS
Enjoy the next section back to Brotherilkeld.

RIVER ESK 1

Walking up Eskdale   *Stuart Miller*

Great Gill Falls, Upper Esk   *Stuart Miller*

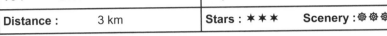

SECTION 2	The Upper Esk		
From :	Tongue Pot 227 035	**Grade :**	IV / V
To :	Brotherilkeld 212 015	**Maps :** O.S. 96, Explorer OL6	
Distance :	3 km	**Stars : ★ ★ ★ Scenery :** 🏵 🏵 🏵	

SUMMARY
A fantastic high valley adventure where continuous shingle and boulder rapids are interspersed with several granite bedrock falls and gorges. Similar in character to Borrowdale's Langstrath Beck.

INDICATORS
The river needs to be in spate and covering all the boulders across the full width of the river at Brotherilkeld. If in doubt a walk up the river for about 1 km to Birk Dub, which is the last fall on the section. This will give a good indication as the water is split into many channels around rocks and if a clear route looks possible then the rest of the river will be ok. Many say, however, that the higher the water, the better !!

START
Park as before at the bottom of Hardknott Pass and walk up past the farm on the left bank of the river to Tongue Pot . This is the flat gorge below the obviously nasty fall of Vicars Swa.

DESCRIPTION
B) IV / V   A small drop out of the flat gorge starts a continuous rush down the valley with all the falls being quite obvious and viewed on the walk in.
3)   III   A small drop out of Tongue Pot.
4)   IV   Two small drops soon after the start.
5)   IV   Great Gill Falls. A long twisty rapid through bedrock leads to a 2 m fall.
6)   V   Heron Pot. A narrow slot containing a **hidden rock** .
7) IV / V Kail Pot. 100 m of powerful water. A photogenic fall with high back loop potential leads into a fast flush through the narrow gorge below.
8)   IV   Birk Dub. Just after the confluence with Scale Beck this complicated fall splits the water into several channels and usually involves bouncing off rocks.

EGRESS
To avoid climbing over fences it is best to egress at the footbridge by Brotherilkeld farm and walk back along the track.

↩ Map on previous page.

RIVER ESK 2

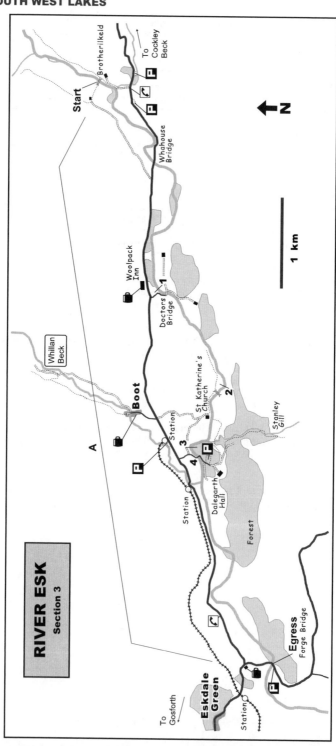

RIVER ESK
Section 3

N

1 km

To
Cockley
Beck

Brotherilkeld

Start

Whahouse
Bridge

Woolpack
Inn

Doctors
Bridge

1

Whillan
Beck

Boot

St Katherine's
Church

2

Stanley
Gill

A

Station

Station

3

4

Dalegarth
Hall

Forest

Station

To
Gosforth

Eskdale
Green

Egress
Forge Bridge

SECTION 3	The Main Esk	
From : Brotherilkeld 212 015	**Grade :**	II / III
To : Forge Bridge 149 995	**Maps :** O.S. 96,	Explorer OL6
Distance : 7.5 km	**Stars : ✶**	**Scenery : ❀ ❀ ❀**

SUMMARY
The classic Esk flows down this pretty and popular western valley to the sea at Ravenglass. It is mainly a fast flowing grade II with a few short sections of III but much of the river is lined by trees making low branches a problem in high water.

INDICATORS
Although a main valley river, the Esk has not cut a deep channel into the hard rock and remains fairly shallow for most of its length, requiring a good downpour to bring it up. At Forge Bridge the water needs to be flowing over the shingle below the bridge. At the top of the run a bend in the river comes right next to the road just above Whahouse Bridge where it runs over shingle rapids. If these are navigable the rest will be also. In flood conditions the river can provide (for the experienced paddler) an interesting blast in big powerful water. On one trip we were even able to paddle into the church yard at St Katherine's .

START
Park at the grassy lay by at the bottom of the Hardknott Pass (GR 211 011) close to the Phone Box and track to Brotherilkeld Farm. Walk up the track towards the farm then take the footpath up the side of the river to put on at the footbridge.

DESCRIPTION
A) II / III   Right from the start the flow is swift and tree branches in the river can pose a problem. There are no real falls on the river and the main difficulties consist of standing waves, strong currents, and folding waves where the water is squeezed through gorges in the bedrock..
1) III Doctors Bridge. The first of the grade III rapids on the approach to the bridge.
2) III Gill Force. A kilometre after Doctors Bridge the river bends right into a rocky gorge 100 m long, this can produce some powerful curling waves, and strong eddies. Followed by a good rapid down to the church.
3) II There is an island on the corner just above Dalegarth Bridge, Beware of the water flowing through trees, especially in the right channel.
4) III Dalegarth Bridge. Again the river is forced to flow through a short narrow gorge under the bridge with a boulder rapid following.

EGRESS
Egress is on the left bank, just after Forge Bridge, where there is access to a large lay by.

RIVER ESK 3

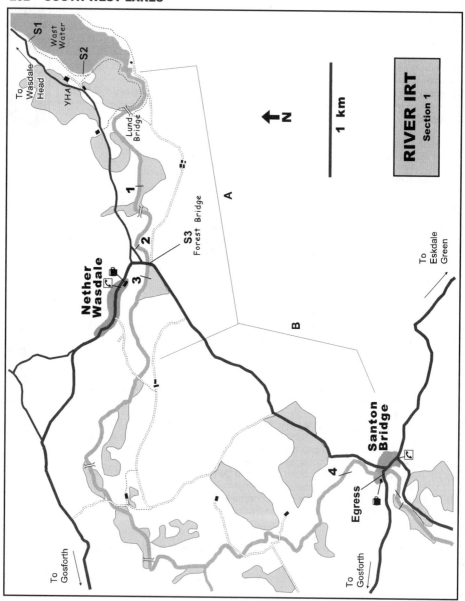

RIVER IRT
Section 1

IRT

SECTION 1

From :	Wast Water	148 048	**Grade :**	I, II
	Forest Bridge	128 037		
To :	Santon Bridge	110 016	**Maps :** O.S. 89, Explorer OL6	
Distance :	9.5 km		**Scenery :** ✿✿✿	

SUMMARY
One might expect the valley that hosts the largest mountain and the deepest lake in England to produce a spectacular river. Unfortunately this is not the case and the Irt which drains Wastwater, although passing through some lovely scenery, is spectacularly flat. The river passes through fairly remote farmland with the only access at the start and finish points, giving a pleasant get away from it all drift through the countryside. Trees are the main hazard of the river and could cause serious problems for beginners in places.

INDICATORS
This needs heavy rain in the hills to raise the level of Wastwater, but the lake helps it stay up for a short while. Much of the river is channelled and deep but there are shallow shingle sections which would be a scrape in low water. The level is best indicated at Santon Bridge where the water should be up to within at least 10 cm of where the arch of the bridge meets the vertical side walls.

START
A dramatic start to the trip begins from beneath the large crags and screes at the end of Wastwater. The road comes close to the lake about 1 km from the outflow where there is a small parking area **(S1)**. There is also a footpath to the lake shore through the grounds of the Youth Hostel which is slightly nearer to the river **(S2)** but has no public parking. Finally a slightly shorter trip can be started at Forest Bridge near Nether Wasdale **(S3)**.

DESCRIPTION
A) II The first part of the river is fairly fast flowing with continuous easy rapids and low tree branches to avoid. The weirs are straightforward but the current often leads under **dense sweeping branches** which can be awkward to avoid. After Forest Bridge another short section of dense rhododendron bushes encroaching from the bank soon gives way to pleasant open fields where the river meanders gently down to Santon Bridge.
1) W   A small angled gauge weir which should normally present no problems.
2) W   A small boulder weir with tree branches guarding its top.
3) II   Just after leaving Forest Bridge the main current sweeps below a curtain of bushes growing from the left bank which can present a serious danger to beginners.

B) I   Mainly flat water meandering through open farmland.
4) W   Another small easy angled weir.

EGRESS
Egress to the left bank just below Santon Bridge .

RIVER IRT 1

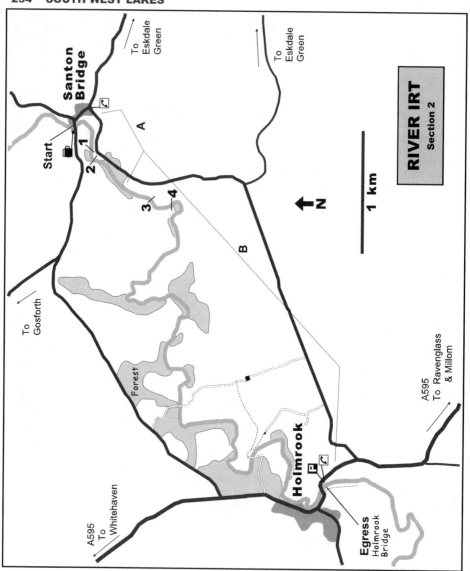

SECTION 2

From : Santon Bridge 110 016	Grade : I, II, (III)
To : Holmrock Bridge 080 995	Maps : O.S. 89 / 96, Explorer OL6
Distance : 6.5 km	Scenery : ❀ ❀

SUMMARY
More endless meandering through peaceful and remote countryside, with great opportunities for wildlife watching. An awkward **blocked rapid** 500 m from the start prevents this otherwise easy section being accessed by those who would enjoy the mainly grade I water the most.

INDICATORS
The river should be obviously flowing and covering the whole river bed at Holmrook Bridge, but the best indicator is as for Section 1 at Santon Bridge.

START
Put in just below Santon Bridge from the left bank.

DESCRIPTION
A) II (III) Easy rapids with the occasional large boulder lead round a couple of right hand bends to an angled boulder weir where an island splits the river. Just below the weir, on the next corner, there is a short rapid which at the time of writing is blocked by trees, presenting a considerable danger.

1) **W** The main channel leads to the left of the island with an easy ramp at the top and slightly more bumpy rocks at the end of the island.
2) **III** Under normal conditions this would be a short straight forward rapid, but trees currently form a river wide dam. At low to medium water it is possible to duck under a trunk into a grabby stopper before avoiding the next tree sticking into the current, but in higher flows this would be a river wide strainer. A private garden on the left and a cliff on the right prevent portaging, making this a serious problem. This may change with time.

B) I The river soon eases and meanders through pleasant open countryside and short wooded sections down to Holmrook.
3) **W** A small but steep weir. Care should be taken in high water.
4) **W** Another small steep weir which should not be a problem at normal levels.

EGRESS
At Holmrock egress 50 m after the bridge to the right bank. A public footpath leads back up to the bridge with parking on the opposite side.

RIVER IRT 2

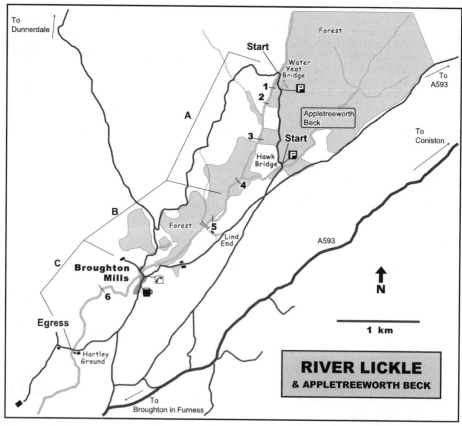

RIVER LICKLE
& APPLETREEWORTH BECK

Description after colour plates ⇨

Logan Beck (the easy bit). *Steve Rogers*

Pen-y-ghent Ghyll. *Andy Plimmer collection*

Bleng Falls. *Stuart Miller*

Mill Falls, Whillian Beck.

Stuart Miller

Kail Pot on Upper Esk.   *Stuart Miller*

Rescue at Heron Pot, Upper Esk.   *Stuart Miller*

LICKLE

From :	Water Yeat Bridge 238 930	Grade :	IV / V
To :	Hartley Ground 214 898	Maps :	O.S. 96, Explorer OL6
Distance :	4.5 km	Stars : ✶	Scenery : ❀ ❀

SUMMARY
This beck lies in a much forgotten part of Lakeland hidden behind the Dunnerdale Fells. At the start it is quite small but is soon joined by tributaries to grow substantially over the first 1.5 km. There are some entertaining falls and rapids amongst lovely scenery but unfortunately the constricted nature of many of the falls and the large amount of tree blockages means that a disproportionate amount of time is spent inspecting and portaging rather than paddling, which makes for an exhausting and frustrating trip. This may change with time.   (⇦ Map is found before colour plates)

INDICATORS
Quite a lot of rain is needed to bring the beck up. At Water Yeat Bridge there should just be enough to scrape a line between the boulders. Low water at the start is considered best as it grows considerably meaning better conditions lower down and if there is too much water it can quickly get out of hand. It may even be worth walking down the first part. The best place to get an overall impression of the water level is Broughton Mills, where all the boulders in the river should be covered, but as for many of these becks, experience, local knowledge and common sense are the best indicators.

START
Water Yeat Bridge is found at the head of the Lickle Valley by following the road up either side of the valley above Broughton Mills. It is best to park at a Forestry gate opening 200 m towards Appletree Worth Beck. Alternatively if the water is very high and you want even more intense steep tree infested paddling it is possible to start down `APPLETREE WORTH BECK` at a hard V+ from Hawks Bridge.

DESCRIPTION
A) IV / V   Steep bouldery rapids lead past a double fall and then a wire fence. More rapids and several tree blockages then lead to a section of very narrow and enclosed chutes which can have strong holes and / or tree blockages. These lead to the confluence with Appletree Worth Beck where just after the confluence there is another series of rapids and a narrow fall before the river eases for a short while.
1) IV / V The double fall.
2) F   Wire fence.
3) V   The Lickle Steps. A long series of intermittent narrow chutes and constricted bedrock steps. These can be pleasant in low water but become desperate in high water. Several narrow sections may need portaging.
4) IV   The confluence rapid.

B) III (V)   The beck now becomes wider and eases except for a dangerous fall under Lind End Bridge, while trees remain a problem.
5) V Lind End Bridge. This nasty fall is hidden under the old packhorse bridge at Lind End which forms a deep and powerful recirculating hole. It is essential to get out well before on the left bank , as there is nowhere to stop directly above it. Egress where the river makes a sharp left turn and the right bank steepens.

C) II (IV)   From Broughton Mills to Hartley Ground the river is flat apart from one good long rocky rapid of grade IV.
6) IV Lumholme Falls. Some narrow twisty drops lead into a series of rocky steps.

EGRESS
Egress to the right bank just after the bridge at Hartley Ground.

RIVER LICKLE

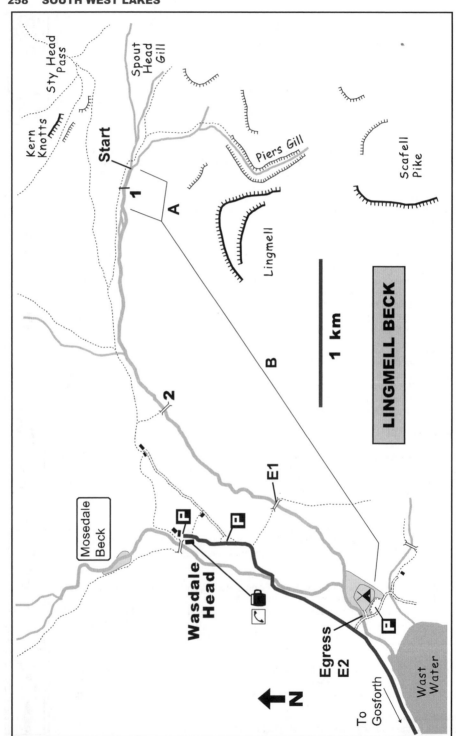

Sty Head Pass

Spout Head Gill

Kern Knotts

Start

1

A

Piers Gill

Lingmell

Scafell Pike

B

1 km

LINGMELL BECK

2

E1

Mosedale Beck

Wasdale Head

Egress E2

N

To Gosforth

Wast Water

LINGMELL BECK

From :	Piers Gill	212 091	Grade :	III, IV
To :	Campsite Bridge	181 076	Maps : O.S. 96, Explorer OL6	
Distance :	4 km		Stars : ✱	Scenery : ❀❀❀

SUMMARY
Formed by the confluence of Piers Gill and Spouthead Gill, Lingmell Beck starts in the very heart of Lakeland close to Styhead Pass. The initial gorge is fast and hectic and then the only fall indicates a step down in grade for the more straightforward bouncing back down to the valley bottom. Really just one long rapid of continuous boulders .
The second part is one of the few mountain streams that may be suitable for Grade III paddlers as an introduction to beck bashing. When everything else is too big head up here for a blast.

INDICATORS
Big, Big rain. A tiny catchment area means a lot of water is needed to make this beck navigable. As the bed of the river is continuously steep and made of small boulders there is nothing to hold any water so it must be done in the storm. Common sense will tell you if it is possible as the white fronds of storm drainage tumble off all the fells around while looking up the valley a continuous white line needs to cover the boulder bed.

START
Park at Wasdale Head (GR 186 084) and take the path up the valley towards Sty Head Pass. Leave the main path as it starts to climb away from the beck and keep to the path which follows the right bank. At the confluence of Spouthead Gill with Piers Gill waterfalls from both Gills fall into a pool at the start of a 100 m gorge. Climb down and start in the pool.

DESCRIPTION
A) IV Once the starting pool is left hang on for the ride down the gorge as there are no eddies and plenty of large boulders to create chaos. After 100 m the gorge walls ease back but the large boulders keep things rough down to Bursting Pot.
1) IV Bursting Pot. There are possible breakouts just above the fall which needs some element of boat control on the entry drop to avoid a big hit on the front end.

B) III From below the fall the beck eases off and there are no particular hazard needing any inspection, but the bed of the beck remains steep and bouldery forming a very continuous bouncy ride back to the valley.
2) F Beware of a sheep fence hanging below the first bridge.

EGRESS
It is possible to egress at the second bridge **(E1)** and carry back along the footpath 400 m to the car park at Wasdale Head, or continue to the bridge at the entrance to the National Trust Campsite, and car park **(E2)**.

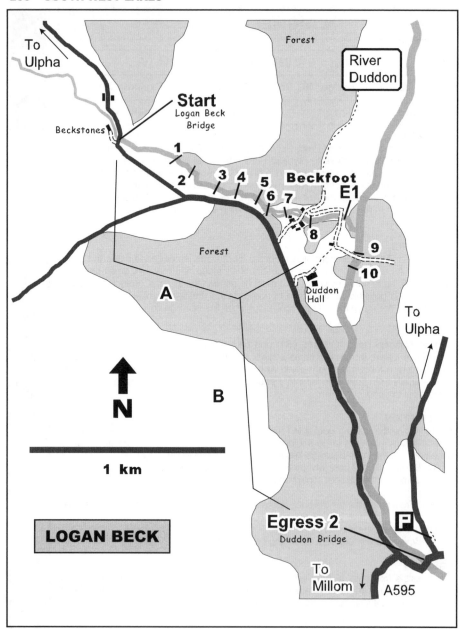

To
Ulpha

Forest

River
Duddon

Beckstones

Start
Logan Beck
Bridge

1

2

3 4

5

6

7

Beckfoot

E1

8

9

10

Forest

A

Duddon
Hall

To
Ulpha

B

↑
N

1 km

LOGAN BECK

Egress 2
Duddon Bridge

P

To
Millom

A595

LOGAN BECK

From :	Beckstones	183 902	**Grade :**	V / VI
To :	Duddon Bridge	199 881	**Maps :** O.S. 90, Explorer OL5	
Distance :	1 km + 2 km on Duddon		**Stars :** ✶✶✶ **Scenery :** ❀❀	

SUMMARY
A very challenging little river. With continuous hard rapids and powerful water this `Duddon Ditch` will be a test for any paddler. A superb and hectic paddle with interest all the way to its confluence with the river Duddon. Rather than walking out from the confluence, it is worth continuing down the Duddon to Duddon Bridge as there are two good rapids and a play wave.

INDICATORS
Quite a bit of rain and common sense is needed for this. High water is good to cover the boulders but makes the falls harder. Parts of the beck can be viewed easily from the road. But if you are considering this run you know the score anyway.

START
From Duddon Bridge head up the west bank, just after a cattle grid bear right at a fork and soon the bridge at Beckstones is reached.

DESCRIPTION
A) V / VI For the whole kilometre down to the Duddon there are many rapids and falls which require almost continuous inspection and protection.
1) V   The beck starts to steepen through twisty bedrock falls with slides, small drops and tight corners
2) V+   A stepped fall with a dramatic 2 m drop through a narrow rocky portal.
3) V   Continuous small stepped drops.
4) IV   A small island with stepped drops around boulders either side.
5) IV   A pool with a man made dam wall on the right leads to a 4m slide.
6) V+   A 150 m long rapid through a rocky knoll with pine trees on the right has a 2 m fall in the middle.
7) V+   Immediately following the last rapid is an island with two possible routes over a 4 m drop. The right hand route is far easier.
8) IV   After passing under a stone bridge the beck turns sharply into the final gorge which contains a boulder mid stream in low water.

B) III / IV   This last section of the Duddon is fun in high water with a fall just after the confluence, followed by two weirs. The first weir is playful but the second can be nasty. There is a further grade III rapid halfway down to the egress.
9) III / IV Duddon Hall Falls.
10) W   The Weirs

EGRESS
It is possible to egress to the right bank just after the second bridge **(E1)**. A footpath leads back over the bridge and up to Beckfoot, where a track is joined leading to the road. It is possible for one car to park just up the hill from the track entrance by an old gate. A shuttle is not really needed as this is less than a kilometre from the start.
However it is much better to continue down the Duddon to egress at Duddon Bridge **(E2)**. (See Lower Duddon ,Section 4, Pg 245).

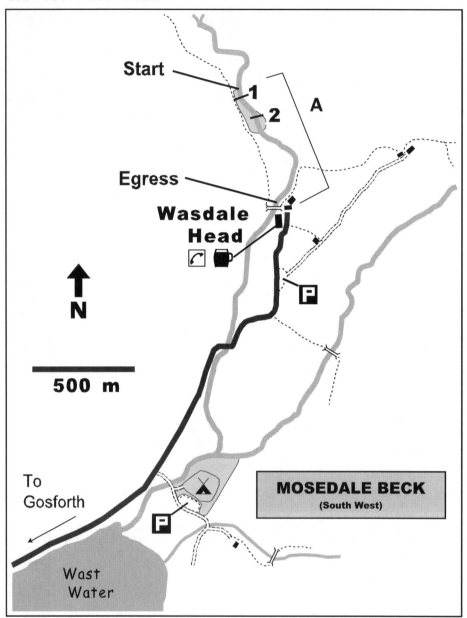

Start

1

2

A

Egress

Wasdale Head

N

500 m

To
Gosforth

MOSEDALE BECK
(South West)

Wast
Water

MOSEDALE BECK (SW)

From :	´ Top of Falls	185 094	Grade :	V

To :	Wasdale Head	186 088	Maps : O.S. 96, Explorer OL6

Distance :	500m	Scenery : ❀ ❀

SUMMARY
A very short section where the beck drops out of the upper valley into Wasdale. It contains a rocky twisty rapid and a portage round Ritson's Force. Not worth a special trip but if you are up exploring the other possibilities in this valley then this makes a finale to end up at the pub.

INDICATORS
Check the beck behind the Wasdale Head Inn and if it is flowing well with the boulders covered then it may be worth a walk up to the falls. Beware of too much water as this will make getting out above Ritson's Force very awkward.

START
Park at the Wasdale Head Inn and go through the gate just right of the public bar. Cross the old packhorse bridge and follow the path up Mosedale. An excursion to Ritson's Force on the way up makes sense. Check out the pool at the base of this fall, confirm not to run it and find the place to egress above it. Continue up the path for another 200 m to where the valley flattens out and the beck swings away from the path. Put in just above the first falls.

DESCRIPTION
A) V   The beck immediately drops into a mass of boulders leading to a small fall. There is then a short section of flat water before the lead into Ritson's Force. After Ritson's it is an easy drift back to the pub.
1) V Twist And Shout. The first fall weaves through boulders with a great deal of pinning potential. A line left of the largest boulder leads to a 2m fall into a flat pool .
2) X Ritson's Force. The main fall has a very shallow pool at the bottom, less than a metre deep and requiring a portage.
   In low water levels the drop into the first pot can be done before exiting quickly to let your boat carry on alone !!!.

EGRESS
Get out at the packhorse bridge and into the pub.

MOSEDALE BECK (SW)

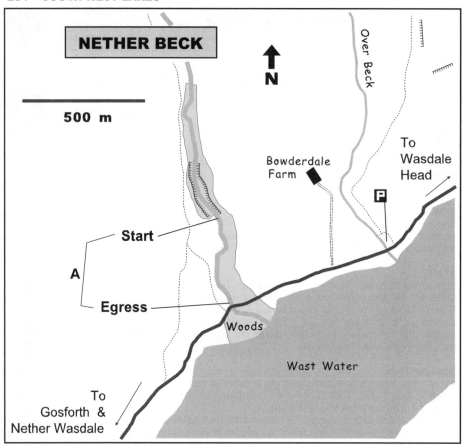

NETHER BECK

From :	Gorge Exit	160 070	Grade :	IV
To :	Nether Beck Bridge	161 066	Maps :	O.S. 96, Explorer OL6
Distance :	500 m		Scenery : ❀ ❀	

SUMMARY
A short section of river with continuous interest. Several bedrock falls and boulder rapids lead from the bottom of a tree covered gorge back to the road. A quick hit to be combined with the other heavy rain options in the area. The gorge above the put in looks tempting, but an entertaining scramble in low water will reveal large falls with no plunge pools and evil sumps amongst huge boulders, enough said.

INDICATORS
Look, walk up it and use your loaf. A lot of rain is needed to bring all the Wasdale becks into condition.

START
Park by the bridge and walk up the right bank to where the beck flows out of a tree covered gorge.

DESCRIPTION
A) IV This will hold no surprises as you have walked up the whole section, but as you do watch out for any trees and branches in the river. The falls are all obvious and easily protected.

EGRESS
At the Bridge.

Bursting Pot, Lingmell Beck   *Stuart Miller*

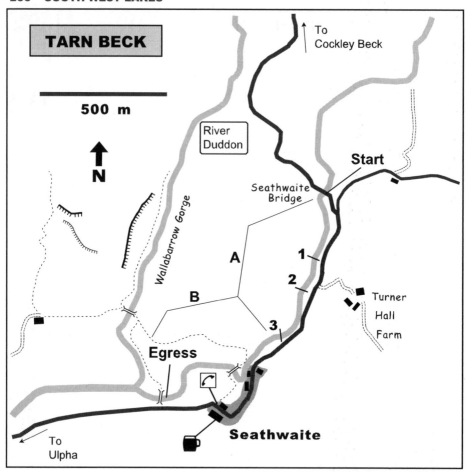

TARN BECK

500 m

N

River Duddon

To Cockley Beck

Start

Seathwaite Bridge

Wallabarrow Gorge

A

B

1

2

3

Turner Hall Farm

Egress

Seathwaite

To Ulpha

TARN BECK

From : Seathwaite Bridge 232 968	Grade : V
To : Footbridge 225 960	Maps : O.S. 96, Explorer OL6
Distance : 1.5 km	Stars : ✴ Scenery : ❀❀

SUMMARY
The first half of this section is plagued by trees then a short section of difficult falls over bedrock lead down to an easier finish. The falls are right next to the road and are probably more often paddled as a one off. By putting in below the falls the lower section can be used as a high access point for the Duddon for those not wanting to tackle Wallabarrow Gorge.

INDICATORS
Plenty of rain is needed and it easy to inspect the main falls by the car park at GR 231 963. Do you want to do it?

START
The road up Dunnerdale leaves the River Duddon at Seathwaite as it by-passes the Wallabarrow gorge and follows Tarn Beck instead. About a kilometre above Seathwaite the Road crosses the beck at the access point, Seathwaite Bridge.

DESCRIPTION
A) IV (V) A short flat section amongst reeds and bushes immediately below the bridge soon leads to a swift narrow channel through the trees with one fall. A slight easing allows a cul de sac on the left to be reached just above the main fall. The main fall is about 50 m long and is followed very shortly by another single 3 m drop.
1) IV First fall
2) V The main fall is a long narrow chute leading to a sharp drop into a pool with a blocked exit.
3) IV A curved 3 m fall.

B) III The river then flattens and eases to grade III, with a couple of nice rapids before the confluence with the Duddon.

EGRESS
Many will carry on down the Duddon but those who wish to get out should do so at the second footbridge below the falls where a path gains the road just below Seathwaite.

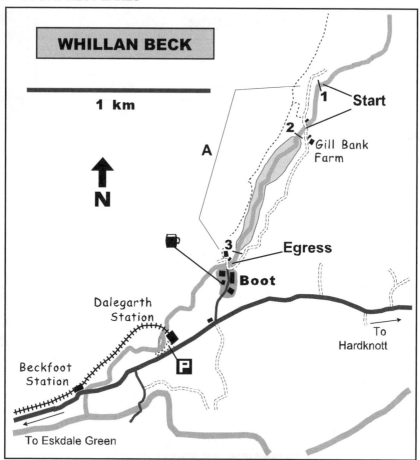

WHILLAN BECK

1 km

N

A

1 **Start**

2

Gill Bank
Farm

3 **Egress**

Boot

Dalegarth
Station

To
Hardknott

Beckfoot
Station

P

To Eskdale Green

In the middle of
Whillan Beck.
Stuart Miller

WHILLAN BECK

From :	Large Fall	181 021	Grade :	V
To :	Boot	176 011	Maps : O.S. 89 / 90, Explorer OL6	
Distance :	1 km		Stars : ✷✷ Scenery : ❀❀❀	

SUMMARY
The ultimate tree infested ditch. Love it or hate it. Continuous, problematic paddling leads through a narrow tree lined vale cutting from Eskdale Moor down to Boot. Losing 80 metres of height in only a kilometre this beck contains all manner of rocky horrors to test your nerves, with twists, slides, blocked drops, narrow chutes, boiling cauldrons, and tree ducks. However with plenty of climbing around on slippery rocks most of the falls can be adequately protected and the necessary low water conditions usually make this an entertaining and amusing jaunt. Remember your elbow pads.

INDICATORS
Unusual for a Lakeland beck in that it is best paddled in low to medium water, and as it is also fed by a large tarn it remains possible for several days after rain. If there is enough water to cushion the rocks then the straight drops into undercut boiling cauldrons will become too dangerous to paddle. The best place to get an idea of the level and the nature of the paddling is at the egress in Boot Village. There should be just enough water to scrape under the bridge at the egress, and If you walk up the road on the left bank for 50 m then the last rapid of Mill Falls can be inspected.

START
Park at Boot considerately, then walk up the road on the left bank. Follow the footpath which bears left through Gill Bank Farm and down to a small bridge over the beck, best to put in here. There is one fall above here found by crossing the bridge and going up a path on the right bank for a further 200 metres, but this top fall has a constricted entry and a ledge partially blocking the plunge pool, which most people wisely avoid as a warm up.

DESCRIPTION
A) V The whole section is a continuous adventure of awkward falls, many with twists and slides and several blocked by trees. Those falls that are straight and clean usually end up in boiling cauldrons with smooth overhanging sides. Constant bank support is necessary and as each fall will be thoroughly inspected by all paddlers before committing themselves to it there is no need for a full description. In low water there is arguably only one portage, but higher water levels, blockages by trees, and a sense of self preservation may induce several more.

1) V   The intimidating fall above the bridge.
2) IV / V The main rapids and falls start just below the bridge.
3) V   Mill Falls. The final long complicated series of falls finish down a narrow gully leading into a pool just above the bridge in Boot.

EGRESS
The best place to egress is from the pool at the end of Mill Falls, where the road on the left can be gained.

SUMMARY TABLE

Name of Run	Page	Grade	WW Stars	Scenic Stars	Km	Water	Notes
Artle Beck	273	4	★★	✿✿✿	4.5	Med	deep isolated gorge
Barbon Beck	275	4(5)	★★	✿✿✿	3.5	Med	continuous + falls
Cowside Beck	277	3		✿	6	High	remote spate run
Doe - Section 1	334	6		✿✿	0.5	Low	nasty narrow falls
Doe - Section 2	334	4		✿✿	1.5	High	high water blast
Gayle Beck	279	5	★★	✿	1	Med	avoid the cave !!
Greta (Ingleton)	281	3(3+)		✿	10	High	fun high water run
Hindburn	283	3(4,5)	★★	✿✿	8	High	large fall near end
Leck Beck	285	4+	★★	✿✿	4.5	High	remote narrow gorge
Lune (Lower river) - Section 3	287	1(2)		✿	35	Med	intro touring
Lune (Lower river) - Section 4	289	3	★★		0.4	Low	park & play rapids
Lune (Lower river) - Section 5	291	1			16	Low	big weir, tidal estuary
Pen-y-ghent Gill	293	4(5)	★★★	✿✿	5	High	remote gorge + falls
Ribble (Upper river)	295	4(5+)	★★	✿✿	7	Med	long rapid + portages
Roeburn	299	3(4)	★★★	✿✿✿	5	High	continuous gorge run
Stainforth Beck	335	4(5)	★	✿		High	steep boulders
Twiss	**334**	6		✿✿	3	Med	mad low volume falls
Wenning	301	2(3)		✿	21	High	flat with weirs
Wyre - Section 1	303	3	★	✿	3	High	continuous spate run
Wyre - Section 2	305	2		✿✿✿	6	High	awkward access

Otters

RIVERS OF NORTH LANCASHIRE AND YORKSHIRE

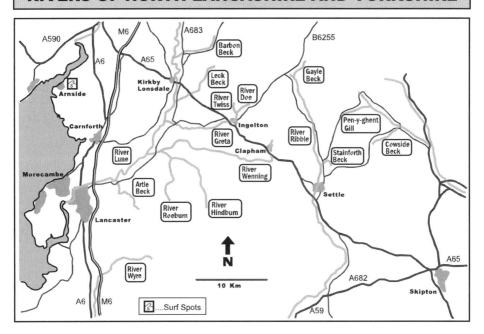

Main Fall, River Hindburn.   *Andy Plimmer*

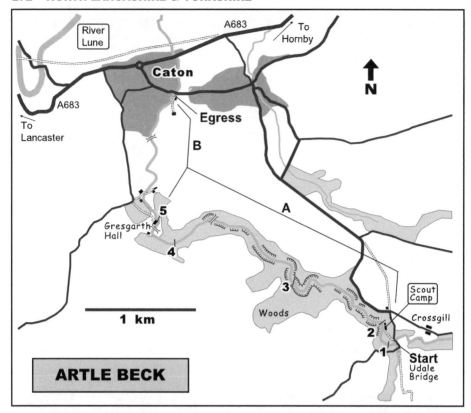

continued from opposite page ⇦

4) F   A fence marks the end of the gorge and entry into the grounds of Gresgarth Hall.

5) W   Take care as you pass the main building of Gresgarth Hall because lurking just around the corner is the massive funnel shaped weir which drops some 15 m in total. Vertical at its top, the weir becomes a slab and then almost horizontal at its base, where it funnels all the water into a narrow chute over a 1.5 m drop at its end. The concrete at the end is undercut and broken on the right which can form a dangerous boil and eddy in high water. At any level this weir is a serious proposition, yet it is awkward to protect or portage due to being surrounded by cliffs and private land. This therefore ups the ante on the whole trip, which should only be considered by experienced and competent teams.

B) II / III   Although still confined by cliffs for a short distance the river immediately ease off after the weir for the final section down to Caton.

EGRESS
Egress is to the right bank just upstream from the bridge to a track.

ARTLE BECK

From :	Udale Bridge 554 622	Grade :	IV
To :	Caton Bridge 534 644	Maps :	O.S. 97, Explorer OL41
Distance :	4.5 km	Stars : ✱✱ Scenery : ❀❀❀	

SUMMARY
A unique experience at the bottom of a deep gorge lined with steep vegetated cliffs up to 60m high. Excellent paddling, although never hard, keeps the adrenalin flowing while wondering what is around the next bend. The rocky base of the gorge gives a mainly clean and unobstructed run with few places to escape. A big fall at the start and a massive 15 m weir at the end add to the fun in this little gem found only 4 km from Lancaster City centre. However, the river passes through the private grounds of Gresgarth Hall, where paddlers should be both considerate and discrete after obtaining prior permission. The **large weir** can not be portaged without difficulty and tramping through private land, therefore running it is almost mandatory for those considering paddling this beck. So only the bold should venture forth in small numbers.

ACCESS NOTE
The present owners of Gresgarth Hall are Lord and Lady Lennox-Boyd, who are landscape gardeners of some repute and whose gardens it is certainly a privilege to travel through. **They request that any canoeists thinking of paddling the beck inform their head gardener in advance.** A preliminary request via their personal assistant on 01524 770313 will reveal his current phone number. Please respect these wishes or go elsewhere.

INDICATORS
Needs heavy rain to bring it up and the run off is quick. But the confined nature of the gorge between rocky banks holds the water well so very high levels are not required and in fact too much water would make parts of the gorge and the final weir very serious. At Caton Bridge if the water is just touching the bottom of the vertical sides of the bridge then it is an enjoyable low level. If the Roeburn is running then this usually will be also, as it has a very similar catchment.

START
Follow Littledale Road out of Caton to a junction at New House Farm where the right turning leads down to the river and Udale Bridge, close to a Scout Camp. There is room to park one car between the bridges and put on at the confluence with Udale Beck.

DESCRIPTION
A) IV   A large fall after only 50 m leads almost immediately into the confined gorge. A continuous and exciting series of small falls, rapids and slabby chutes through the bedrock lasts for the next 3 km. Most of the gorge is grade III but the rock strata does not allow landing for rescue or inspection so competent read and run tactics must be employed with an acute awareness for tree obstructions. The large weir at Gresgarth Hall can not conveniently be portaged and gives an intimidating finale to the run.

1) IV   This big 6 m fall starts the trip with a bang. A smooth slab on the right or a stepped channel with most of the water on the left.

2) III+   The first entry channel into the gorge ends with a small drop.

3) IV   About half way down the gorge as the beck twists between large cliffs a massive tree blockage comes into sight. Fortunately it is possible to land here and inspect this from the left bank. The trees lead the water into a narrow channel past an undercut boulder on the left where a quick cut back right avoids a second tree dam. An interesting problem that is more serious than it is hard, but which is difficult to portage.

⇦ *continued on opposite page*

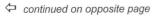

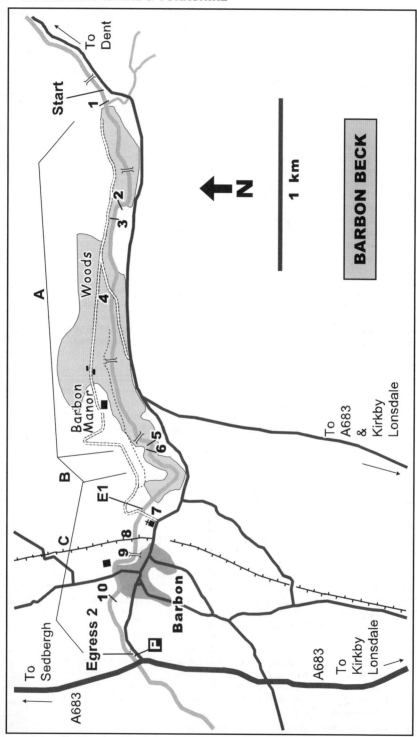

BARBON BECK

From :	Ford	656 828	Grade :	III, IV (V+)
To :	Barbon Village	635 766	Maps : O.S. 97, Explorer OL2	
Distance :	3.5 km		Stars : ✱✱ Scenery : ✿✿✿	

SUMMARY
A great paddle with continuously interesting rapids hidden in a small tree-lined valley and a difficult set of big falls in a cliff-lined gorge to finish it off.

INDICATORS
Heavy rain is needed to start this flowing but then the confined nature of the main bed of the gorge keeps its level up well. The beck is at its widest and shallowest at the start and egress so if looks navigable at these points the rest will be fine. There should be enough water to get over the first fall at the put in.

START
Start at a ford in Barbondale just where the beck leaves the road to enter the woods.

DESCRIPTION
A) III / IV A small fall at the starts gives a taster of the fun to follow. There is then 600 m of gentle beck through open woodland before a bend right channels the water over some rocks and the beck changes character to become narrower and deeper. Trees and bushes are a problem in places, while the rapids are fun and continuous but nowhere hard. Go on down past a stone bridge and two footbridges to a sharp corner and obvious horizon line at the entrance to `The Witches Cauldron`. In high water this section goes up a grade.
1) III   The small rocky reef at the start leads into a pool which is partially blocked by a fence with a gap in the middle.
2) III   The next fall which concentrates the flow is guarded by a tree on the right.
3) T   A large tree blocks the whole beck and needs portaging.
4) III   A series of small bedrock steps lead down under the stone bridge followed by a kilometre of sustained rapids.

B) V   The **Witches Cauldron** poses an interesting problem to complete the trip. A triple drop surrounded by cliffs which requires bold paddling or an awkward portage to gain the base of the final gorge. A degree of rope work skills can be useful in here.
5) IV   Just below a footbridge a bend right signals the top of the first fall. This is a steep 4 m chute into a large pool. Make sure you can egress in the pool to the left bank to inspect the second drop. It is possible to portage by climbing down the right side of the fall but you then have to cross the pool to the left bank.
6) V+   The second fall is a narrow slot falling 5 m into the scary boiling cauldron from which escape over the last smaller drop is difficult. Alternatively lower boats down the mossy slab on the left to a small ledge where a seal launch can be made.

C) III The last part of the gorge is easy again but with more tree hazards. The beck then opens out as it passes Barbon village with several fences to negotiate and a final fall just before the second egress.
7) F   A fence under the first bridge. Possible to egress here to the road by the church.
8) F   A fence under the old railway bridge.
9) F   A fence under a footbridge behind the village.
10) III Just after leaving the village the final fall is a 2 m drop through a narrow chute.

EGRESS
E1) It is best to egress to the right bank just above the first bridge in the village, by the church, to avoid all the fences. However there is better parking just off the A683 at **E2**.

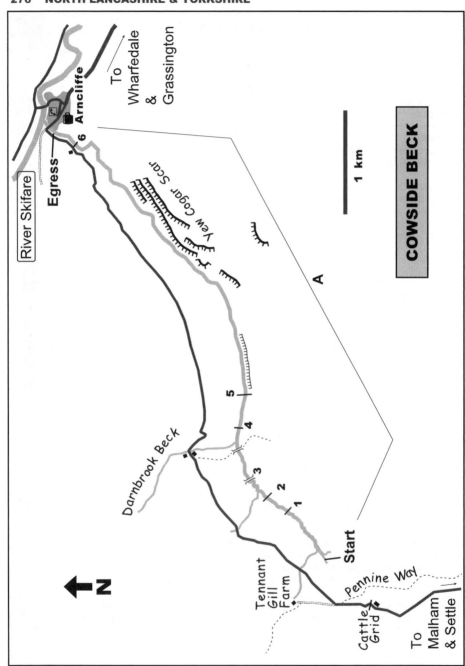

COWSIDE BECK

From :	Source	888 692	**Grade :**	III
To :	Arncliffe Bridge	930 719	**Maps :**	O.S. 98, Explorer OL2
Distance :		6 km		**Scenery : ❀**

SUMMARY
This beck is a narrow twisty channel for much of its length and is fairly straightforward. It starts from a stream resurgence in a grassy valley and runs through pleasant Yorkshire Dales scenery. It contains a nice little gorge section and offers a good introduction to Yorkshire beck bashing. It just sneaks into this guide due to its proximity to the Ribble and ease of access from Settle. The Skifare and Wharfe which this eventually joins are beyond the remit of this book and can be found in the *Yorkshire Rivers guide book* or the *Canoeists Guide to the North East*.

INDICATOR
For this trip the more water the better and it should have been raining plenty with all the springs spouting water down the valley sides as you drive to Arncliffe. From Arncliffe as you cross the bridge and turn up the valley the road runs right next to the beck for a distance and where the road begins to climb the hill by a barn there is a fall hidden behind the wall (GR 927 716) . If the water is flowing over the full width of this fall, including the rocks to the left of the main flow and is covering all the boulders in the river above with that brown ale colour then the river is canoeable.

START
Park at a bend in the road (GR 884 688) between a cattle grid and the entrance to Tennant Gill Farm at the head of the valley, taking care not to block the road. Follow the Pennine Way path through a gate and drag your boat down the dry valley leading to the source of the stream to put on as soon as possible.

DESCRIPTION
A) III Follow the beck around many twisty turns through grassy banks as it grows and fills. There are very few breakouts so watch out for the **fences and bridge** which need portaging. After the footbridge is passed and Darnbrook Beck enters, the gradient eases until the start of a brilliant little gorge section. After this it eases again for the pleasant run down to Arncliffe and the final fall.
1) F Portage the fence.
2) F Another fence.
3) B A very low footbridge which will need portaging in high water.
4) F After passing the second footbridge and the confluence with Darnbrook Beck there is one more fence before the gorge.
5) III An excellent gorge section for about 500 m which contains a series of small chutes and falls with the possibility of a fallen tree in the last drop.
6) III The final fall next to the road, viewed on the way up the valley. This is bigger than it looked from the road and can have quite a deep meaty stopper in high water.

EGRESS
Egress to the left bank just above the bridge in Arncliffe. Watch out for the fence just above this which may have a way through, it or egress before it.

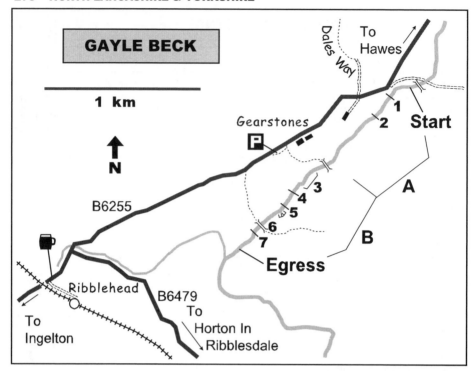

GAYLE BECK

1 km

N

Gearstones

B6255

Ribblehead

B6479
To
Horton In
Ribblesdale

To
Ingelton

Dales Way

To
Hawes

Start

1
2

A

3
4
5
6
7

B

Egress

Cowside Beck in very low water.   *Stuart Miller*

GAYLE BECK

From :	Ford	787 803	Grade :	IV / VI
To :	Gorge end	776 794	Maps : O.S. 98, Explorer OL2	
Distance :	1 km		Stars : ✷ ✷ Scenery : ❀	

SUMMARY
This is the main source stream for the river Ribble high up at Ribblehead and it gives a mini classic through a memorable limestone gorge containing all sorts of sharp rocks, undercuts and caves to avoid. The gorge gives 500 m of very sustained and challenging paddling with numerous difficult drops needing constant inspection and support.

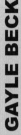

INDICATORS
Heavy rain is needed to start this flowing but too much actually running down the beck will make it very dangerous. The river Ribble at Settle should be at a medium high level with the Twin Bridges rapid looking good but not monstrous. The beck at the put in should still have plenty of rocks showing but be OK to float down and have a brown ale colour rather than hot chocolate.

START
Drop off boats and gear at a bend on the B6255 north of Gearstones where the Dales Way leads down a track to a ford and footbridge over the beck. Then drive 1 km back down the road to a large lay-by just below Gearstones Lodge at GR 778 798. This is at the end of the path leading to the middle bridge and 200 m up from the egress path. Run / walk back up the road to the start. It is important to use rights of way in this area and not to park in the car parks of the Gearstones houses.

DESCRIPTION
A) III A few gentle rapids as the beck twists and turns with a short narrow section.
1) F A fence near the start is portaged on the right.
2) III A nice narrow section with a bush halfway down.

B) IV / VI Egress above the footbridge on the left bank to inspect the first half of the gorge. Once you drop into the gorge there is no escape and the grade is very dependent on water level. At a low level when it is only just possible then it is a technical IV but with more flowing it gets exciting and far more dangerous. The first section starts with a series of drops leading to a nasty stopper and big undercut. A tree then needs portaging before the second series of difficult falls under another footbridge. The final set of falls are more straightforward.

3) V A few tiny drops lead to a rocky ramp, then around a corner is a straight drop followed by small double drop with the nasty stopper at the bottom. Immediately below this the river bends right with another drop containing the serious undercut on the right wall and swimmers must be protected from this.

4) T From the pool by the undercut a shallow section leads past a huge boulder into a gun barrel and over another small drop to egress and portage the tree.

5) IV Inspect the next fall which has serious pinning potential. The main flow then disappears down a cave **(Extreme Danger)** which must be avoided at all costs on the right before bony rapids lead down to the next set of tight drops.

6) V God's Bridge. A narrow chicane followed by three drops into basin with an undercut right wall. These can be inspected from the footbridge.

7) IV The final gorge is narrow but straightforward once past the first drop which contains a sump on the right and a head banging overhang on the left.

EGRESS
Carry back up to the car park using the path from God's Bridge.

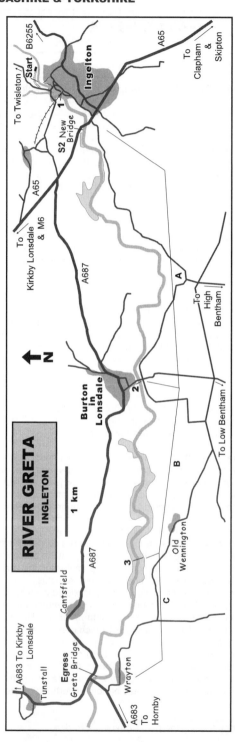

GRETA (Ingleton)

From : Ingleton, River Doe 695 734	Grade :	II, III (IV)
To : Wrayton, Greta Bridge 611 726	**Maps :** O.S. 91, Explorer OL19	
Distance : 10 km	**Scenery :** ✿	

SUMMARY
The River Twiss and the River Doe drain much of the water running off and out of this area of prime limestone caving country. They combine at Ingleton to form the River Greta which can rise and fall quickly after rain but gives a fun high water run.

INDICATORS
View the river from the A65 road bridge by Ingleton and if the river is obviously running with enough water to paddle under the bridge then it will be OK. The more water the better.

START
A steep hill leads down from the centre of Ingleton to a double bridge over the two rivers. Between the two bridges a minor road leads north towards Twisleton and 100 m up this road a track leads off to the right where the bank of the River Doe **(S1)** can be accessed, although the parking here is private. It is also possible to start from the playground beside the swimming pool.
An easier start can be made to avoid the first complicated weir by putting in at New Bridge on the A65 **(S2)**.

DESCRIPTION
A)   III (IV) The river is immediately fast flowing and full of small boulders. The River Twiss soon joins from the right to add more volume and power for the **awkward weir** which lies under the viaduct. After leaving Ingleton the river eases as it flows through open fields with shingle rapids and the occasional bedrock shelf, which in high water can give fun surfing on some of the large standing waves.
1) W   At the viaduct the river is split by one of the supports. Most of the water flows through the left side where there is another division of the flow. Next to the support in the middle of the river is an angled slope into an enclosed stopper between concrete walls, the flat pool which follows then falls over a second vertical weir with boulders in places and a strong stopper in high water. The alternative route hugs the left bank through a series of 7 fish steps. This intimidating, awkward and potentially dangerous weir is usually at least grade IV and can not be portaged due to fences and private land on both banks. It can be inspected from the lane beside `Ingleton Pottery` before starting and put on below if you don't like the look of it, at New Bridge.
2) III   At Burton in Lonsdale there is a bridge with two arches. both arches have small stoppers on the downstream side which are usually no problem. The stopper below the right arch can be a fun surf wave with good eddies on either side.

B) III+ Below the bridge a series of bedding plane ledges are a fun ride in high water before the river enters woodland. A few interesting rapids lead eventually to a 1.5m shelf across the whole river which is soon followed by a small rocky reef.
3) III+ The large bedrock shelf can produce a strong stopper in high water and should be inspected / portaged on the left.

C) II   The last two kilometres are easy with occasional shingle rapids.

EGRESS
Egress to the right bank on the outside of the bend just above Greta Bridge.

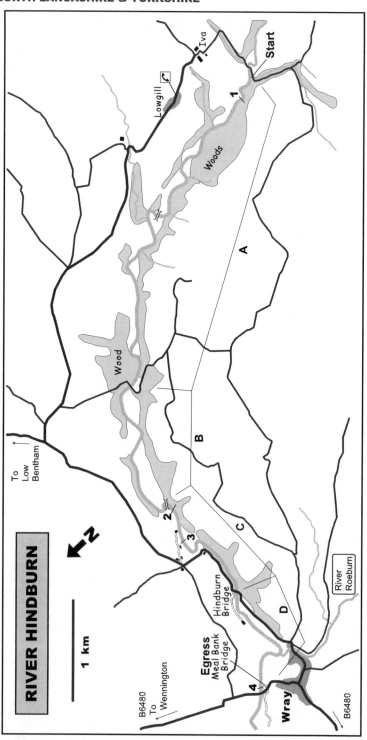

HINDBURN

From :	Millbeck Foot	649 640	Grade :	III, IV, (V)
To :	Wray	604 680	Maps : O.S. 97, Explorer OL41	
Distance :		8 km	Stars : ✶✶ Scenery : ❀❀	

SUMMARY
A good trip in a variety of water levels with some steep slabs near the start, plenty of grade III and then a **hard triple fall** near the end. Unfortunately there are a great many trees in the river, several of which may require portages.

INDICATORS
Heavy rain is needed as this rises and falls quite quickly. However it is still a pleasant run just off the spate. The best place to view the river is from Hindburn Bridge at GR 613 676. Looking upstream from here the water should cover the full width of the fall that is visible. This bridge is also a useful egress. In high water some big stoppers develop, pushing the grade up a bit.

START
The road crosses the river at a bridge close to Lowgill Village. Just west of the bridge it follows the left river bank for 100 m to another bridge over a small side beck and a sharp bend. From this bend there is access down to the confluence.

DESCRIPTION
A) III / IV   Easy at first but after only a few bends a section of steep bedding planes are reached. Things ease off again after these to give pleasant grade III paddling down to the first road bridge.
1)   IV   There are three steep bedding planes in a row with pools between. These are straight forward in low water, can have grabby stoppers at high flows, and give entertaining play waves somewhere in between.

B) II   A kilometre of easy water leads down to a footbridge. Land above the bridge to inspect/ portage the hard fall which follows immediately.

C) III / IV (V) The big fall then several smaller drops with some playful stoppers give a good section down to Hindburn Bridge.
2) IV / V This triple drop loses some 4 m in height. Inspect or portage on the right bank. There is a ramp to regain the river 50 m past the falls.
3) III / IV A long series of small drops over bedding planes up to 1.5 m in height leads down to the bridge.

D) II   After the bridge the river eases right off to grade II down to the confluence with the Roeburn and then a small weir at the egress. A the time of writing a large tree forms a river wide strainer on this section soon after the bridge ,which needs portaging, so many may choose to finish at Hindburn Bridge.
4)   W   A small weir at the egress.

EGRESS
Egress to the left bank at the weir just above Mealbank Bridge. This is on the road north out of Wray where there is a lay by beside the weir.

RIVER HINDBURN

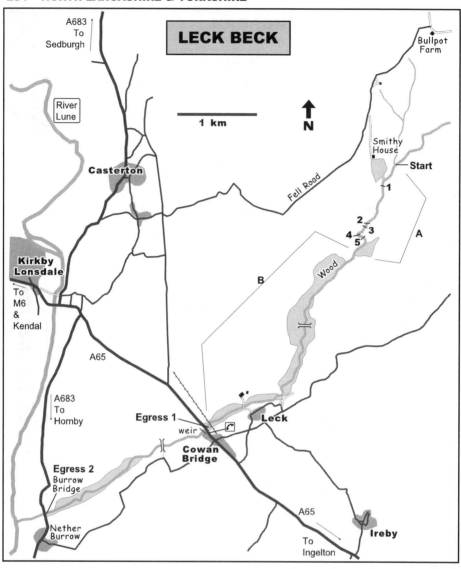

LECK BECK

LECK BECK

From :	Smithy House	658 798	Grade :	IV+ / V
To :	Cowan Bridge	635 766	Maps : O.S. 97, Explorer OL2	
Distance :		4.5 km	Stars : ✶ ✶ Scenery : ❀ ❀	

SUMMARY
A great little beck with an awkward twisty gorge and a set of big falls before settling down to an easy run through the woods. Although the difficulties are short-lived, this is a worthwhile and unusual expedition as all the water in this beck emerges from the subterranean passages of the great Easgill Caving system. The resurgence is only a few hundred metres above the put in.

INDICATORS
Quite a lot of recent rain is needed to fill the caverns that feed this beck. Look over the bridge at the egress in Cowan Bridge. The beck is fairly wide and shallow here and if it is running and looks paddleable without a scrape then it will be fine above. Very high water should be avoided as the narrow gorge will become extremely serious.

START
From Cowan Bridge head back towards Kirkby Lonsdale but take the first turning right to Casterton. Then take the first turning right again (at a cross roads), which is the fell road to the Bullpot Farm Caving hut. After climbing the fell the road takes a sharp bend left and contours along the side of the valley. Approx 1.5 km after the bend there is a track which doubles back and heads down the hillside to Smithy House. There is room for one car to park carefully by the entrance to this track. Carry boats from here straight down the fell side into a tiny sub valley which soon joins the main beck. Put in at the confluence.

DESCRIPTION
A) IV+ / V At first the beck is open and shallow but after a few hundred metres (and a fence) the banks start to close in to form a gorge. A single fall marks the start of the difficulties through the gorge which last for about 200 m and end with a fine series of complicated falls and a large drop.
1)   F   A fence 300 m below the put in.
2)   IV   The first fall is a 1.5 m drop into a rocky pot with a restricted exit.
3)   IV+   Leck Beck Gorge follows with a technical series of small falls and awkward twists around large boulders.
4)   IV+   Double Dilemma. This awkward three tier fall has a pool before the last drop with a choice of exits either side of central rocks.
5)   IV+   Going Under. The last 3m drop follows immediately.

B) III   Around the corner below the series of falls the beck soon enters woodland and continuous bouldery rapids lead down to Cowan Bridge with the only hazards being from tree branches or fallen trees blocking the river.

EGRESS
At Cowan Bridge egress to the left bank after passing under the old railway bridge and above the road bridge where a path leads to the road **(E1)**.
A weir immediately follows Cowan Bridge, then the river continues gently through more woodland for a further 2 km to another possible egress at Burrow Bridge **(E2),** before it joins the Lune.

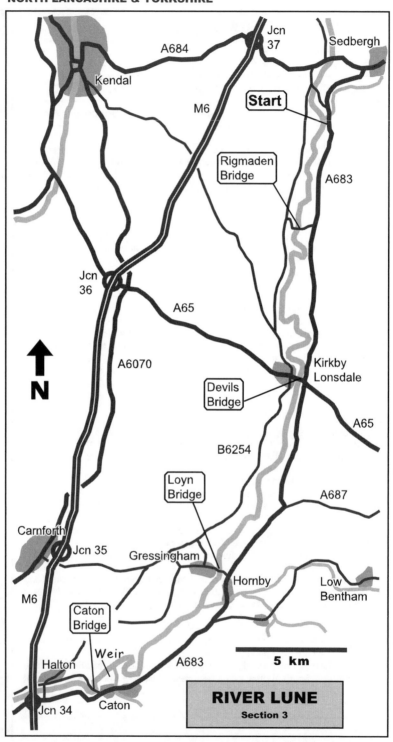

LUNE (Lower Lune)

After its confluence with the river Rawthey just below Sedbergh the Lune calms down significantly and winds its way gently to the sea. These lower parts give some good long easy grade trips, at first through pleasant farmland then the unusual traverse of Lancaster which can be made into a long round tour by returning on the Lancaster canal. By contrast the short section of rapids at Halton give some interesting water on the outskirts of Lancaster that are suitable for beginners at low water and experts at higher flows. Most of this part of the river runs through Lancashire after leaving Cumbria at Kirkby Lonsdale. The higher reaches of the river lie totally in Cumbria, and so the Tebay Gorge and the classic Crook of Lune to Rawthey confluence sections are to be found in the *East Cumbria South* chapter.

SECTION 3   Rawthey Confluence To Caton

From : Lay-by on A683 630 892	Grade : I / II+
To : Bridge below Caton 522 647	Maps : O.S. 97, Explorer OL2 / 41
Distance : 35 km	Scenery : ✿

SUMMARY
From the Rawthey confluence down to Kirkby Lonsdale the river is mainly grade I / II, with the occasional shingle rapid noticeable in low water. However the last kilometre down to and through the Devils Bridge at Kirkby Lonsdale is II+ and powerful currents can make it grade III in high water. Below Kirkby Lonsdale the river becomes quite flat and meanders across open fields with only a weir just above Caton to be aware of. There are several bridges along this long section which can be used for access. Positions and distances are given in the description below.

START
Just beyond the bridge over the River Rawthey the A683 enters a wood and climbs a hill. There is a lay-by on the left close to a gate and bridleway on the opposite side of the road which leads down to the river.

DESCRIPTION
Rigmaden Bridge....................................... 616 848.   5 km.
Kirkby Lonsdale (Devils Bridge)............... 615 782   10 km
Loyn Bridge... 581 697   10 km
Caton Bridge................................. .... 522 647   10 km
1) W   On approaching Caton the river swings away from the road to run down the far side of the valley. Just after the confluence with Artle Beck there is a weir. Footpaths on either side of the river provide inspection or portage.

EGRESS
A kilometre below the weir the river passes under an old railway bridge and a road bridge. Egress to the right bank above the railway bridge. This is close to a car park beside some public conveniences. These are found by turning right off the A683 just after leaving Caton, signposted Halton Green. The car park is on the right after crossing the river.

RIVER LUNE 3 (Lower Lune)

Devil's Bridge at Kirkby Lonsdale, River Lune.   *Thomas Allom 1836*

SECTION 4   Halton Rapids

Parking : Car Park 503 645	Grade : III / IV
by Lancaster University Boathouse.	Maps : O.S. 97, Explorer OL41
Distance : 400 m	Stars : ✶ ✶

SUMMARY
Halton rapids are a few hundred metres long and are situated between two weirs at Halton on the outskirts of Lancaster. They are formed by a series of stone walls sticking out into the flow from both banks. They can be paddled at all water levels and vary from a good introductory training ground for beginners in low flows to a full on epic surf spot in spate. The holes formed by the walls are only playable at low to normal levels and form dangerous stoppers as the level rises. Finally, severe access restrictions limit paddling to November, December and January.

INDICATORS
If access agreements permitted, then Halton could be paddled all year round at all levels. The boathouse weir beside the car park gives a good indication of the level.

Low and rocky : If water is only flowing through a channel in the centre of the weir.
Normal levels : When water is flowing above the centre channel but well below top of the stone walls to the sides.
High Water : When water is approaching the top of the stone walls at the side. (Best Level)
Very High : When water is flowing over the stone walls at the side.
Spate : When the whole weir is closed out bank to bank with massive recirculation.

START
The large car park beside Lancaster University Boathouse is found by following the A683 east from Lancaster. 600 m after passing under the M6 motorway (Junction 34) there is a turn off to the left down a small steep lane to the river. At the bottom of the hill on the right, before crossing the bridge to Halton, is the site of an old railway station which is now used as the university boathouse. The car park is on both sides of the road. The top of the rapids are reached by walking up the pathway along the old railway track. Do not go right up to the top weir as this will interfere with a fish counter. At normal levels it is also possible to paddle upstream from above the boathouse weir.

DESCRIPTION
At normal levels there are many small waves, eddies, and holes to play on and it makes a fine area for an introduction to, and training on, moving water. However as the water rises the power increases quite markedly with good surf waves forming and the stone walls generating huge stoppers which need avoiding.
In spate, for experts only, there are some challenging surf waves produced which are hard to get onto, while the stoppers are obviously definite no go areas.

EGRESS
Egress to the left bank well above the boathouse weir which is **dangerous** at all but extremely low levels.
Paddling the weir and the river down to the bridge is strictly forbidden.

See map overleaf ⇨

RIVER LUNE 4 (Lower Lune)

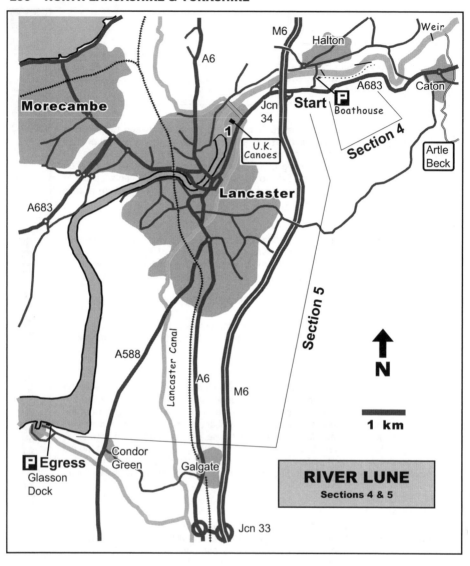

SECTION 5		Lancaster Ramble	
From : Halton Bridge	503 645	**Grade :**	I (Tidal)
To : Glasson Dock	447 561	**Maps :** O.S. 97, Explorer OL41	
Distance :	16 km		

SUMMARY

An unusual trip through the centre of Lancaster on mostly tidal waters. Best timed with a falling tide it can be quite enjoyable with plenty of bird life on the estuary. The main hazard is portaging the large and **lethal Skerton weir**. It is also possible to double the length of this trip by returning to within 2 kilometres of the starting point by paddling back up the Lancaster canal.

INDICATORS

This can be paddled at any time. However, in very high water Skerton weir becomes lethal and very hard to portage so the trip should then be avoided. Check beforehand if in doubt.

START

A large car park beside Lancaster University Boathouse is found by following the A683 east from Lancaster. 600 m after passing under the M6 motorway (Junction 34) there is a turn off to the left down a small steep lane to the river. At the bottom of the hill before crossing the bridge to Halton, is the site of an old railway station which is now used as the university boathouse and there is car parking on either side of the road. From the car park follow a path down to put in below the bridge on the left bank.

DESCRIPTION

Flat water leads from the bridge at Halton underneath the M6 and then under the canal viaduct as the outskirts of Lancaster are entered. Watch out for the weir which is about 300 m below the viaduct, and keep to the right side of the river ready to egress and portage.

1) W   This is Skerton Weir which usually consists of evil pourovers either onto concrete ledges or into massive stoppers. It has been run in very low summer levels when it is reported to be a risky grade IV run which can not be protected, but it is normally a mandatory portage on the right side. At normal levels it is best to land by some boat houses 50 m above the weir on the right bank and walk down the road a short way to a lane which leads back to the river below the weir.

After the weir the river flows past Lancaster Quay, with some easy rapids appearing at low tide, and then out into the estuary. The estuary is quiet and featureless but can be relaxing and teeming with bird life. At Glasson Dock a sea wall appears on river left as the estuary bends rightwards. The quayside or sea wall on the left should be gained, which often necessitates a struggle through mud and an awkward climb.

EGRESS

The Egress at Glasson Dock is found by following the A 588 south from Lancaster to Condor Green, where a turn off right leads to the village. Follow the signs to the East Dock where there is car park opposite the Victoria Inn. The sea wall can be gained from the estuary just to the right of the pub behind the bowling green.

RIVER LUNE 5 (Lower Lune)

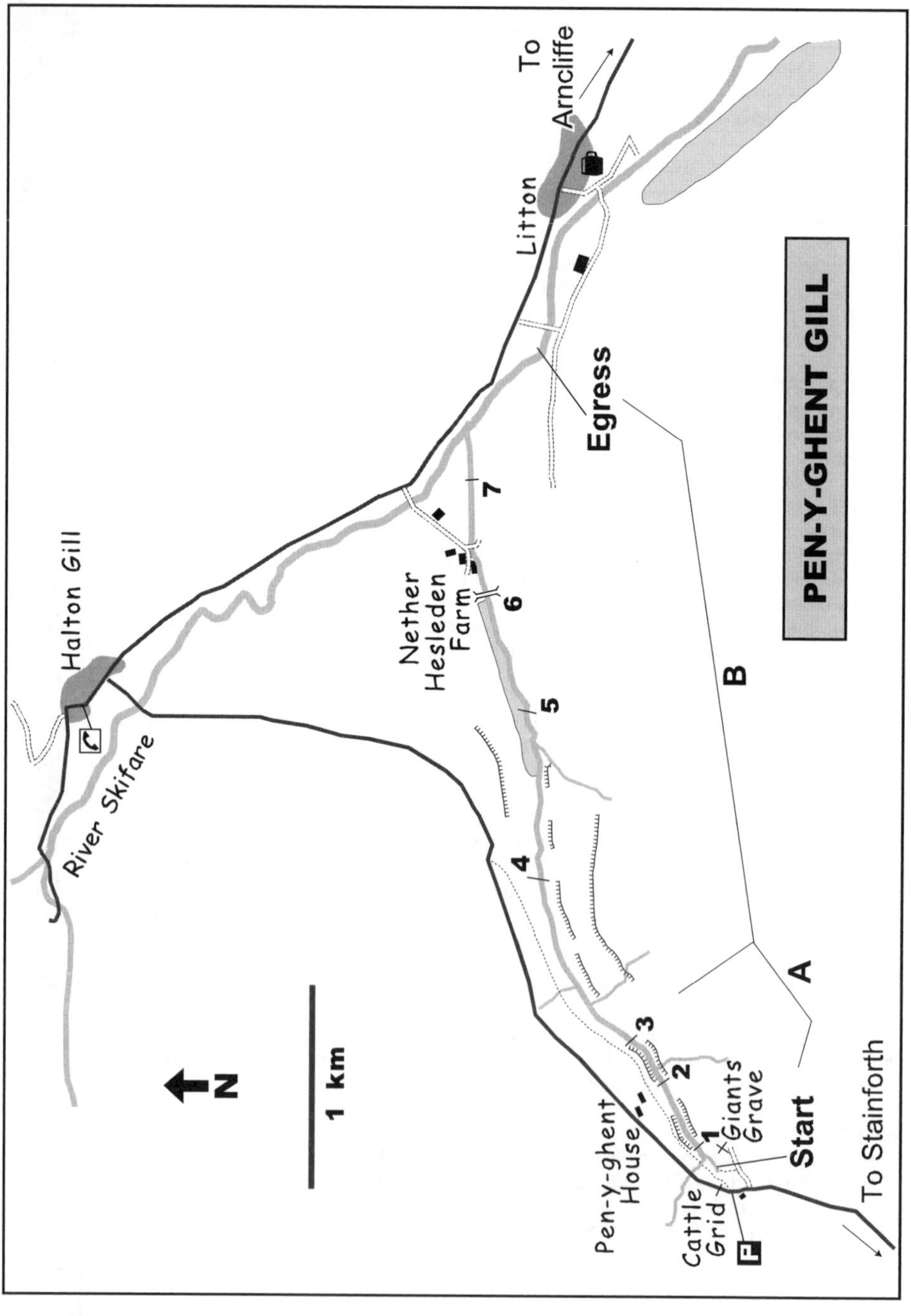

PEN-Y-GHENT GILL

To Arncliffe

Litton

Egress

Halton Gill

River Skifare

Nether Hesleden Farm

7

6

5

4

3

2

1

B

A

N

1 km

Pen-y-ghent House

Giants Grave

Start

Cattle Grid

To Stainforth

PEN-Y-GHENT GILL

From :	Resurgence 856 733	Grade :	IV / V
To :	Bridge on Skifare 898 742	Maps : O.S. 98, Explorer OL2 / 30	
Distance :	5 km	Stars : ✱✱✱ Scenery : ❀❀	

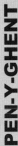

SUMMARY
A brilliant little river hidden in a deep and narrow valley to the south east of Pen-y-ghent which gives excellent beck paddling through an isolated valley in limestone gorges .

INDICATORS
Only possible after heavy and prolonged rain to fill up all the limestone caves and get the resurgences flushing. If all the springs in the area are spewing white water down the fells then this should be OK. As with many other becks the grade can change dramatically with water level. If the level is low and it is just possible then it can be a grade IV with portages but more water means more excitement. From the road in Littondale just above the egress check the level at the confluence with the Skifare as the beck flows underground and becomes totally dry in low water here. It should be flowing well out of the confluence.

START
Start from the resurgence of the beck at the head of the valley. This is found on the minor road from Stainforth to Littondale where near the top of the pass there is a cattle grid and a small building with plenty of room to park nearby. A Giants Grave is marked on the map and if the path towards this is followed through a gate then another gate almost immediately on the left leads to a jumble of boulders from where the beck appears.

DESCRIPTION
A) V   The beck immediately starts dropping very steeply with water both gushing from and disappearing down various holes in the ground. The first 700 m is continuously challenging with **two hard falls** hidden in gorges.
1) V   A steep ramp leads over the first small fall then be ready to get out as the big drop into the first gorge follows in only 50 m. It is an angled 3 m fall into a nasty narrow slot. Inspect / Portage awkwardly on the right.
2) V   More small falls lead out of the gorge to where the angle eases for a short way below Pen-y-ghent House, seen high on the left. A fence marks the entrance to the second big fall. A narrow chute leads underneath the fence and over a 3m drop into a deep enclosed pool. Inspect / portage on the left where the river can be regained in 50 m.
3) IV   The gorge below the main fall contains some more bedrock steps and the last of these is a 2 m fall into a shallow pool with a bony landing.

B   IV   The gorge opens out and the beck runs through the narrow but open valley for a while with numerous small falls and mini gorges. These continue down to and through the woods with a couple of larger falls and an awkward fence to watch out for.
4) IV   A narrow twisty gorge spouts into a large pool.
5) IV   Soon after the entrance to the woods is a nice 2 m river wide fall.
6) F   A metal footbridge has a nasty metal and wire fence beneath it which is hard to avoid so take care and egress 50 m above it to the right bank and portage.
7) IV   After the farm the river becomes very narrow and fast as blind bends rush you over the final surprise, a 3 m easy angled ramp. Low branches lead to the.

EGRESS
Continue down the Skifare to egress 50 m above the first stone bridge. Make sure to get out on the left in good time before committing to the last rapid which leads into a nasty wire fence under the bridge. Park considerately in the lane to the bridge.

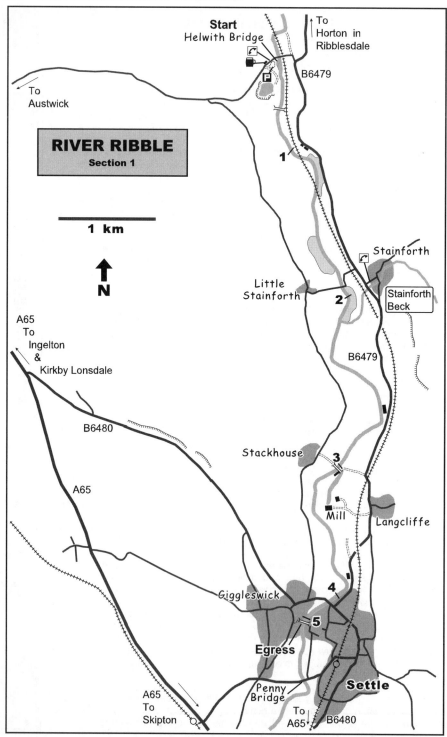

Start
Helwith Bridge

↑ To
Horton in
Ribblesdale

P

B6479

← To
Austwick

RIVER RIBBLE
Section 1

1

1 km

↑
N

Stainforth

Little
Stainforth

Stainforth
Beck

2

A65
To
Ingelton
&
Kirkby Lonsdale

B6479

B6480

A65

Stackhouse

3

Mill

Langcliffe

4

Giggleswick

5

Egress

Settle

A65
To
Skipton

Penny
Bridge

To
A65

B6480

RIBBLE

A river of strange contrasts, the Ribble is often referred to as a Yorkshire river yet it flows west and mainly through Lancashire. It starts high in limestone country yet its main rapid is through gritstone and in its upper section it has two rapids that are at their best at widely opposing water levels.

In its seventy five kilometre trip from Ribblehead to the coast just below Preston it passes mostly through pleasant and gentle farmland with plenty of opportunity for flat water touring but there are two more lively sections which are paddled regularly. The first and harder of these sections is close to its source where the river loses much of its height as it tumbles out of the high Yorkshire limestone country through a jumble of boulders between Horton in Ribblesdale and Settle.

The second section is found much lower on the river close to Clitheroe where the Ribble is well established in Lancashire and is described separately in the *South Lancashire and Yorkshire* chapter of this guide. This lower section is a pleasant easy grade trip with straightforward shingle rapids often used as an introduction to moving water for beginners. It is improved greatly by high water levels when more experienced paddlers can find some entertainment.

SECTION 1   Above Settle

From : Helwith Bridge 811 695	Grade : III / IV, (V)
To : Settle 814 639	Maps : O.S. 98, Explorer OL2
Distance : 7 km	Stars : ✷✷ Scenery : ❀❀❀

SUMMARY
A great section of the river where it loses some 70 m in height on its way down to Settle. The river runs through pleasant limestone scenery with the long Twin Bridges rapid being the main interest and **Stainforth Force** being the main worry. A couple of quite serious weirs also liven up the lower part of this run.

INDICATORS
At Settle the river is wide and looks like a big river yet we are still close to the source and plenty of rain is needed to get the run off from the limestone fells and caves, which goes up and down quickly. At Settle the last rapid by the egress should look possible either side of the large rock, with a haystack on the left, to be at its best. However the river can be run at lower levels and if water is just starting to flow to the right of the rock, but still not navigable, the rest of the river will be low but ok. If no water at all is flowing to the right of the rock then the river will be a scrape in places. Another place to look is from a lay-by a kilometre north of Stainforth which overlooks Twin Bridges rapid, but it is some distance away to get a true feel for the volume unless you already know the river.

START
Helwith Bridge is the most convenient starting point where to the west of the bridge there is a parking and picnic area next to the river.

DESCRIPTION
A) IV (V)   A few rocky shelves produce some easy rapids at the start as the river bends around a small hillock. A footbridge marks the run into Twin Bridges which continues to below the second railway bridge where the rive eases again down to Stainforth Force.
1) IV Twin Bridges. This long continuous rapid runs down over large gritstone
        boulders for some 500 m as it passes under the two railway bridges. In low water

continued on next page ⇨

⇨ *continued from previous page*

it is pool drop style with technical twists and turns amongst the boulders, while in big water it is a roller-coaster ride with little chance of respite, relief or rescue until below the second bridge.

2) V+ Stainforth Force. Egress should be made immediately below the small stone bridge to portage this **dangerous fall**. In low water there are hidden potholes while in high water the final drop becomes a killer as an extremely powerful enclosed stopper develops between cliffs from which rescue would be difficult. It is occasionally paddled at low medium levels, but great care must be taken. The portage necessitates continuing down the right bank for 100 m to get round the cliffs immediately below the fall.

B) III   From here interesting rapids lead down to the first weir. There is another weir at the entrance to Settle and then a final rapid at the egress.

3) W   Stackhouse Weir. This is found just above a footbridge and can have a very **dangerous** tow-back in high water. Inspect / portage river right.

4) W   Settle Weir. On the approach to the A65 road bridge. Always **dangerous** and a portage is advised again on river right. This is a big drop onto rock and only possible in flood conditions when it gets serious for other reasons. The fish ladder on the left is also dangerous and definitely not an easy option.

5) III / IV Queens Rock. Otherwise known as Municipal Falls is a few hundred metres after the main road bridge where the river divides around a large central rock just above a footbridge. In high water there is a choice of lines giving a final fling before the egress.

EGRESS

Get out river right immediately below the last falls and carry back over the footbridge to a lane between the council works yard and the Kings Mill housing development. This point is found by turning off the A65 close to the centre of Settle down the road past the station towards Penny Bridge. Just before the bridge turn into the Sowarth Field industrial estate by a Land Rover garage. Continue through the industrial estate until the mill development is on the left and a housing estate is on the right. Park in this vicinity and the footbridge is found further along the road at its end by the council depot. Change discreetly, if you have to, in this very public area.

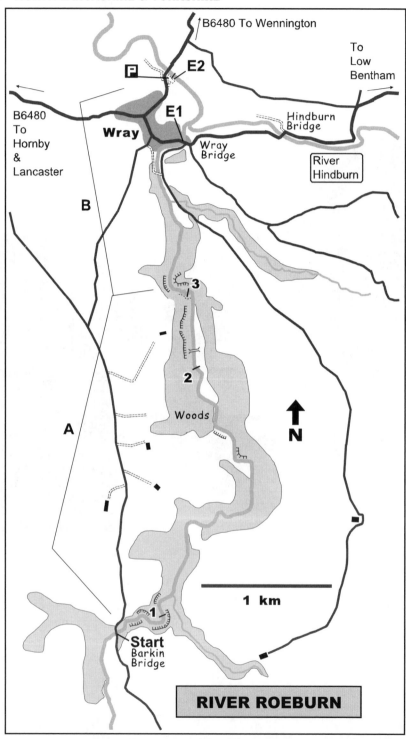

B6480 To Wennington

To
Low
Bentham

E2

P

E1

B6480
To
Hornby
&
Lancaster

Wray

Wray
Bridge

Hindburn
Bridge

River
Hindburn

B

3

2

Woods

A

N

1 km

1

Start
Barkin
Bridge

RIVER ROEBURN

ROEBURN

From :	Barkin Bridge	600 637	Grade :	III / IV
To :	Wray Bridge	605 674	Maps :	O.S. 97, Explorer OL41
Distance :		5 km	Stars : ✶✶✶ Scenery : ❀❀❀	

IV

SUMMARY
A pleasant run through a hidden valley giving a continuous and challenging grade III, with one fall in a gorge reaching grade IV in high water and which is awkward to portage. The river and parking areas are not suitable for large groups.

INDICATORS
Look at the river at the egress in Wray village. If there is enough water to pass under the bridge it is worth paddling but it is even better if it is fat, brown and in spate.

START
From the centre of Wray village follow the minor road towards High Salter from beside the Post Office, marked Roeburndale West. Follow this road to where it crosses the river 2 km beyond a junction. There is parking for one car by the bridge.

DESCRIPTION
A) III / IV The rapids start immediately and are fairly continuous all the way back to Wray.

1) III   After 500 m a small waterfall down the cliff of the right bank signals the approach of a series of slides. An awkwardly fallen tree partially blocks the first slide.

2) III   At the end of a more open section of fields the river bends right by a barn and a large piece of concrete has fallen into the river with a tree on top of it. Beware that the main current flows into and under the concrete.

3) III / IV A long straight section of good rapids leads under a footbridge and down to where the river flows against a small undercut cliff as it bends sharply left to enter a short gorge. A 2 m drop at the end of the gorge can develop a strong tow-back in high water. It is best inspected by landing on seeing the first cliff and climbing up to a terrace which runs along the left bank above the fall. However, safety cover or portaging are awkward to organise.

B) II+ The river now eases but trees can remain a problem to the end.

EGRESS
Egress to the left bank just below the road bridge on the east side of Wray village **(E1)**. Or continue past the confluence with the Hindburn to the car park by the weir on the north exit from Wray on the B6480 **(E2)**. (See Hindburn Egress Page 283)

RIVER ROEBURN

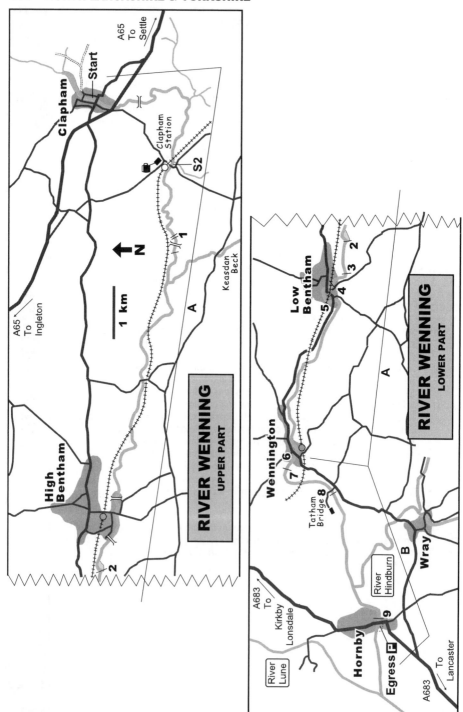

WENNING

From :	Clapham	744 692	Grade :	II (III)
To :	Hornby	585 684	Maps : O.S.97/98, Explorer OL2/41
Distance :	21 km		Scenery : ✿

SUMMARY
A pleasant grade II river with no major difficulties that collects the water from the limestone cave area south east of Ingleborough. The main interest is derived from the large number of weirs on this section, which usually pose no problems at normal levels but should be treated with the usual caution in high water.

INDICATORS
Heavy rain is needed to bring this up as much of the water is held back by underground cave systems and a small reservoir above Clapham. These can cause a delay of about 12 hours before the river rises. Check the level at the bridge beside the Punch Bowl Inn at Low Bentham. Enough water is needed to paddle under the bridge here.

START
It is possible to start in the centre of the village at Clapham where the river is still known as Clapham Beck **(S1)**. Otherwise the bridge at Clapham Station (GR 733 677) is 3.5 km lower down the river, and gives access just above the bridge from the left bank **(S2)**. From here it may have more water as a couple more becks have joined it to form the Wenning.

DESCRIPTION
A) II (III) From Clapham to Bentham the river is mainly grade II with some bushes to avoid at Clapham Station and a few weirs.
1) W   After some meandering bends there are several small weirs creating waves and possible play stoppers. However care should be taken as the weirs are made of wire baskets which are breaking up causing debris and spikes in the stoppers.
2) II / III   A kilometre below the bridge at High Bentham the river bends left around some woodland leading to a river wide reef just before the river bends back right sharply. The fall is about 1 m high at the right and lower on the left.
3) W   Just before the river bends right again on its approach to Low Bentham there are two weirs. The first is about 1 m and vertical, which is normally quite easy but could be nasty in high water. The second is much larger at 4 m in height with a single angled slope on the right and a series of steps on the left.
4) B   Above both the road bridges at Low Bentham there is a pipeline which can collect log jams sometimes blocking the whole river. Best to inspect before hand when also checking the water levels near here.
5) B   Punch Bowl Bridge. The lower road bridge on exit from Low Bentham. This is a place to check the levels and is often used as an egress.
6) W   Under the bridge at Wennington is an angled 2 m weir, followed by an unsettling wave and then flat water to another small weir with a strong tow-back.

B) I The river now eases to grade I to the Lune confluence, but with still more weirs.
8) W   200 m to yet another weir.
9) W   Tatham Bridge weir. This is horseshoe shaped but can still be taken anywhere.
10) W   Hornby Weir. This large angled weir is just above the bridge and can be shot in several places, but again be wary in high water, especially in the middle. Bushes on the right and private land on the left make portaging awkward, and it is best inspected before starting.

EGRESS
Egress on the left bank below the bridge to a car park. Or continue easily to the Lune.

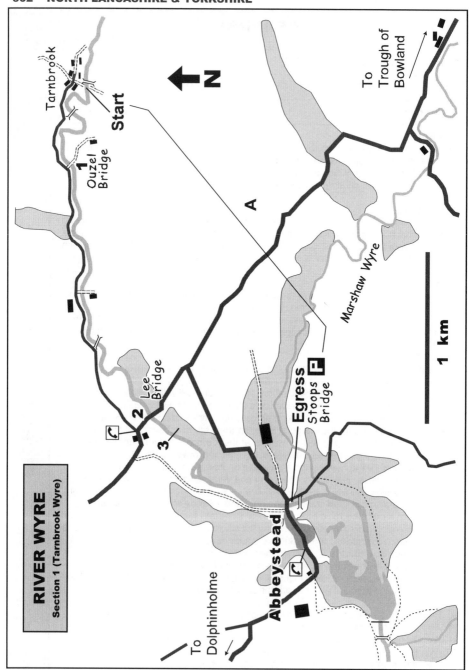

RIVER WYRE
Section 1 (Tarnbrook Wyre)

WYRE

Unfortunately, although the Wyre is a major river of the area it is not canoed very often due to restricted access in its upper reaches while lower down much of its water is held back by reservoirs. Garstang Canoe Club use a short section where it flows through Garstang by the Discount Centre car park. However, if access was easier it is the upper reaches described here which offer the best paddling in high water conditions.

SECTION 1   Tarnbrook to Abbeystead

From :	Tarnbrook	586 557	Grade :	III
To :	Abbeystead	583 543	Maps : O.S. 102,	Explorer OL41
Distance :	3 km		Stars : ✶	Scenery : ❀

SUMMARY
Known as the Tarnbrook Wyre, this section gives a good run in high water, of continuous bouldery rapids in a shallow gorge which runs next to the road for much of the way. Be aware that at present canoeing appears to be actively discouraged in this area and avoiding confrontation may be the most challenging part of a trip into this lovely valley.

INDICATORS
Heavy rain is needed to bring this into condition. It will be obvious at the egress in Abbeystead if it is running and a good view is obtained where it runs along side the road.

START
It is easiest to access the river at a ford in the hamlet of Tarnbrook, but parking can be awkward so make sure to find somewhere completely off the road.

DESCRIPTION
A) II / III Continuous bouldery rapids lead back to Lee Bridge.
1) W   A small weir beneath Ouzel Bridge.
2) W   At Lee Bridge the river runs down a man made brick chute and over a small vertical weir. This can be inspected from the bridge before starting.

B) II After Lee bridge the river eases slightly and becomes more open as it leaves the road to pass through woodland down to Abbeystead.
3) W   Another small weir is passed soon after Lee bridge.

EGRESS
Egress to the road at Stoops Bridge in Abbeystead.

The **Marshaw Wyre** which joins just below this egress has also been paddled in high water conditions down to the confluence, from the Trough of Bowland road.

RIVER WYRE 1

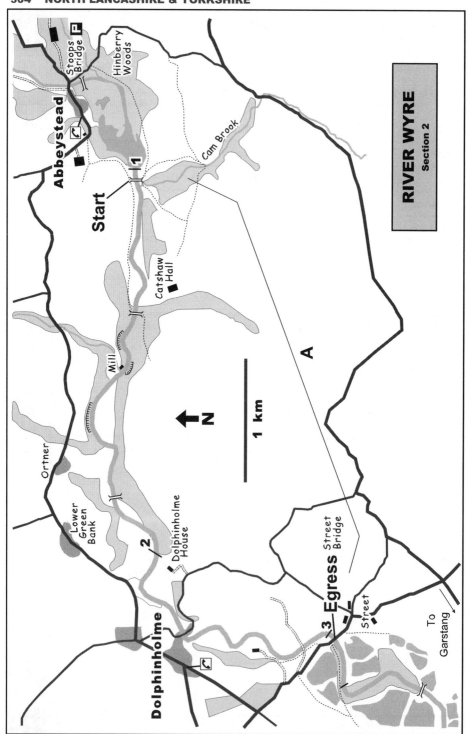

RIVER WYRE
Section 2

Stoops Bridge

Hinberry Woods

Cam Brook

Abbeystead

Start

1

Catshaw Hall

Mill

N

1 km

Ortner

Lower Green Bank

2

Dolphinholme House

Street Bridge

Egress

A

Street

3

Street

To Garstang

Dolphinholme

SECTION 2		Abbeystead to Street		
From :	Footbridge	555 538	**Grade :**	II
To :	Street Bridge	518 522	**Maps :** O.S. 102, Explorer OL41	
Distance :		6 km	**Scenery :** ❀ ❀ ❀	

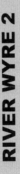

SUMMARY
Awkward to access and hard to find a suitable water level but once established on the water it is an nice section of river through pleasant countryside.

INDICATORS
Very heavy rain is needed to bring this into condition as much of the water is held back by the dam at Abbeystead Reservoir. Best place to look is from the egress at Street Bridge, where the whole river bed should be covered and obviously running well.

START
If it was allowed, a start from Stoops Bridge in Abbeystead would be the easiest point of access with a paddle across the reservoir to **portage the dam** and gain the river below. An alternative is to follow a footpath from the bridge over the Marshaw Wyre through Hindberry woods and around the south edge of the reservoir to reach a footbridge below the dam.

DESCRIPTION ???
A) I / II Straightforward paddling.
1) X   The large dam at the end of Abbeystead Reservoir should be portaged on the left if approached from above. Make sure to stay away from the overflow which ends in a large vertical drop onto concrete
2) W   A weir near Dolphinholme House
3) W   The weir just above Street Bridge is easy angled.

EGRESS
Egress at Street Bridge to a footpath on the right bank. Parking is awkward here and it is better to park a few hundred metres away at the Street crossroads.

RIVER WYRE 2

SUMMARY TABLE

Name of Run	Page	Grade	WW Stars	Scenic Stars	Km	Water	Notes
Brock	335	2(3)		❀ ❀		Med	quiet woodlands
Calder (Halifax)	335	2(3)				Med	urban + weirs
Calder (Whalley)	309	2(3)		❀	4	Med	wild swans !
Cragg Brook	311	5	★ ★	❀	6	High	very steep & deep
Darwen	315	2(4)			15	Med	dirty grey fluid
Douglas - Section 1	317	2			4	Med	urban introduction
Douglas - Section 2	319	1			8	Low	flat touring
Hebden Water	321	3(3+)	★ ★ ★	❀ ❀ ❀	7	High	brilliant spate run
Hodder	323	2		❀ ❀ ❀	24	High	scenic fishing area
Irwell	325	3	★ ★	❀	7	Med	good urban boating
Lead Mines Clough	329	4	★ ★	❀	1.5	High	moorland flume ride
Ribble (Lower river) - Section 2	331	1		❀ ❀			scenic touring
Ribble (Lower river) - Section 3	331	2		❀ ❀	9	Med	intro touring
Yarrow	333	1			7	Med	flat tour

RIVERS OF SOUTH LANCASHIRE & YORKSHIRE

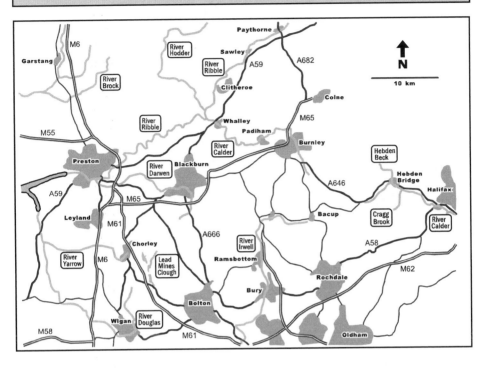

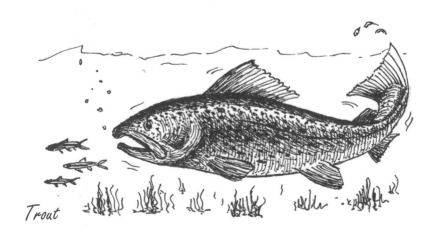

Trout

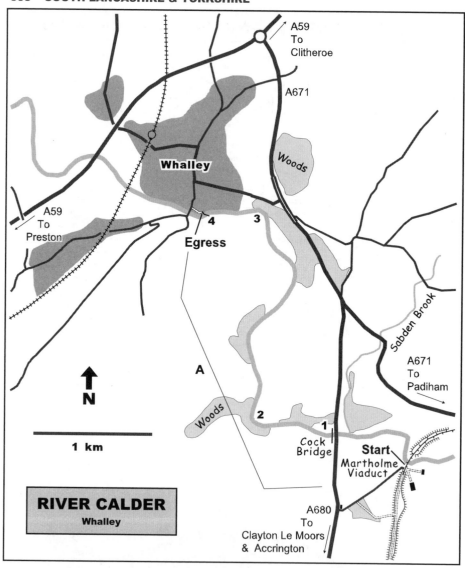

A59
To
Clitheroe

A671

Woods

Whalley

A59
To
Preston

4

3

Egress

Sabden Brook

A671
To
Padiham

A

N

1 km

Woods

2

Cock
Bridge

Woods

1

Start
Martholme
Viaduct

RIVER CALDER
Whalley

A680
To
Clayton Le Moors
& Accrington

CALDER (Whalley)

This Calder runs from above Burnley down to join the Ribble just below Clitheroe, flat and urban for much of its length it is another river through industrial Lancashire with a reputation for dubious water quality. However things are supposed to be improving and the building of a new weir at Padiham with facilities for both canoeing and fishing may see a new era of cooperation between different sets of water sport enthusiasts making the best of these improvements to the water. The only stretch that is regularly canoed is a short section just above Whalley. The Padiham Weir Project should however provide a useful local training resource and park and play spot.

Padiham Weir Project
At the time of publication this is still in its planning stages but if it all goes ahead this will provide a short white water course with three pools separated by small drops and stoppers. There will be coaching, car parking, toilets and changing facilities. It can be found and accessed from the Shuttleworth Mead Business Park which is on the A687 Blackburn Road out of Padiham, close to a junction with the A6068 which leads from exit 8 on the M65. It is also possible to start from the leisure centre in Padiham and paddle down to this site.

River Calder at Whalley

From : Martholme Viaduct 751 769	Grade : II / III
To : Whalley Weir 735 359	Maps : O.S. 103, Explorer OL287
Distance : 4 km	Scenery : ✾

SUMMARY
The water quality may leave something to be desired but the river flows through this fairly pleasant section of countryside just above Whalley and is of interest to local paddlers.

INDICATORS
There is a small island visible at the put in at normal levels. It is at the foot of the supports for the bridge in the middle of the river, and for a good level this island should be covered.

START
From Whalley follow the A671 to a junction with the A680 which is then followed towards Clayton Le Moors. The river is soon crossed at Cock Bridge and the next left is taken, which is a sharp bend by an Italian Restaurant. This road is then followed down to its end underneath an old railway bridge. Park under the bridge and the river is over a small wall.

DESCRIPTION
A) II / III A fairly easy section with only a few rapids and a weir at the end, but some play spots develop in high water.
1) II   Under the road bridge there is a small rapid with a big boulder on the left. In high water this can produce some play spots.
2) III Where the river bends right some sections of grade III are found followed by a part where trees can block part of the river.
3) I   The river eases off and becomes flat, but there are some notoriously territorial swans which appear to inhabit this area.!!
4) W Whalley Weir. This is a 6 metre slope and should be treated with extra caution as the centre of the weir has collapsed forming a man made siphon. When it is run a line hugging the left wall is usually taken.

EGRESS
Egress either immediately above or below the weir (avoiding the gardens) to the right bank where a footpath and lane lead to Whalley town centre with car park and pubs.

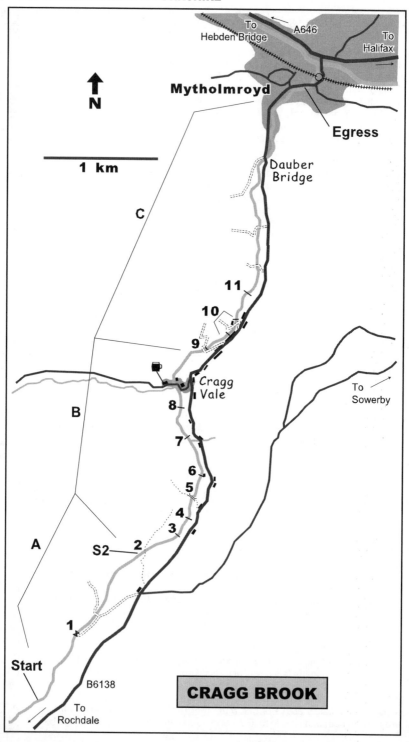

CRAGG BROOK

CRAGG BROOK

From :	Turvin Clough	988 205	Grade :	V
To :	Library Bridge	011 258	Maps : O.S. 103 /104, Explorer OL21	
Distance :	6 km		Stars : ✶✶ Scenery : ✿	

SUMMARY
A brilliant high water white knuckle ride through the deep and narrow valley of Cragg Vale running off Soyland Moor down to Mytholmroyd. The deep valley and dense vegetation make this valley difficult to explore except by kayak. The concentration of hard falls and nasty weirs make it equally difficult to explore in a kayak. The top section of the run begins as a small flume ride on the moors before entering the woods with continuous rocky rapids and falls down to Cragg Vale where escape can be made. The lower section becomes more industrial with the main difficulties involving some large and nasty weirs and a tunnel containing a fall which cannot be portaged.

INDICATORS
Heavy or prolonged rain is needed to give the high water required for this run. At Mytholmroyd it can be viewed at Dauber Bridge to see if the beck is running and navigable but a better idea, to see if it is at a level you wish to run it, is to look upstream from the bridge by the Church in Cragg Vale, where all the boulders should be covered. It is also a good idea to check the Tunnel and the following weir before starting.

START
It can be started high on the moors where the road comes close to the beck which is known as Turvin Clough at this point. It is also possible to join the beck at the stepping stones just before the woods start by parking at the Sowerby junction off the B6318 and following a public footpath across the fields 100 m below the farm house.

DESCRIPTION
A) III   The beck starts as a narrow flume ride as it collects more water from springs and streams and rushes over small slides giving a good warm up for the fun below.
1) W   Watch out for the water works pumping station and weir just after a wall which comes down from the road on the right bank. This needs portaging.

B) V   The beck flows over some stepping stones where a path crosses, but these should be covered and hardly noticed at a good level for the run. It then enters the woods as it drops deeper into the valley and the next 1.5 km offers little respite from sustained rapids and falls all threatened by tree hazards which will need continuous inspection and protection for a safe descent. At Cragg Vale there is a short level section after the bridge where escape can be made to a field and public footpath on the right bank if you have had enough.
2) IV   100 m below the stepping stones a tree on the left indicates the first angled fall. An old and broken aqueduct runs along the right bank from this point giving an opportunity to inspect part of the gorge.
3) V   Passing under a fallen tree marks the run-in over some smooth slabs to a large 2 m drop. This is followed immediately by a complicated set of boulders. Land just past the tree on the left bank to inspect or portage.
4) V   Passing under another fallen tree indicates the approach to a set of large and awkward boulders with a slide under a large flake. Inspect / portage on left bank.
5) X   A narrow passage between boulders indicates a low stone footbridge. Portage.
6) W   Tree problems and small rocky shelves lead to a weir by a concrete structure. It is best to egress at the weir to inspect a holly tree blocking most of the river below.

continued on next page ⇨

CRAGG BROOK

⇨ *continued from previous page*

7) W   A walled bank on the right and a small stream indicate a 1 m horseshoe weir which can develop a strong stopper.

8) IV The beck bends right around a goose farm before more boulders and a long slide where the water piles into the left wall at the bottom.

C) V   The first stone bridge indicates the village of Cragg Vale where egress / access is possible to a field on the right and the Hinchcliffe Arms is nearby to calm the nerves. The second stone bridge indicates the start of further wild adventures amongst historical features from the industrial revolution. There are **three dangerous weirs** and an unavoidable **tunnel** section containing falls which must be run once committed to this section, so be prepared or get out while you can.

9) W   Egress to the left bank immediately below the bridge to portage the first weir. A 2 m affair onto rocks and then another 2 m of rocky falls.

10) V   The next 200 m starts with the river being channelled between old stone walls as it passes under two old brick arches and over a small fall which leads to a second vertical weir dropping 1.5 m onto rocky steps. This is the entrance to the Tunnel, which contains another small fall at its exit with a protruding rock on river right. Immediately afterwards are two bridges and a tree blockage before the last nasty weir which has a large brick arch on its right side. This will probably need a difficult portage on the steep left bank as the main drop is 4 m into an ugly slot containing rocks and trees while the route through the arch is a 2 m drop with a very shallow landing. A difficult problem made more awkward by the surrounding private land and difficulty in portaging. Ropes will definitely be of help.
The exit from the tunnel can be inspected from the bridge below it by walking down from the road at GR 005 237, before starting, but the paths are not clearly marked and are hard to find. Private land on the roof of the tunnel prevents easy inspection or portage from the river except by climbing a very steep bank from the weir to a public footpath high on the left, which then leads back down through the garden of the house on the left to the bridge. Another footpath leads back up beyond the bridge which may help in portaging the lower weir but the steep bank, noisy dogs and alert inhabitants may deter you.

11) T   More tree blockages but the angle of the beck eases off.

EGRESS
After entering the outskirts of Mytholmroyd the beck runs behind a series of factories and workshops before egress is made to the left bank just above the road bridge by the Library and the car park of the Shoulder Of Mutton pub. A small bank to land on here allows a climb over the wall to the road.

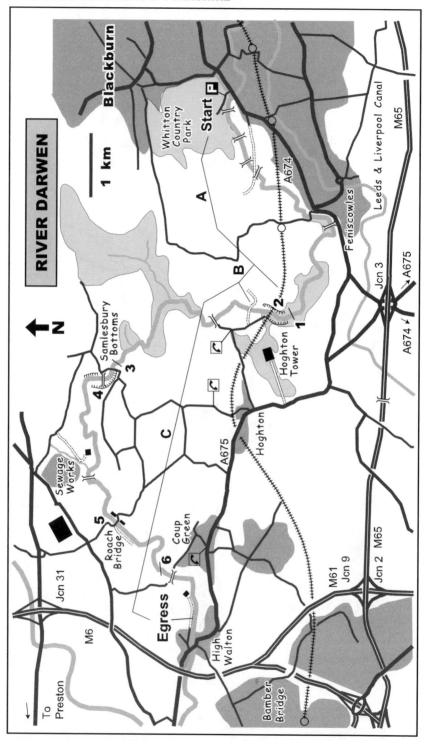

DARWEN

From :	Witton Park	661 270	**Grade :**	I / II (III / IV)
To :	High Walton	580 276	**Maps:** O.S.102 / 103, Explorer 286 / 287
Distance :		15 km		

SUMMARY
A rather surprising journey through the heart of Lancashire which although travelling through some short sections of nice countryside and containing a couple of interesting rapids is spoilt by the oppressive accompaniment of rubbish and a water quality which can only be described as hazardous to health. The grey and smelly liquid is enough to put off all but the most desperate or twisted of enthusiasts but some local paddlers have been known to take the plunge and even survive a swim. Not really recommended. Mainly a flat and easy paddle at grade I / II interspersed with **large and dangerous weirs**.

INDICATORS
Heavy or prolonged rain is needed to get this flowing. If the whole river bed is covered and looks navigable at Whitton Park or at the egress in High Walton then the rest should be OK. The bridge at Feniscowles is another convenient place to view the river. The rocky gorge at Hoghton Bottoms needs a higher level to cover the boulders.

START
There is a large car park at the entrance to Whitton Country Park off the A674 on the outskirts of Blackburn, from where the river is easily accessed.

DESCRIPTION
A) I / II   The river remains flat and fairly gentle through the park and the first gorge at Feniscowles. On the approach to Hoghton Tower the valley sides steepen and be ready to egress for the weir at the start of the viaduct gorge.
1)   X   A large nasty 3 m weir which falls vertically onto rocks. Egress is awkward at the top of the weir so get out in good time 100 m above to the left bank.

B) III / IV   The narrow viaduct gorge beneath Hoghton Tower is about 300 m long where the river is squeezed between gritstone cliffs.
2) III / IV   Access to the gorge is gained immediately below the weir where large boulders and other obstacles give an interesting section of rapids. In high water with all the boulders covered this becomes impressive and much harder. The whole gorge can be portaged by a footpath on the left bank.

C) I / II   The river returns to a more gentle state and runs through a narrow wooded valley before more large weirs and a sewage works interrupt the journey to Walton.
3)   X   On the approach to Smalesbury Bottoms a large vertical 4 m weir must be portaged on the right bank.
4) II / III   In the gorge at Smalesbury Bridge there is a small natural rocky shelf just below a suspension footbridge. This should be ok at most levels.
5)   X   Another large vertical 5 m weir must be portaged at Roach Bridge on the right bank. Descent into the gorge below is awkward and intimidating down the steep bank surrounded by boiling frothy water and pungent odours!
6)   W   A complicated semi-natural weir in the fields behind Coup Green with a large vertical drop on the right and dangerous narrow channels containing undercuts and strong stoppers elsewhere. Portage on the right bank.

EGRESS
Egress to a road which runs from Shop Lane along the right bank above the A675 road bridge at High Walton. Get out in good time as it is channelled by walls near the bridge.

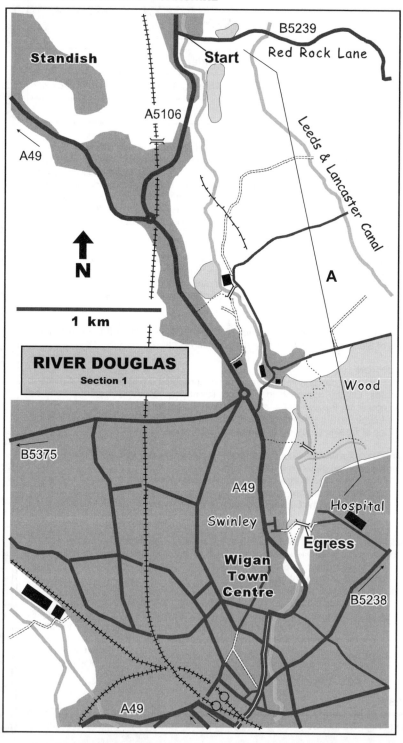

Standish

B5239

Start

Red Rock Lane

A5106

A49

Leeds & Lancaster Canal

N

1 km

A

RIVER DOUGLAS
Section 1

Wood

B5375

A49

Swinley

Hospital

Egress

Wigan Town Centre

B5238

A49

DOUGLAS

The Douglas has its source in the moors above Bolton but it is not until it begins to loop around Wigan that it is used as a resource for canoeing. It is flat and gentle in these parts and is only of interest to those looking for an easy introduction to moving water skills or for flat water touring amongst countryside to escape the otherwise urban environment. However both these sections suffer from trees and branches lining the banks and murky water of dubious quality.

SECTION 1

From :	Red Rock Lane	579 098	Grade :	I / II
To :	Swinley Footbridge	587 066	Maps : O.S. 108 , Explorer OL276	
Distance :	4 km			

SUMMARY
4 km of grade I / II paddling through pleasant countryside with the main hazard being trees to avoid. It finishes close to Wigan town centre in Swinley Park.

INDICATORS
It should be obvious at the start or the egress if it is flowing and there is enough water to make this trip worthwhile.

START
Take the A49 north out of Wigan to the second roundabout where then the A5106 goes off right towards Chorley. Follow this for a kilometre to another right turn onto the B5239 to Red Rock. Almost immediately the road crosses the river where access can be gained.

DESCRIPTION
The river meanders gently down to and then around Leyland Mill Brow. Here it passes under a road bridge before entering the parkland of Bottling Wood.

EGRESS
Egress at the second footbridge which marks the end of the park. It is possible to park close to this footbridge by taking the first turning right onto Penson Street after crossing the river when leaving the town centre on the A49. Penson Street leads to a right turn onto High Street and then a left onto Coppull Lane which runs down to the footbridge. Below here the river takes a somewhat urban and at times subterranean passage through the town and factories, which should be avoided, until Martland Mill.

RIVER DOUGLAS 1

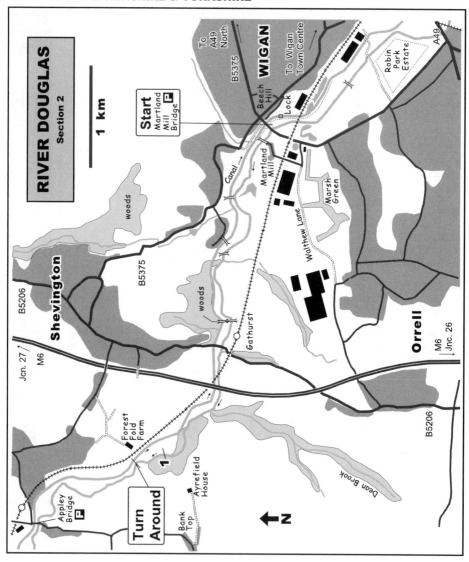

SECTION 2

From : Martland Mill Bridge 561 068	Grade :	I
To : Appley Bridge 523 092 or round trip back to Martland Mill	**Maps :** O.S. 108, Explorer OL285	
Distance : 8 km round trip		

SUMMARY
This easy grade I tour is usually done as a round trip by returning along the Leeds & Liverpool canal which runs alongside for the whole time. Not the prettiest of rivers but gives a welcome escape from the otherwise built-up environment in this area.

START
Martland Mill is found by driving west out of Wigan through Beech Hill, where a road turns left passing over the canal and the river. Parking is possible on an area of land between the two bridges.

DESCRIPTION
The river is followed as far as one wishes on flat and quite murky water with the main consideration being tree branches and bushes which overhang from the banks in places. It is possible to paddle some 24 km to Tarleton, close to the Ribble estuary, and still return via the canal but the normal turning point is where the river comes within a few metres of the canal after 4 kilometres at GR 529 082. This is just short of Appley bridge which is a useful egress for a one way trip.

1) W   The only place to watch on this part is a sloping weir a kilometre after passing under the M6 motorway, and only 400 m before the turning spot. This may need portaging in higher flows.

EGRESS
Normally done as a round trip to egress back at Martland Mill.
However Appley Bridge is a further kilometre past the turning point where egress is best to the right bank on a corner 50 m above the bridge, just after passing under a pipe. There is parking here on land between the canal and river.
It is possible to continue to the sea on a further 20 km+ of grade I paddling along mainly flat estuarial river. This too can be done as a long round trip by returning via the canal from Tarleton. How far do you flat water junkies want to paddle?

RIVER DOUGLAS 2

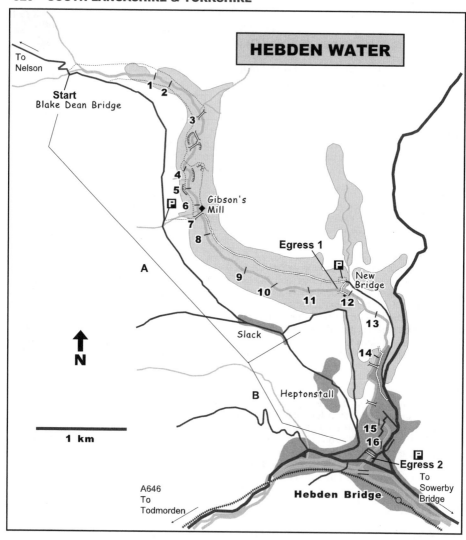

continued from opposite page ⇦

EGRESS

If you find difficulty parking or changing in the centre of town then the spacious National Trust car park at New Bridge **(E1)** is a good alternative for a shorter trip which takes in the best of the run through the woods. Egress **(E2)** is in the centre of Hebden Bridge at some steps immediately below the cobbled stone footbridge opposite the White Hart Pub in Bridgegate. This is found by turning off the main A646 at some traffic lights by the tourist information centre with the Yorkshire Bank on the corner. There is a convenient car park by the riverside but it is usually very busy.

HEBDEN WATER

From :	Blake Dean	958 313	Grade :	III
To :	Hebden Bridge	992 272	Maps : O.S. 103, Explorer OL21	
Distance :	7 km		Stars : ★★★ Scenery : ❀❀❀	

SUMMARY
A great little river which runs for the most part through the delightful woods of Hebden Dale with continuous rapids, tight boulder gardens and runnable weirs before descending into the very bowels of old mill territory to finish in the centre of Hebden Bridge. This old Yorkshire mill town has now shrugged off its dark industrial past and is an interesting busy tourist centre in the heart of the Pennines. A fantastic run in high water.

INDICATORS
Heavy or prolonged rain is needed to bring this into condition as much of the water is held back by reservoirs. A good river wide flow at the egress will give an indication of a suitable level but it is worth a drive up to New Bridge to check the level above the confluence of Crimsworth Dean Beck and see the river in a more natural environment.

START
From the centre of Hebden Bridge drive west on the A646 to a turning circle on the edge of town which allows a U turn to be made so a side road heading north to Heptonstall can be taken. Follow this road past Heptonstall to branch right at Slack onto the moors road towards Nelson. It eventually drops down to cross the river at Blake Dean. Start from the bridge or just below at the confluence with Alcomden water.

DESCRIPTION
A) III Quite narrow and open at first, the beck soon enters the woods with continuous bouldery rapids interspersed with small weirs.
1) III+ 100 m into the woods, at the end of a clearing on the left bank, a collection of large boulders creates a narrow channel with small drops.
2) III A second boulder garden follows shortly with a swift route down the centre.
3) W The first footbridge is followed by a small vertical weir best taken in the centre.
4) III+ A sharp bend left with large boulders on the right creates an awkward chicane.
5) W A small 50 cm vertical weir.
6) W On the approach to Gibson's Mill is an easy angled weir with a small drop onto rocks at its base.
7) SS Just below the stone bridge at the mill are some small stepping stones.
8) SS 100 m lower are some larger stepping stones with a broken route in the centre.
9) SS More stepping stones.
10) W An easy angled weir, but followed by a tree blockage.
11) W Another easy weir followed by a good bouldery rapid, after which it is possible to egress (**E1**) to the left bank and National Trust car Park at New Bridge.

B) III From New Bridge the river leaves the woods to quickly pass through the fringes of the town and drop deep into mill country.
12) W Below the bridge there is a weir with two small steps by the Midgehole Hut.
13) W A small 50 cm vertical weir.
14) W Passing under Lee Mill bridge the river is confined between walled banks and shoots easily over a weir made of three small shelves.
15) W At Nutclough another easy angled weir leads the river under a short tunnel and then between high walled banks behind the mills.
16) W The last weir is angled but again straightforward and soon leads to the bridges at the egress.

⇦ *continued on opposite page*

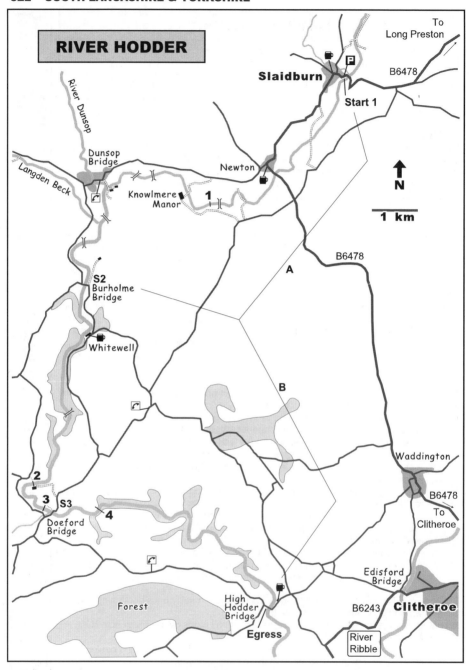

RIVER HODDER

HODDER

| From : | Slaidburn | 714 524 | Grade : | I / II |
| | Burholme Bridge | 658 479 | | |

To : High Hodder Bridge 697 411 | **Maps :** O.S. 103, Explorer OL41

Distance : 24 km | **Scenery :** ❁ ❁ ❁

SUMMARY
A large and very pretty Lancashire river collecting water from the southern edges of the Forest of Bowland. However a large dam holds back much of the water and zealously guarded private land and fishing rights make access a problem.

INDICATORS
The river is quite large, shallow and wide and needs a lot of rain to make it navigable. From Slaidburn down to Dunsop Bridge most of the water is held back by Stocks Reservoir but then a couple of major tributaries help to fill the lower section. If the river looks navigable at the egress at High Hodder Bridge then it should be OK from Burholme Bridge down but the top section can only be judged at the put in at Slaidburn.

START
This is a long section of river which is crossed by several bridges where there are paths along the river bank giving access. However, there are also many signs indicating that canoeists are not welcome in places. Slaidburn **(S1)** is the highest access point where there is a large car park and picnic area next to the river but water levels are likely to be better below Burholme Bridge **(S2)**. Here the river can be easily accessed from a footpath on the left bank and parking is possible by the road junction on the opposite side of the bridge.
A much shorter trip can be started at Doeford Bridge **(S3)**.

DESCRIPTION
A) I / II The first 10 km of the river flow through open farmland with only one weir to watch out for.
1) W   The weir is found 200 m after a footbridge on the approach to Knowlmere Manor .

B) II / III Soon after Burholme Bridge the river passes a hotel at Whitewell and enters a narrow tree lined valley with mainly flat water and gentle rapids. There is a more open section past Doeford Bridge before a second tree lined gorge which lasts almost all the way to the egress.
2) SS   Stepping stones may be exposed at low levels.
3) II   Two small river wide shelves a couple of hundred metres above Doeford Bridge.
4) II / III The river narrows slightly and some rocky shelves lead into the start of the second
        gorge. There are three main rapids ending in a small fall in the gorge which
        can become grade III in high water.

EGRESS
Egress to the right bank and a public footpath just below High Hodder Bridge.
It is also possible to carry on for another 4.5 km to join the Ribble and then continue a further 7 km to Ribchester, but care is needed at a weir 1 km above Low Hodder Bridge GR 705 399.

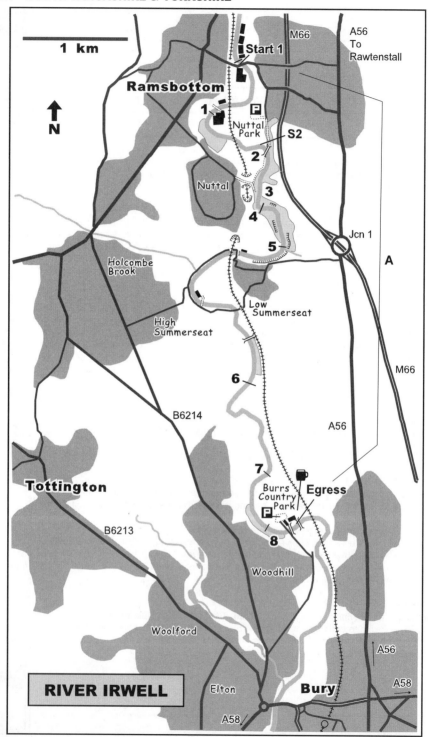

1 km

N

M66

A56
To
Rawtenstall

Start 1

Ramsbottom

1

P

Nuttal
Park

S2

2

Nuttal

3

4

5

Jcn 1

A

Holcombe
Brook

Low
Summerseat

High
Summerseat

M66

6

B6214

A56

7

Egress

Burrs
Country
Park

Tottington

P

8

B6213

Woodhill

Woolford

A56

Elton

Bury

A58

A58

RIVER IRWELL

IRWELL

From :	Ramsbottom 793 168	Grade :	II / III
To :	The Burrs 799 127	Maps : O.S. 109, Explorer OL287	
Distance :	7 km	Stars : ✶✶ Scenery : ✿	

SUMMARY
A river through the heart of Lancashire mill country which helped drive the industrial revolution. Although separated by long flat sections there are several rapids of interest and some weirs which can become quite fearsome in high water. The water quality is a bit dubious, but supposedly improving. It has been paddled above Ramsbottom in flood, but a long canalised section with many obstacles between Bacup and Rawtenstall will deter all but the most determined. The most popular section is described, which is surprisingly scenic, and includes the short but useful managed site at Burrs Country Park, in Bury.
The Burrs Outdoor Centre manage the training site in the Burrs Country Park and for a small fee the changing, toilet, and shower facilities can be used. The site has had some manual sculpting and is a good resource for introducing basic white water skills with a few surfing waves and play spots available. If you are running the river from Ramsbottom and just using the car park to egress no fee is required.

INDICATORS
The best place to get a good idea of the levels is to look downstream from the bridge at `The Burrs`, where there is normally an island visible. If a line of rocks are also visible parallel to the bridge and there is hardly any water in the right hand channel then the level is low and paddling is only possible on the Burrs site. If the rocks are almost or just covered then it is medium levels and the trip from Ramsbottom will be possible but a scrape. If there is water flowing either side of the island but no obvious rocks showing then it is high water and the trip from Ramsbottom will be fine. If the island is covered then it is in flood and a trip from Nuttall park is possible for experienced paddlers but the **nasty weir** in Ramsbottom should be avoided as well as the Burrs Weir, while all the features at the Burrs will be washed out.

START
To start from the main road bridge in Ramsbottom town centre, put in just upstream of the Peel Bridge where the bottom of the weir can be gained from the right bank **(S1)**. In high water starting at Nuttall Park **(S2)** (GR 797 161) is advised to avoid the dodgy weir. The put in at Nuttall Park is found by crossing the bridge from Ramsbottom town centre past the first put in and up a slight hill. Where the road bends left take the first right, down Nuttall Road, which leads to a car park. The river can be easily accessed from the park by a footbridge at the end of the lane.

DESCRIPTION
A) II / III Flat water separates the rapids and weirs in a fairly industrial setting. As usual high water makes the section becomes more serious and it can become a grade IV.
1) W   After the road bridge the river bends right and passes under a railway bridge and another road bridge. Just after this second bridge is a small but very **dodgy weir** which has to be run as it is enclosed between concrete walls and security fences prevent portaging. This weir has some small metal spikes protruding from it and fallen concrete at its base. A line near the left side where the weir ledge protrudes should avoid the main stopper. If in any doubt avoid this and start at Nuttall Park.
2) B   Below the weir the river is obstructed by willow trees and goes under another railway bridge down to a footbridge which marks the start of Nuttall Park Gorge.

continued on next page ⇨

⇨ *continued from previous page*

3) III   Nuttall Park Gorge. A 300 m rapid with few eddies but several holes and waves.

4) III   There is a pipe on stilts in a large pool at the bottom of the gorge. Take the left hand side of the right channel which leads to another pool.

5) III   Watch out for a waterfall on the left which marks a rock step which can form a river wide stopper. In flood a good surf wave forms just above this feature.

6) W   Taylor's Weir. After passing under a restaurant and a road bridge at Summerseat the river goes around a loop then through another stone bridge and a short gorge before a large white house marks the position of Taylor's Weir. This weir contains exposed steelwork but can be shot in low water by a chute on the left and a possible line centre right opens up in high water, but treat with caution and take the usual care by inspecting and portaging if in doubt.

7) W   Burrs Weir. This is a huge 6 m slope which is usually no problem in normal flows. It is smooth in the centre and stepped on the right. The stopper may hold a boat sideways but is relatively safe in low water. Best over the steps in higher flows and should be **avoided in flood**. Inspect and portage on the left.

8) II / III The Burrs Site. This 800 m section provides several safe features to learn river running and is a grade II at low to medium levels. In higher water many of the features wash out but there is a good surf wave under the road bridge at the end and a pop out spot.

EGRESS

Egress is obvious to the ramp on the left by the last surf wave and before the second bridge at Burrs. The car park at Burrs is found by following the B6214 from Bury towards Ramsbottom then turning right at the signs to Burrs Country Park.

`Old Skool` pop out at the Brathay Looping Pool.   *Ian Wilson collection*

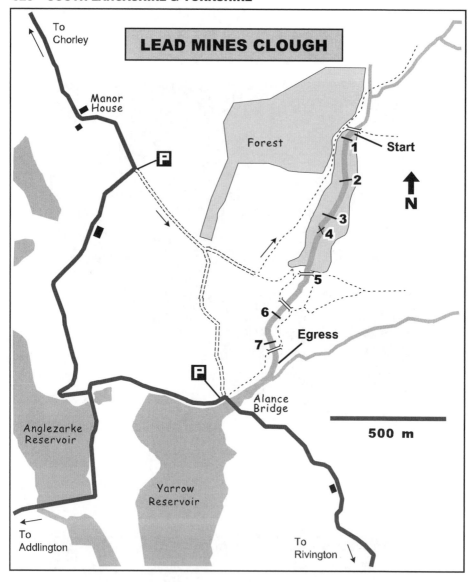

LEAD MINES CLOUGH

From :	Footbridge	634 173	Grade :	IV
To :	Alance Bridge	627 160	**Maps :** O.S. 109, Explorer OL287	
Distance :	1.5 km		**Stars :** ✶✶ Scenery : ✸	

SUMMARY
A steep little bobsleigh run with fast knuckle grazing drops and no eddies which falls off Anglezarke Moor into Yarrow Reservoir. Short boat territory.

INDICATORS
Plenty of heavy rain needed to give the flood conditions necessary for this little horror to be at its best. If there is enough water to slide down the final section of man made canal to the reservoir without scraping on the cobbles then the rest is running.

START
From Chorley follow the road past White Coppice around the west side of Anglezarke Reservoir, up a steep hill and past a sharp bend at Manor House. Soon there is another sharp bend right where the road heads back towards the reservoir and a track continues straight on contouring around the hillside. Park here (GR 624 169) and walk along the track for 700 m, turn north east and continue another 700 m through some pine trees and some gates until you reach the beck at a small footbridge above a 4m angled fall. Cross the bridge where a stile allows access to the base of the fall.

DESCRIPTION
A) IV Extremely narrow at the start, the beck continues in this log flume style for most of the way shooting over several small drops. Keep alert for the **large 7 m drop** which needs portaging, yet is hard to stop for !

1) IV   The beck immediately rattles off over many small shelves and bedrock slides.
2) IV   A 2 m drop where the beck narrows slightly.
3) IV   The bank on the left starts to rise and several more smaller drops lead down to a fast 1.5 m drop near where pine trees appear. Eddy out and make sure you stop in the pool immediately after this drop as it is difficult to stop any further on before the portage of the big fall. In high water it is useful to have a catcher to field you from the bank !!!
4) X   50 m below the last fall this large 7 m drop falls into only a few centimetres of water and is a mandatory portage, The tempting slides lead straight over the fall with no eddies so make sure you get out in time and portage on the left bank.
5) B   A few smaller drops lead down to a low footbridge, where the valley begins to open out. This may need portaging in high water.
6) IV   A fast rocky slide just after the 2nd footbridge which can have a grabby stopper at its end in high water.
7) III   The shallow man made slide leads under the last footbridge, and egress as soon as you can to the left bank before the reservoir.

EGRESS
Egress to the left after the third footbridge and then walk back up and over it to a path on the right bank down to the road by Alance road bridge where there is parking.

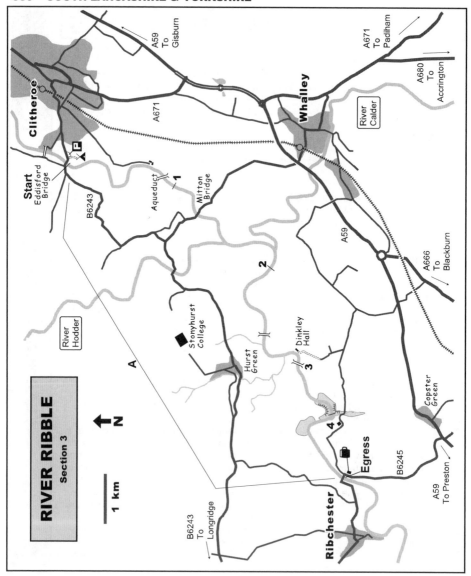

RIBBLE (Lower River)

Below Settle the Ribble calms down greatly and flows through gentle farmland for 20 km or so offering little in the way of interest or scenery for the touring paddler. It then enters Lancashire and near Paythorne the scenery starts to improve as the banks become lined with trees and there are several easy sections of river which are paddled interspersed with weirs. The river grows greatly in volume as many of the other rivers of the area join it on its run down to Preston.

Higher up the river above Settle there is a good section of harder rapids which are described in the **North Lancashire and Yorkshire** chapter of this guide.

SECTION 2   Paythorne To Sawley
This easy touring section of river gives a peaceful grade I / II paddle through pleasant countryside and contains no rapids of note but several small weirs are encountered just above Sawley. Access and egress can be made from the `Ribble Way` footpath which runs on the left bank at Paythorne Bridge and the right bank at Sawley Bridge. Parking at both points is awkward and needs to be considerate to other users.

SECTION 3   Clitheroe to Ribchester

From : Eddisford Bridge 726 414	Grade : II
To : Ribchester Bridge 662 356	Maps : O.S.103, Explorer OL41 / 287
Distance : 9 km	Scenery : ❁ ❁

SUMMARY
An fairly straightforward and attractive stretch of river through pleasant countryside with one nasty weir and a short section of unsettling boils. In a head wind parts can become a long slog.

INDICATOR
This section is best paddled in medium to high flows and as the Ribble is large and mature at this point it holds its level here for a few days after rain. If there are shingle banks visible at the put in but they are passable with a scrape then the river is low but possible. If no boulders are showing at Eddisford bridge then it is high water and this section is at its best, but as the level goes up the weir becomes more dangerous, while the boils at Marls Wood get more interesting.

START
Follow the B6243 out of Clitheroe and there is a car park at Eddisford Bridge on the left.

DESCRIPTION
A) II Mainly flat and straightforward with occasional shingle beds which form easy rapids in low water but get washed out a higher levels.
1) W   The weir is found about 3 km from the start soon after passing under an aqueduct and can be spotted by a small building on the left bank. It has a dangerous tow-back and should be portaged on the left.
2) II   Just after the confluence with the Calder and under a cable is the start of a rapid
3) II   Dinkley Bridge rapid. A short rapid under a suspension bridge.
4) II / III Sale Wheel. Roughly 2 km above the finish the river is constricted between high wooded banks and rock formations at Marls Wood, leading to a huge eddy on a sharp right bend. Strong currents and boils can form here which are unsettling to beginners and in big water can even back loop boats.

EGRESS
At Ribchester bridge egress to the left bank after the bridge. There is a car park by the pub that can possibly be used if permission is sought. The continuation on to Preston is flat.

RIVER RIBBLE 2 & 3 (Lower River)

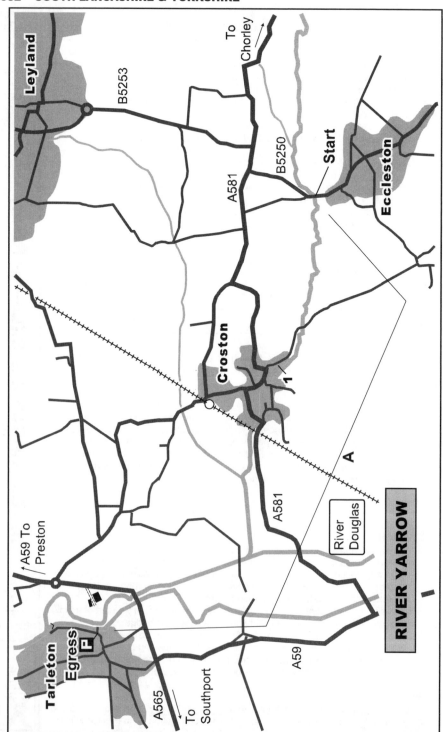

YARROW

The section described on the lower river is a gentle ramble. However there is an upper section starting from Carr Lane off the A6 close to the centre of Chorley which looks promising in high water which may reach grade III with many tree obstacles. It runs through a wooded valley for some 6 km down to Pincock and a further 4 km to Eccleston Bridge. Something to explore for those living locally.

From :	B5250 Bridge	512 174	Grade :	I
To :	Tarleton	456 208	Maps : O.S. 108, Explorer OL276	
Distance :	7 km			

SUMMARY
An easy and somewhat dull flat water trip with an unusual canalised section through Croston.

INDICATORS
Some rain is needed to bring it up to a paddleable level at the start. If able to float through Croston village the rest will be ok.

START
Put in at the B5250 road bridge where there is a car park next to the river. This is found by turning off the A581 between Croston and Chorley signposted for Eccleston.

DESCRIPTION
A) I Flat water leads to Croston where the river enters an old man made gorge about 3m below ground level. This unusual feature is probably of more interest than any paddling that is encountered. Soon after the village the river Douglas is joined for the last kilometre to Tarleton.
1) W A tiny weir by the churchyard at the entry to Croston should not be a problem.

EGRESS
Egress in Tarleton where the river meets the canal and a road runs down from the town to a small bridge over the canal.

RIVER YARROW

OTHER RIVERS

There are several other rivers and many becks in the area that have been paddled but I have either been unable to obtain full information or they are not considered worthy of a full description. However the following brief notes may be of interest.

EAST CUMBRIA NORTH

River Petteril
This river flows through flat farmland between Penrith and Carlisle and is of no interest to canoeists for most of its length. A short section from close to the Motorway roundabout junction 42 through Carlisle to join the Eden has been paddled at grade II and contains a couple of weirs.

NORTH EAST LAKES

Grisedale Beck
The last few hundred metres of this beck fall from out of the valley to the south of Striding Edge on Helvellyn down to Patterdale. There is a 500 m section through the private grounds of Patterdale Hall which has been paddled. This is mainly grade III / IV bouldery rapids with two harder falls of IV and V respectively. There is considerable tree hazard along the whole beck requiring several portages and the landowners request that canoeists do not paddle the beck. There are much better things to do in the area so best to go elsewhere.

NORTH WEST LAKES

River Ellen ???
This runs through Maryport to the west coast. It has been paddled from Ellenhall Bridge near Gilcrux down to Maryport for 9 km of grade I / II but it is not recommended for either its canoeing or scenic qualities.

NORTH LANCASHIRE & YORKSHIRE

River Doe
The river Doe is one of the two rivers that join in Ingleton to form the river Greta. They both have sustained sections of impressive waterfalls which can be viewed from a popular tourist path known as the Ingleton Waterfalls walk. The Doe flows from below the Twisleton Scars over a series of difficult falls between Beezley Falls and Snow Falls. This top section is grade VI and is started at Beezley's Ford (GR 706 748) accessed from Oddie's Lane. Low levels will be wanted for these falls and paddle or portage as bravery permits. Several sections remain unrunnable.

The gorge from below Snow Falls (GR 703 743) back to Ingleton gives a good grade IV blast in high water and can make an interesting start to the Greta if you carry up from Ingleton village by the footpath. Egress in Ingleton at the playground by the open air pool (GR 695 734).

River Marshaw Wyre ???
This runs from the Trough of Bowland road down to join the Tarnbrook Wyre at Abbeystead and can be paddled in high water after heavy rain. The main hazards known to be encountered are the eager bailiffs keen to discourage canoeing in this area.

Stainforth Beck
Make sure to get on below Catrigg Force (GR 832 671). This is best approached by carrying down from the minor road between Langcliffe to Malham Tarn. Catrigg Force is a large multi tiered drop which falls initially into a horrible narrow slot. Some of the lower falls may or may not be possible after careful inspection. High water is required for the steep grade III / IV boulder rapids down to Stainforth village. There are three wooden fences in this section and several tree problems, then as the beck becomes walled between stone banks on the entry to the village there is a wire mesh fence covering the right side of the river which is hard to spot. A low pipe at chest level spans the

river just below the main road bridge at the exit from the village (GR 820 672), this can be nasty in high water and should be inspected from the picnic site on the right before starting.

The beck then passes the sewage works with tiny ledges in the bedrock producing continuous interesting rapids until a slabby drop around a corner leads to the top of the final difficult fall. This last drop (IV/ V) is a big 4 m stepped ramp as the beck channels and drops into a short gorge with all the water piling at the bottom into the undercut left wall. The confluence with the Ribble follows shortly. Egress to a footpath on the far side (right bank) of the Ribble and walk back upstream past Stainforth Force to a small road bridge in 300 m. Alternatively continue down the Ribble to Settle.

River Twiss

The Twiss is the other tributary of the Greta falling out of the Kingsdale valley. Another grade VI horror with as many portages as runable falls. Any attempt on this river will undoubtedly attract a major audience from the continuous stream of tourists on the waterfalls walk. A very level dependant trip requiring just enough water to get through some of the narrows but too much will quickly make it dangerous. Start at a footbridge (GR 694 758) found down a lane to the right just after the road enters the Kingsdale valley. Enough water is needed to just be able to paddle from the footbridge. It is 300 m to the next footbridge at Raven Ray and then take great care as it is only another 300 m to the unrunnable Thornton Force. Take out in good time to portage this 15 m drop which falls onto rocks. From below this continue to paddle or portage as you wish down to Pecca Bridge from where easy water leads back to the car park on the edge of Ingleton.

SOUTH LANCASHIRE & YORKSHIRE

Bradshaw Brook ???

Runs from the Jumbles reservoir past Bradshaw to Bolton. It is only navigable in high water but then problems with weirs and low pipes occur. Although only grade I / II it is not recommended for the inexperienced. Start from the car park at the Jumbles Dam. After 1 km there is a low pipe with only 1m of clearance followed by a serrated weir that is normally portaged. A weir below the 2nd footbridge in Bradshaw has a low pipe just below it. The weir just below Firwood Fold is large and is portaged on the right. After Thicketford Bridge the weirs and pipes come thick and fast with some being at a very dangerous 0.5 m level needing portages. You get the picture, Good Luck!

River Croal ???

The confluence of Bradshaw Brook with the river Tonge form the Croal near the centre of Bolton. It is navigable with care for 5 km down to the Irwell confluence. Grade I / II with some unpleasant weirs, the first of which at the start needs a difficult portage and is not recommended for beginners.

River Calder (Halifax)

This river scrapes into the eastern boundaries of the guide by virtue of the quality of its two fine tributaries, Hebden Water and Cragg Brook. The Calder is navigable from Hebden Bridge to Brighouse at around grade II. However, the water quality leaves much to be desired there are several weirs which need care, becoming dangerous in high water. There is a short white water course at Sowerby Bridge where a couple of the falls reach grade III in high water. There is no charge for passing through the course but if you wish to park and play on the course only contact Halifax Canoe Club. A full description of this river can be found in `A Canoeist's guide to the North East` and on www.ukriversguidebook.co.uk

Pendle Water ???

A tributary of the Calder running from Barley on Pendle Hill to join the Calder close to Burnley. The first section from Barley down to Barrowford and the confluence with the Colne Water is very steep and bouldery with some big falls of unknown grade and no confirmed descent.

However things ease up in Barrowford and the river can be run from A682 road bridge close to Newbridge College down past the confluence with the Calder and on to Padiham. It is mostly grade II with some weirs and one small grade III fall. All the weirs should be treated with the usual caution and one weir in particular, 200 m below the New-in-Pendle bridge and behind the Heald Wood sewage works, gets quite nasty and may require a portage.

continued on next page ⇨

↩ *continued from previous page*

River Roch ???
Runs underground through Rochdale but is navigable from behind the Technical College (GR 894 132) to join the Irwell at Bury, although a better place to egress is Heap Bridge (GR 822 103). It can reach grade III at times in high water and has several weirs which need portages. Poor water quality is highly likely and another unpleasant obstacle is a car breakers yard which encroaches on the river at Hooley Bridge helping the pollution levels. Not canoeing as we know it!

River Tongue ???
Another unpleasant Bolton river for the desperate. Only grade I / II but again unsuitable for the inexperienced due to weirs, low pipes and obstructions. Probably unsuitable for anybody actually.

EXPLORATION

Finally, a list of projects and runs we didn't get a chance to check. When you have done everything else or are looking for an unknown adventure or are just plain curious here are some ideas. These rivers are unchecked and in many instances are un-paddled, the list has been developed from rumours, here say, pub gossip and studying maps. They are where we may be found in the future with lumps in our throats in apprehension of what awaits around the corner, grappling with trees and undergrowth amongst dark hidden ditches. One does not have to go abroad for exploration boating, it is here in our back yards!

Do not attempt any of these unless you are fully prepared and able to deal with the unexpected. Impossible falls, rapids of unknown grade, difficult portages, quick exits, dangerous strainers, fights with trees are all the norm in this territory. I absolve myself of all blame if you go looking for these and find them not possible or have an really frustrating day out. You have been warned.

EAST CUMBRIA NORTH

Croglin Water
Runs out of the hills above Croglin to join the Eden at Nunnery Walks. Most of this is a gentle bouldery run through farmland with trees. There is a narrow section where is steepens just after the start known as Caber Leap leading to a weir. Then there is a section through a private estate just before joining the river Eden containing some large and narrow waterfalls which will require portaging. These can be viewed from the Nunnery Walks tourist path which requires paying a fee. Good Luck. No known descent.

Raven Beck
This looks promising and runs from Sickergill Bridge to Kirkoswald through a small tree lined valley with a waterfall just above the village. No known descent.

NORTH EAST LAKES

Dacre Beck
This small beck runs from Hutton, close to the A66 north of Ullswater, down through Dacre to join the Eamont at Dalemain. Some sections look possible while others are clogged with overhanging bushes.

Grains Ghyll
This is one of the source streams for the river Derwent and starts high up in the central fells below Greatend. Follow the path up the valley from Seathwaiite, at the end of Borrowdale, to Stockley Bridge where a fall under the bridge marks the start of the Derwent. The half kilometre above the bridge looks paddleable in very high water. Entry to the confines of the ghyll can be gained from the right bank where Red Beck joins it. Make sure this is below the impassable falls at a footbridge just above. There is immediately a large drop followed by a twisting route through a rocky gully before blasting down the remaining bouldery bed back to Stockley Bridge. It would be wise to scramble up this ghyll in dry conditions and also check for tree blockages prior to any descent.

Hayswater Gill
This short rocky beck flows out of Hayswater to Hartsop just south of Patterdale. There are some large falls half way down but from below these it looks promising in high water. No known descent.

Watendlath Beck
This runs from the picturesque hamlet of Watendlath above Borrowdale down to Derwent Water and contains the impassable Lodore Falls which are an impressive sight in flood. However from Watendlath down to the top of the falls looks promising. At the start there is a steep section of narrow technical falls before a long section along the valley floor. It then has almost a kilometre of good rapids through the woods down to the lip of Lodore Falls. However there are many trees in this which would need clearing. Make sure you can escape before the falls. No known descent.

NORTH WEST LAKES

Mill Beck, Buttermere
A narrow tree filled ditch from the western side of Newlands Hause down to the pub in Buttermere. Often talked about but would probably require a week with a chainsaw to make a descent possible.

Mosedale Beck (Loweswater)
This beck looks promising from where it falls out of the upper valley and down through the woods to Church Bridge by the pub in Loweswater. There are several large falls at the start and a nasty looking sump created by a jammed block on the lip of a fall, with trees also being a considerable hazard. No known descent yet.

NORTH LANCASHIRE & YORKSHIRE

Cam Brook
In high water this could offer a steep alternative start to the 2nd section of the Wyre. It starts from Cam Brow road to the south of Abbeystead and loses 50 m in height in a kilometre down to the footbridge below Abbeystead reservoir dam. Who knows what happens in here?

Keasden Beck
This flows into the Wenning between Clapham Station and High Bentham and runs off the moors to the south. It looks quite promising with a couple of waterfalls marked on the map, although tree and fence obstacles are likely to be encountered. Starting in the vicinity of a water works building on Keasden Road close to Cowsen Gill Bridge and finishing at a road bridge where Hollin Lane crosses the river.

Needlehouse Gill
A tributary of the Upper Rawthey which you cross over on the way to the start of Section 1 (See page 83). It is possible to do sections of this tight beck after heavy rain, from just above the access bridge down to join the Rawthey. Beware of a 4 m drop with a shallow pool, plenty of trees and a final narrow ditch which is a portage until the chainsaw gang go clearing ! Grade depends on water levels, as usual. IV+ / V+.

SOUTH LANCASHIRE & YORKSHIRE

Bottoms Beck
Runs through Gisburn Forest above Stocks reservoir at the source of the river Hodder.

River Brock ???
This looks a promising grade II river in the right water levels. It is a gentle gradient for most of its 5.5 km length, and runs through some pleasant woods with nature trails between Snape Rake Lane and New Bridge, with a couple of weirs. At the end of Snape Rake Lane (GR 554 441), there

continued on next page ⇨

EXPLORATION

⇨ *continued from previous page*

is a very small turning area and room to park a car with a steep rocky track leading down to the river. Soon after the start there is a weir 150 m after passing a bridge.

An alternative and easier start is from the parking and picnic area at Brockmill (GR 549 431). Roughly a kilometre below Brockmill there is another weir on the approach Brock Bottom.

At the egress at New Bridge (GR 523 409) there is a final weir which could be dangerous in higher flows. This cannot be avoided unless you get out 300 m above the bridge to the left bank and a public footpath before the banks of the river become walled in front of some houses. Inspect before starting and if you need to avoid it walk up to check the egress. There is a lay-by 50 m from the bridge.

River Calder (Calder Vale)

A small narrow beck that looks a promising run of unknown grade in high water. Possible to start at Oakenclough and run all the way through the Calder Vale to Sandhome Bridge. There appear to be several small rocky outcrops and gorges to provide interest and also some weirs as it passes the town of Calder Vale. Tree hazards will be present as it runs through plenty of woodland.

There is also difficulty in egressing at Sandholme Bridge due to an awkward weir under the bridge. Inspect before you start and you may wish to climb the steep bank above the bridge.

Colne Water

Flows through Colne to join the Pendle Water at Barrowford.

Dean Black Brook

Flows into White Coppice from Anglezarke moors. Steep beck bashing with a large un-runnable fall at the bottom.

River Dunsop

A tributary of the Hodder out of the Forest of Bowland to Dunsop Bridge. Looks to have a steady gradient but will be a long walk in.

River Douglas (Upper river)

This bears little relation to its lower half as the actual course of the river gets lost amongst the reservoirs and towns hereabouts. However close to its source where it runs off Rivington Moor there is a section of technical grade 3 / 4 as it skirts the southern edge of Lever Country Park past the school.

The Goit

A flat water trip from Brinscall to Anglezarke reservoir. Small sloping fall at end into reservoir.

Langden Brook

Another tributary of the Hodder close to Dunsop Bridge. From where it joins the road below the Trough of Bowland down to the Hodder confluence looks a promising high water run with a couple of fences to portage. May also be worthwhile exploring higher up above the waterworks station.

Sabden Brook

Runs from Sabden down to the River Calder close to Whalley.

River Yarrow (upper river)

As mentioned briefly in the main text the Yarrow looks possible after heavy rain in its higher reaches from the A6 road bridge in Chorley down to Pincock. This is accessed from Copp Lane and it immediately leaves the built up area to run through the pleasant woodland of Yarrow valley park. The first three kilometres give the best gradient and there is a convenient car park at a small bridge in the Valley Park bottom as it passes below Coppull. Trees are likely to be a major hazard.

BIBLIOGRAPHY

"Rivers of Cumbria", Mike Hayward. Cordee 1992.

"Cumbrian Becks", Richard Evans. 1995.

"A Canoeist's Guide to the North East", Nick Doll. Cicerone Press 1991.

"Canoeist's Guide to Yorkshire Rivers", M. Twiggs. Menasha Ridge Press 1992.

"Rivers of North West England", Tony Tickle.

"An Atlas of The English Lakes", John Wilson Parker. Cicerone 2000.

"Westmorland, Cumberland, Durham and Northumberland" Thomas Allom. 1832.

"UK Rivers Guidebook" on the Internet see:-   www.ukriversguidebook.co.uk

The following Ordnance Survey Sheets are required to give a full coverage of the area described:
Ordnance Survey Landranger Series 1:50,000 scale;
Sheets 79, 85, 86, 89, 90, 91, 96, 97, 98, 102, 103, 104, 108, 109

Ordnance Survey Explorer series 1:25,000 scale;
Sheets OL4, OL5 , OL6, OL7, OL2, OL41, OL43, OL19, OL21, OL30, OL43, 276, 285, 286, 287, 303, 315, 323, 324,

Environment Agency Rivercall Service

The Environment Agency gives river level information for several rivers in the region on a recorded message updated daily. A data base of information is beginning to be built up among the Cumbria Canoeists as to how the levels given relate to how the river actually is for paddling. As yet it is early days but it is worth checking out and to see how the levels correspond to your own findings and keep an eye on the Cumbria Canoeists Website as they collate the information.

Rivercall N.W. Region number is - 09066 197733
Rivers covered are Lower Derwent, Eden, Kent, Lune, Ribble and Irwell.

Cumbria Canoeists Website   www.cumbriacanoeists.org.uk

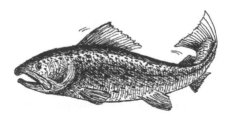

GRADED LIST

This list will no doubt be open to debate as no two persons' memories of a run will be the same even if run at the same time never mind in different conditions. It is meant as quick reference to group rivers of a similar grade, show what else is around of that standard and start arguments. The grade usually refers to the hardest rapids on a particular section and further reference to the main text will show if it is a one-off in an otherwise easy section of river or a sustained run. No attempt has been made to put them in order of difficulty within a grade and they are listed in alphabetical order.

Grade 6
Crosby Gill 231
Esk (section 1).......................247
Little Langdale Beck -
- `Colwith Force` 201
Rawthey (section 1).............. 83
Scandale Beck (Ambleside) ...211
Torver Beck (section 1).........221
Yewdale Beck (section 1).......227

Grade 5
Appletreeworth Beck.............257
Barbon Beck 275
Belah 61
Bleng 235
Brathay - `Skelwith Force` 171
Church Beck (section 1).........175
Cragg Brook. 311
Dee (section 1).......................73
Duddon (section 2)................241
Esk (section 2).......................249
Force Beck 185
Gayle Beck 279
Glenridding Beck 123
Grassguards Gill 241
Irthing, - `Crammel Linn` 43
Lickle 257
Logan Beck.............................261
Mosedale Beck (NE)..............135
Mosedale Beck (SW) 263
Oxendale Beck 207
Pen-y-ghent Gill. 293
Sprint (section 1)...................213
Stock Ghyll 219
Swale (Keld Gorge)................ 91
Swindale Beck 95
Tarn Beck. 267
Wasdale Beck.........................101
Whillan Beck 269

Grade 4
Artle Beck 273
Black Beck..............................233
Birk Beck 63
Borrow Beck. 65
Calder (Cumbria) (section 1) ..147
Caldew (section 1) 107
Church Beck (section 2).........177
Clough (Section 1) 67
Clough (Section 2) 69
Crookdale Beck. 71
Cunsey Beck. 183
Derwent (section 1)...............109

Grade 4
Duddon (section 3) 243
Gatesgarthdale Beck 163
Gelt... 41
Glenderamackin (section 1) ...115
Glenateraterrra 121
Great Langdale Beck 187
Hindburn................................283
Kent (section 1).....................189
Kent (section 3)....................193
Kent (section 4)....................195
Keskadale Beck 131
Langstrath Beck.....................133
Lead Mines Clough................329
Leck Beck...............................285
Leven (section B) 198
Liddle Water 51
Lingmell Beck 259
Liza...165
Low Gill................................... 75
Lune (section 1)...................... 77
Mint (section 2)....................205
Nether Beck............................265
Rawthey (section 2)............... 85
Rawthey (section 3)............... 87
Ribble (section 1)..................295
Roeburn..................................299
Sprint (section 2...................215
Torver Beck (section 2).........223
Trout Beck (North) 141
Trout Beck (South)................225
Upper Eden (section 1 97
Wyth Burn..............................143

Grade 3
Brathay..................................171
Border Esk.............................. 25
Calder (Cumbria) (section 2)..149
Calder (Whalley)....................309
Cocker (section 2)..................153
Cowside Beck.........................277
Darwen...................................315
Derwent (section 2)...............110
Duddon (section 1) 239
Duddon (section 4) 245
Eden (section 2)..................... 37
Greta (Keswick) 127
Hebden Water 321
Irt (section 2)........................255
Irthing (section 1)................. 43
Irthing (section 2)................. 45
Irthing (section 3)................. 47
Irwell.....................................325

Grade 3
Leith....................................... 49
Leven (section A)................... 199
Little Langdale Beck 201
Lowther 53
Lune (section 2)...................... 79
Lune (Halton Rapids) 289
Marron.................................... 167
Mint (section 1).....................203
Newlands Beck......................137
Rawthey (section 3)............... 87
Whitsundale Beck.................103
Wyre (section 1) 303
Yewdale Beck (section 2) 229

Grade 2
Caldew (sections 2).............. 27
Caldew (sections 3).............. 29
Cocker (section 1) 151
Derwent (section 5) 155
Derwent (section 6) 157
Douglas (section 1)...............317
Eamont (section 1) 31
Ehen (Section 1)....................159
Ehen (Section 2)....................161
Glenderamackin (section 2)... 117
Glenderamackin (section 3)... 119
Goldrill Beck 125
Hodder 323
Lune (section 3).....................287
Lyne 55
Lyvennet................................. 57
Ribble (section 3)..................331
Rothay....................................209
Scandale Beck
(Ravenstonedale) 89
St John's Beck.......................139
Upper Eden (section 2)......... 99
Wenning.................................301
Wyre (section 2) 305

Grade 1
Dee (section 2)...................... 73
Derwent (section 3) 111
Derwent (section 4) 113
Derwent (section 5) 155
Douglas (section 2)...............319
Eamont (section 2) 33
Eden (section 1) 35
Lune (section 5).....................291
Yarrow....................................333

INDEX

CARLISLE CANOES

OLD RAFFLES PARADE, WIGTON ROAD CARLISLE, CUMBRIA, CA2 7EX
TEL/FAX 01228 531703
E-MAIL: info@carlislecanoes.co.uk
www.carlislecanoes.co.uk
OPENING TIMES
MON-FRI 9.30 - 5.30
SAT 9.30 - 4.30

HIGHLAND CANOES

7 MYRTLEFIELD CENTRE
GRAMPIAN ROAD
AVIEMORE PH22 1RH
TEL/FAX 01479 810116
E-MAIL: info@highlandcanoes.co.uk
www.highlandcanoes.co.uk
OPENING TIMES
MON-SAT 9.30 - 5.30

STIRLING CANOES

BLOCK 4 UNIT 2, MUNRO ROAD
SPRINGKERSE IND. ESTATE
STIRLING, FK7 7UU
TEL/FAX 01786 478820
E-MAIL: dave@stirlingcanoes.freeserve.co.uk
www.stirlingcanoes.co.uk
OPENING TIMES
MON-SAT 10.00 - 5.30

SUN & BANK HOLIDAYS BY ARRANGEMENT

THE NORTHS PREMIER KAYAK AND OPEN CANOE SPECIALIST

KAYAKS, SEA KAYAKS, OPEN CANOES, PADDLES AND ACCESSORIES FROM ALL LEADING MANUFACTURERS

VISIT OUR WEB SITE FOR SPECIAL OFFERS

www.carlislecanoes.co.uk

INTEREST FREE CREDIT 6 OR 9 MONTHS

MAIL ORDER HOT LINE 0800 0747975 FREEPHONE

Sea kayaks & open canadian canoes For hire

SAME DAY
DISPATCH

SWITCH

NEXT DAY
DELIVERY

VISA

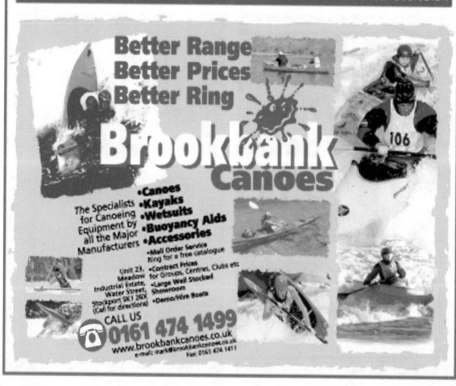

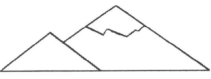

Paddle your own...
or one of ours.

Kayaks

Canoes

Sit-on-tops

Accessories

Demo boats

One to One Instruction

Group instruction

Call in for friendly advice

Windermere
Canoe & Cycle
Bowness-on-Windermere
Tel:015394 44451

get out **more**!

Canoeing & Multi-Activity
Instructors

PGL is the UK's largest employer and trainer of canoeists – every year over 150 of our canoe instructors teach paddling skills and lead river trips in the **UK** and **France**.

Ardèche, Southern Alps, Wales, Scotland...with 25 centres situated in some of Europe's most stunning locations PGL has something to offer to paddlers of all standards. Our season operates from February to November, providing an excellent gateway to a career in the outdoors or the opportunity to spend a few months sharing your love of sport with others.

Each season several hundred star tests are awarded, 200+ coaching awards are gained and more than 35 employees complete Assessor training and WCA/BCU Raft Guide Assessments.

So, if you are vibrant and energetic, love the outdoors and get on well with kids, we'll help you achieve the skills and qualifications you need. For a highly rewarding position, excellent training opportunities, accommodation, meals and the chance for rapid career progression – *get out and get in touch now!*

We also offer the chance for experienced white water paddlers to train as Raft Guides in the **Southern Alps**.

PGL is Britain's leading provider of adventure holidays and courses for children. For over 100,000 children each year, a PGL holiday means the adventure of a lifetime. For more information about PGL – employment, trips for children and families – visit www.pgl.co.uk

www.pgl.co.uk/people
email: pglpeople@pgl.co.uk
phone: 01989 767833
PGL is committed to equal opportunities

learn it | teach it | love it

Other Great Guidebooks

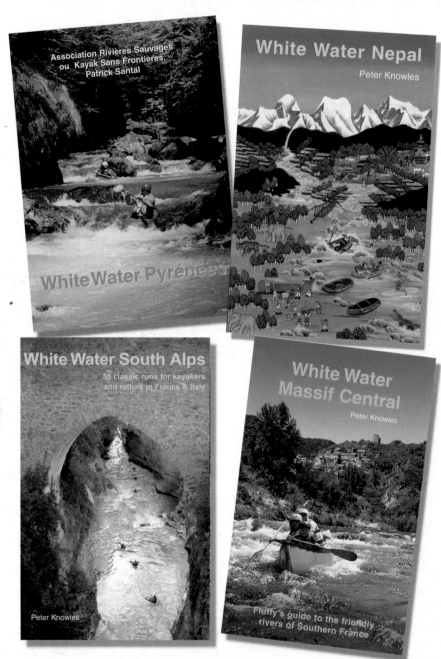

www.riverspublishing.co.uk